TEACHER OF THE YEAR

ALSO BY M.A. WARDELL

Mistletoe & Mishigas

Napkins & Other Distractions

Husband of the Year

TEACHER OF THE YEAR

M.A. WARDELL

FOREVER

NEW YORK   BOSTON

Cover design by YY Liak. Cover illustrations by Myriam Strasbourg. Opening illustration by Ian Leone. Inside illustrations by Mayhara Ferraz. Closing illustration by Jorge San Martín. Cover copyright © 2025 by Hachette Book Group, Inc.

Forever
Hachette Book Group
1290 Avenue of the Americas, New York, NY 10104
read-forever.com
@readforeverpub

Originally published by M.A. Wardell in April 2023
First Forever trade paperback edition: June 2025

Forever is an imprint of Grand Central Publishing. The Forever name and logo are registered trademarks of Hachette Book Group, Inc.

The publisher is not responsible for websites (or their content) that are not owned by the publisher.

The Hachette Speakers Bureau provides a wide range of authors for speaking events. To find out more, go to hachettespeakersbureau.com or email HachetteSpeakers@hbgusa.com.

Forever books may be purchased in bulk for business, educational, or promotional use. For information, please contact your local bookseller or the Hachette Book Group Special Markets Department at special.markets@hbgusa.com.

Library of Congress Cataloging-in-Publication Data
Names: Wardell, M. A., author.
Title: Teacher of the year / M.A. Wardell.
Description: First Forever trade paperback edition. | New York : Forever,
    2025. | Series: Teachers in love ; 1 | Identifiers: LCCN 2024059808 |
    ISBN 9781538774625 (trade paperback) | ISBN 9781538774632 (ebook)
Subjects: LCGFT: Romance fiction. | Queer fiction. | Novels.
Classification: LCC PS3623.A7357 T43 2025 | DDC 813/.6—dc23/eng/20241230
LC record available at https://lccn.loc.gov/2024059808

ISBNs: 9781538774625 (trade paperback), 9781538774632 (ebook)

Printed in the United States of America

LSC-C

Printing 1, 2025

AUTHOR'S NOTE AND
CONTENT GUIDANCE

Dear Reader,

While *Teacher of the Year* may be about a kindergarten teacher, it is an open-door romance intended for mature audiences. Hey, kindergarten teachers deserve love too.

The characters in the story are consenting adults, and there is explicit, on-page sexual content. It also contains explicit language and adult situations.

While I hope to present an uplifting, sweet, and hilarious story about the healing power of love, it's a journey. Along our way, the characters deal with alcohol recovery, traumatic memories of an alcoholic parent, severe anxiety, panic attacks, infidelity (not by main characters), and a pregnancy scare.

The topic of recovery looms large in *Teacher of the Year*. If you or someone you know is struggling with addiction, there are ways to get help. Please visit my website for online resources at MAWardell.com.

Peace and love,

M. A. Ward

CHAPTER ONE

Dear Families,

Happy New Year! I hope everyone had a restful break filled with cozy family time, hot cocoa, playing in the snow, and lots of good books! Your child is undoubtedly as excited to return to school as I am to see them. Our first day or two will be spent reviewing routines and procedures and thinking about our New Year's resolutions for school. We also have a new student joining our kindergarten community, and I know everyone will welcome her with open arms. As always, I'm grateful for the opportunity to teach your children.

Warmly,
Marvin Block

"Nice of you to show up," Jill quips.

"My damn gas light came on. Again. Hence my post-crack-of-dawn arrival."

"Marvin Block, you had the entire break to get gas. Why do you always risk one more drive when there's a serious chance of being stranded?"

"I honestly forget. And panic. Plus, I like to think of each trip with barely any gas as a Chanukah miracle. Not enough oil but look, made it anyway!"

Jill delights in teasing me. She may be the embodiment of petite, but Jill Kim commands a room like a boss. Technically, she stands at four eleven and a half, but I round up the extra half-inch when describing her because we all deserve a friend who embellishes. Jill and I joke that we both have two minority tallies (her: Vietnamese and tiny, me: Jewish and gay). We've bonded over being outsiders, particularly at our school, where the staff resembles a nineteen-fifties housewife's Tupperware party (white, straight, Christian, relatively tall, and female). We were drawn to each other from the moment we met at my interview nine years ago, when we locked eyes across the conference room table, she winked at me, and I knew our friendship was destined. She's like the bratty older sister I never had, and I adore her to bits.

"Well, Baruch ata Adonai, I'm blessed you're here," she delivers in surprisingly accurate Hebrew.

"Yeah, I figured I better come in and do your job for you."

She turns toward me and swishes her shoulder-length jet-black hair.

"Be my guest. I'll gladly send my entire class over to you and go shopping."

Our banter is routine, playful, and expected. As Jill whips around preparing her classroom for the day, her ankle-length flannel dress appears caught in a flurry.

"I mean, you *are* a contender for Teacher of the Year."

Jill loves to mock me about the nomination. Heck, she likes to tease me, period.

"Listen, if it wasn't the first day after vacation and I didn't have a new student starting, sure, I'd gladly take them all," I say.

This reminder shifts her demeanor, and her eyebrows gather.

"Right. What do we know about them?"

"Not much, just her name. A single dad, I think. I'm not actually sure. The mother's phone number is out of state, and 'lives with dad' is scribbled on my paperwork, so who knows?"

"Oh, a single dad. Maybe he's cute."

Jill loves to bait me. She's trying to spruce up my desolate dating life, and thinks that any single man with a pulse could be my Mr. Right.

"Ah yes, just what I'm looking for, a straight father whose child is in my class. Sounds like a match made in heaven."

As she scribbles her morning message, the marker squeaks against the whiteboard. She sets it down and wraps her fingers around her hip.

"You do know to have a relationship, you actually have to put yourself out there, right? And why do you assume everyone is straight? That's heterophobic."

"Heterophobic? You made that up."

"No. Google it. In any event, staying home watching movies with your cat isn't the way to find a guy. You're a catch. Adam was an asshole. Not all men are. Someone would be incredibly lucky to be your boyfriend."

My relationship with Adam crumbled because I made the colossal mistake of thinking I could count on someone. Jill was my central pillar of support. She sat with me in silence and brought me strawberry ice cream and Junior Mints, my depression noshes of choice. The breakup with Adam crushed me. Walking in on him boning a stranger in the laundry room probably had something to do with the melancholy. Loving someone isn't supposed to lead to immense hurt. The three years since the breakup have been a gradual reemergence from darkness, and I couldn't have done it without Jill. Her friendship means the world to me, but her eagerness for me to date has caused her to be quite the *yenta*. Right now, dating doesn't interest me. I'm fine by myself. Me and Gonzo. Our own boys' club. A sweet furball lying on my chest, staring up at me, and voraciously purring, who needs more than a snuggly cat? Jill knows me well, knows I'm not ready, but still wants me to have someone to lean on the way she has Nick.

"Put myself out there? Have you watched *Dateline* lately?"

Jill gives me her I'm-not-buying-your-bullshit stare. I recognize it almost as well as she recognizes my jokes-as-diversion strategy.

"Why are you dancing, Marvin? Focus."

"This isn't my ADHD. I'm listening. Mostly. I need to pee. Badly," I tell her, hopping from one foot to the other.

"Go!" she yells, and I dash out.

Having a men's room in a building where typically no more than two grown men work makes little to no sense. I've pushed our principal, Dr. Knorse, to consider making it a gender-neutral bathroom, and she said she'll "think about it." Which means, not happening in this lifetime. Much to everyone's chagrin, Jerry, the male PE teacher, and I joke it's our personal powder room.

Rushing in, I pee quickly and proceed to wash up. I position my hands under the automatic faucet. Nothing. Out and back under. Still nothing. While the tree-hugger in me understands these sinks are meant to conserve water, their inability to function in a timely and reasonable manner often leaves me wanting to scream with frustration. As I'm fighting with the damn sink, about to actually yell, a blur zooms toward the urinal.

Hurrying to finish, I throw my hands under the faucet one last time, and it erupts to life. A stream of water sprays my arms and gushes all over the front of my gray joggers. And now I appear to have thoroughly pissed myself. Lovely.

Glancing over at the urinal, I see that the man peeing clearly isn't a white, short, rotund redhead. Jerry wouldn't be at school this early anyway. From the back, I can see he's almost as tall as me, with rich brown skin and hair springing from his head in tight coils. The urge to escape embarrassment washes over me, but I also need the bathroom's air dryer to attempt to rectify the large splash on the front of my pants.

The urinal flushes with a swoosh and I quickly finish washing. The zip of his pants and his crisp footsteps on the tile floor inform me he's en route. My forehead begins to sweat, and I know I'm about to be caught with what appears to be pissed pants.

The stranger strolls over, and I rush to cover the lower portion of my body, throwing my wet hands over myself to hide the awkwardness but only making the offending splotch worse. He scrutinizes me with deep, hickory eyes. And maybe because my hands attempt to cover the area, his gaze lowers, landing on my crotch. My eyes widen with humiliation and the confirmation I'm a complete *schmuck*.

"It's water from the sink. Be careful. They're automatic. And relentless. And well…" I move my hands away, revealing the source of my mortification.

Without a word, he slowly places his hands under the sink, and the faucet magically comes to life with no histrionics or fanfare. He looks at me, gives the faintest grin, and washes his hands.

I turn to the air dryer and do my best to position myself under it, thrusting my hips forward to get the airflow right. I'm now gyrating in the bathroom in front of a handsome stranger like a complete putz. The man finishes and, as I'm bogarting the dryer, wipes his hands on his pants and gives me a nod and exits. Standing there, hot air blowing my nether regions, I wonder, who was that gorgeous man, and why am I so damn flushed?

As I return to my classroom, my heartbeat begins to return to normal. The scorching air from the dryer erased the water on my pants, but why am I still flooded with warmth? That man. His eyes. The way he looked at me. Down there.

I snap on the lights and wait for the harsh fluorescent glow and the low hum they create. The quiet purr whirs in the spare moments before and after children take over the space which is filled with their work and writing, bursting with life, even without them present.

Edginess creeping in, I close my eyes, and Caron Wheeler's bright, distinctive alto joins the drone from the lights. The opening harmonies of "Back to Life" take over my headspace. Her rich a cappella voice singing about returning to routine and reality cues me to take long, deep breaths. In through the nose, out through the mouth. One, two, three. I pause, making the break last slightly longer than usual. In moments when my emotions feel heavy and my anxiety bubbles, my brain's DJ cues up the perfect song. When the music starts up, it's my cue to pause. A few minutes of meditative gulps of air along with centering on the music and lyrics, and I'm usually ready for reentry.

I open my eyes. Without the noisy energy of the children, the classroom feels mournful, almost melancholy—even with all the evidence of their presence. My first task, cracking a window because even in the middle of frosty Maine winters, the onslaught of germs from five-year-olds necessitates a modicum of fresh air. Children have literally coughed and sneezed directly in my face and thought nothing of it. Do you know what that feels like? Sticky, wet, and warm—and not in a good way. All the hand sanitizer and face wipes in the world won't help. Crisp, clean air provides a curtain of freshness until I'm able to scrub down in a Silkwood shower the minute I'm home. Dropping my backpack by my table, I glance at a small pile of items I'd procured for my new student before the break.

She starts today, and though I could have dragged my *tuchus* in over the holiday break to label and set her things up, I needed the respite. As I formulate a plan of attack to prepare for the nutty day ahead, Kristi Brody, the school guidance counselor, pops her head into the doorway like a small prairie dog searching for her pack.

"Morning! Have a good break?" Kristi trumpets, her hair bouncing with each step. Her voluminous curls swing and sway, unlike mine, which were a gift from my Jewish ancestors—small and tight, more like corkscrews shooting from my head in a wild fashion. As a child, my mother occasionally referred to me as "pubic head," which explains a lot about our relationship.

Conflicting feelings about returning to work swirl in my *keppie*. I adore my job. Specifically, the children bring me great pleasure. It's hard not to cherish their sweet faces, quirky smiles with missing teeth, and the often random, confusing, but hilarious tidbits that pop out of their mouths at the most inopportune times. Like the time I attempted to explain the concept of addition, and Roberta confessed, "When I grow up, I want to marry a taco." For the record, me too, kid, me too.

I'm trying to figure out how to answer Kristi. When someone asks if you had a "good break," they rarely want complete honesty. They don't want to hear you spent most of your break in solitude, watching subpar rom-coms on Netflix, overeating store-brand strawberry ice cream containing no actual strawberries, and feeling elated to only have the company of your cat whom you secretly refer to as your "kitty boyfriend." A super snuggly and sweet cat eclipses most men, and—with my history and fear of commitment—may also be my best prospect at the moment. No, people want politeness and pleasantries. But as a guidance counselor, Kristi deals with emotions for a living. And though she rarely joins Jill and me in socializing outside of school, we're rather tight in the building.

"Pretty good. Chilled…a lot. Happy to be back. How about you?"

"Same. Spent time with family, baking cookies, watching movies, all of that holiday magic," she says with her signature calm kindness that puts people at ease. Kristi's main character flaw? Her love of running. Always trying to get other people to run with you is not welcome or cute. I wouldn't run unless zombies were chasing me, and even then, after a block, I'd probably relent and offer myself up as a tasty kosher snack.

"Ready for your new student?"

Here's the thing about getting new students in the middle of the school year: it's always a crapshoot. Families moving their children during the school year are usually experiencing some sort of significant life change. A new job, marriage, or divorce, whatever the circumstances, you can bet it will impact the student in a way sure to upset the microcosm of serenity I've carefully curated since September. Steadying myself with another deep breath, I remind myself that, returning from vacation, revisiting rules and routines happens organically. This will lessen the impact of the wildcard about to be dealt in.

"I think so," I say, patting the stack of items to prepare for her in the next hour.

I glance at the neon green sticky note on top of the pile containing the little information I have about her until her paperwork arrives.

"Well, remember, we have the parent welcome meeting at seven forty-five."

"Oh right, I better get to it," I say, standing and moving into action.

Of course I remember. How could I not? Coming back from break, reentering the atmosphere, a new student, and a meeting to kick off the day, you remember such things when you're already anxious about returning. I've mastered overthinking, and my body finds bolting awake in the middle of the night the perfect time to hone my expertise. A whole night's sleep? Why rest when my mind can ping-pong about multiple topics and increase my bubbling anxiety simultaneously? I've taken to grabbing Gonzo, waking him from his peaceful slumber, and singing to him. What do cats dream about anyway? Chasing giant mice? Swimming in lakes of creamy milk? Playing volleyball with giant balls of yarn? Typically, after a few minutes of my quiet singing, we're both back to dozing.

Rationally, my being anxious about returning to school makes no sense. The number of life skills I'm horrible at (remembering my car requires gas to function, keeping food in my apartment—and not just sweets—walking without tripping) helped confirm my ADHD diagnosis years ago. Teaching kindergarten? That's my jam, but anxiety comes so easily to me, like blinking or stumbling over my own feet. To be clear, generalized anxiety provides a soft churning of dread fueled by DNA, reaching back thousands of years to people constantly on the run and/or being persecuted. As a Jew, a pervasive low hum of anxiety is my birthright. Being closeted and bullied for being overtly fabulous in school only amplified it. Returning to work after a break shakes sprinkles on the anxiety sundae I prepare and devour daily.

"Okay, see you in a few," Kristi says, smiling and—taking my blur of activity as a hint—she vanishes.

As I look up at the clock above the door, the lipstick-red second hand glides around the numbers like a bird catching a wave of wind. With only thirty minutes to prep for the day, including finishing all the materials for my new student, I grab the sticky note from the pile of folders and labels and read her name. Illona Stone. In almost ten years of teaching, I've never encountered the name Illona. Uncapping a fat black marker, the comforting scent of paint thinner and diesel fuel takes over the room. I begin scrawling "Illona" on the stack of items, letting the aroma of the ink and the swoosh of the marker's tip on paper soothe me as I write her name. I'm not sniffing markers, but if the chemicals force my body to relax, even a little, so be it. One thing I know for sure about student placements, there are no accidents. The universe planted this little girl in my class for a reason, and I'm about to find out why.

CHAPTER TWO

"Good morning, sunshine. Welcome back!" Jean shouts, arms open for an embrace.

As I step into the mundane school office, Jean's round, cheerful face greets me with a smile. Crinkles pool around her sparkly eyes, and her collection of bracelets creates a tinkling orchestra. As our secretary and the school's point person, Jean welcomes everyone. In her sixties (nobody dares ask her actual age) and closing in on retirement, maternal love permeates everything she does. Like a teddy bear with slightly too much stuffing, she spills out of the seams of her cheery cobalt-blue romper. There's a general understanding among anyone associated with the building that Jean, and not Dr. Knorse, runs the school. I glance at my mailbox (empty, winning!) and head over to her.

I wrap my arms around her body, and she squeezes me like someone trying to get the last bit of juice out of a lemon. Her fragrance, a combination of apples and hairspray, along with melting into her soft body, is comforting. She hugs me with ferocity, giving me some much-needed love. Peeking over her shoulder, I notice the closed conference room door. The meeting attendees are awaiting my arrival. As I pull out of my hug with her, Jean reaches over and grabs a thick manila envelope.

"This came for you over break. It's from the Teacher of the Year folks," she says, beaming with pride.

"Ah, thank you." I tuck it under my arm. I knew there would be forms to fill out and more information about the process. Being in the office, I'm reminded this nomination means much more than me receiving an award, and I must focus on and prioritize it. I must ensure all my ducks are in a row. My ducks typically dance at a rave, so I've got my work cut out for me.

Jean steps toward me and whispers, "Your new student." She nods toward the gray fabric chair at the end of her desk where a girl sits. Her swinging feet don't even come close to touching the floor. Understanding she's probably more anxious than me, I mindfully approach her.

All I know about her comes from the information on that sticky note. Illona Stone is five and moved from a small school in California that I've never heard of because, well, California. Her hair almost resembles my own, if mine were much longer. Tight, dark brown curls jut out from her head in all directions in a way that frames her round, adorable face and connects us immediately. A black knit dress covered in yellow sunflowers complements her warm khaki skin. She'd probably dressed up to make a good impression, which I adore. Illona appears to be a child any teacher would be thrilled to have in class.

As often happens with parent meetings, Jean will keep an eye on Illona while I meet with her father, Dr. Knorse, and Kristi. I take a knee, so I'm on her level, and introduce myself.

"Hi there. I'm Mr. Block. I'm going to be your teacher."

I give her my best smile, one I hope lets her know that, if nothing else, I'm on her team now.

Illona looks cautious as she colors with the crayons Jean has given her. What appears to be a horse, pony, unicorn, or perhaps a dog? I've become an expert at deciphering kindergarten handwriting, but the drawings still often stump me. She looks up at me with wide eyes, trying to decide what to make of me.

"You're a boy teacher."

A statement, not a question.

"Ha, yes, I am. Did you not know you'd be having a boy teacher?"

"Uh-uh. My daddy didn't tell me."

"Well, I'm delighted you're here, and I can't wait for you to meet the class. They're going to love you. I'm going to meet with your dad for a few minutes, and then we'll head down to the classroom together. Sound good?"

Illona smiles and nods quickly and goes back to her unidentifiable drawing. Her body softens, relaxes into her chair, and she begins to hum as she colors. Teaching is part craft and part energy. For whatever reason, I have incredible kid energy. For most of my life, I had an inkling I would end up working with children in some capacity. This quality allows me to spend my days in a room full of children and enjoy myself.

I stand and slip into the conference room at the back of the office, where the other adults are waiting for me. Greeting Jean and Illona set me squarely five minutes late for the meeting. Approaching the snug conference room, I again take three deep breaths, in through the nose and out through the mouth. I don't love meetings, but they're a required part of the gig.

Stumbling into the room, I scamper to my seat. The energy in the room bubbles in a way not typical for these meetings. Squirming into my chair, I blurt, "I'm so sorry. I wanted to meet Illona. We had a lovely chat."

As I settle myself, I glance up, and my stomach drops. The stunning man from the bathroom sits next to me, peering in my direction. *Oy*.

CHAPTER THREE

I'm overcome with embarrassment, and my mouth momentarily fails to function. The times I've been rendered speechless can be counted on one hand, and most of them have to do with my face being full of cake or numb from the Novocain I needed because of all the cake. My anxiety begins to kick in because, apparently, being in the presence of this extremely handsome father muffles me.

Sitting close, the scent of fresh linen and coconut swirls in my nose, and I lick my lips at the idea of a virgin piña colada. Free from the constraints of the embarrassing bathroom situation, I study him. He's wearing a navy V-neck sweater, something soft, maybe cashmere, which I've only gawked over when shopping. The space just below his Adam's apple, a soft groove of tender skin, summons my gaze, and I imagine leaning over and licking him there.

Illona's father turns to me and attempts a smile. His face glows, all jawlines and angles, beaming brighter than the summer sun, with the smallest gap between his two front teeth. My mouth waters thinking about what I could accomplish in that tiny space with my tongue, causing my heart to race and my head to feel woozy. Emotions overtake my speaking ability, and anxiety invades my frontal lobe. Unable to stop it, the thumping bass line and light stringy synths of Cece Peniston's 1991 classic "Finally" begin playing in my head, and her voice, rich and vibrant, sings to me about meeting Mr. Right, and as I close my eyes and breathe in his intoxicating scent, I'm taken away for a beat.

"Mr. Block, Mr. Block..." Dr. Knorse says with a tinge of annoyance, grabbing my attention and prodding me from my stupor. I take another deep inhale to center myself.

If I'm attempting to make a first impression that screams, "I'm a complete dolt, and why would you entrust your child with me for seven hours a day," I'm doing a bang-up job. The problem before me, the man is unnervingly handsome. As a teacher, we get all kinds of parents, and usually, if I'm lucky, every so often, the elusive hot dad appears. Someone to make open houses, conferences, and field trips a little more interesting. It's all innocent fun, and Jill and Kristi love to tease me about them, often giggling outside my closed classroom door, peering in the window during conferences, making me blush.

"Marvin, hello, this is Mr. Stone, Illona's dad, and um..." Dr. Knorse is stammering. She never stammers nor gives any indication of being unsure of anything. She's a doctor, for god's sake! Okay, not a medical doctor, a doctor of education, but still, she insists we all call her "doctor." Only having experience with medical doctors, the kids usually think she's going to examine them and administer shots.

Handsome dads are not uncommon, but this guy? Next level. Did I see him modeling in a catalog, lying on the beach, shirt open, wind blowing the trees, sable skin sizzling in the sun? All right. I need to focus. If I weren't so taken aback myself, Dr. Knorse's squirming would bring me immense pleasure. Clearly, the arrival of this man has shaken our esteemed principal, so Kristi, currently the most levelheaded in the bunch, takes over.

"Yes, this is Mr. Stone."

"Please, call me Olan," he states. His tone suggests nonchalance, but these first words are delivered in a rich bass from his absolutely delicious mouth, causing the bottom of my stomach to drop a little. This can't be good for business.

"He and Illona just moved to Maine," Kristi says.

"Sweet," I say, only able to squeak out a single foolish word because, apparently, my brain and mouth are currently not on speaking terms.

"Thanks?" he replies.

A question to my ridiculous "sweet." His face goes flat, and between the pseudo pee disaster in the bathroom and my lack of coherent sentences, I'm clearly not winning this parent over.

A few uncomfortable moments of silence fester and it becomes clear someone needs to speak. With nobody else jumping in, I choose to be brave. Gingerly placing my hand on the table to steady myself, I take a deep breath, ready to sell myself and the school.

"Welcome. I'm sure Illona will adore our school."

I can now speak in complete sentences. This will be fine. Newly found confidence convinces me to consider him for more than a nanosecond, allowing me to examine him in more detail. Glancing up beyond his mouth, I study his hair. The natural texture creates a crown of stunning, tight coils framing his face. A sliver of sunlight from the window lands near his forehead, causing the soft spongy curls to shine. What product does he use to make it so velvety and touchable? My own Jewfro bird's nest borders on unmanageable, and I've tried almost everything I can find to tame it. As if on cue, a large ringlet plummets in front of my eyes, and I reach up to brush it aside. Studying him, attempting to comprehend Olan Stone, I wonder how a single human can be so incredibly magmatic?

He continues speaking in low dulcet tones. Words tumble out of his mouth about schools and relocating and something about Illona's mother, but it's all jumbled like the randomness of my junk drawer because his rich voice, along with those deep eyes looking right at me, leaves me feeling like a jellyfish on land.

As he talks, the women nod with such enthusiasm their heads almost bop off. He's clearly comfortable addressing a room. Questions fill my head. Why the move in the middle of the school year? Why leave the West Coast, and for Maine, of all places? Would Olan Stone let me give him a lap dance? With his daughter a part of my class now, I'm curious but also want to be respectful...so no lap dances.

"Mr. Stone," I continue.

"Please, Olan," his gaze flicks up toward the fluorescent lights, and my chest tightens.

"Um, right. Sorry, Olan, what brought you here? Not to school. We know why you're here this morning, to meet us, I meant..." I let out a feeble laugh, and it feels like pennies jangling in my throat.

Speaking. Difficult.

"Why here?" he says, rescuing me.

For once, someone besides me interjects, and I'm thankful for his assistance. Thinking it might be best for my mouth to rest for a moment, I nod.

"Illona's mother and I recently separated. We needed a change. I'm an engineer, and there are some prospects here. We've vacationed in the area, and I've heard remarkably favorable reports about the community. Most importantly, a public school with a diverse population like Pelletier Elementary, one that celebrates their students, is critical to me as well."

The more he speaks, the less uncomfortable he seems, and with his last word, Olan Stone smiles. Like a child taking their school photo, he forces his face into it by pulling his cheeks back and revealing his teeth. Displaying a luminous grin with that sexy gap, he uncovers the full magnitude of his magnetic face. It doesn't only light up the room, it illuminates any darkness obscured in the corners of my soul. Olan Stone floods my basement.

Okay, focus. He's separated. Potentially single. Clearly straight. My gaydar registers a big fat zero. He's an engineer, not a model. That might explain his to-the-point attitude. He's blessed with these stunning looks and appears to have no clue. Olan Stone is such a Daphne.

In college, I took an astronomy class because I foolishly thought learning about the solar system would be a way to fulfill a science requirement. And meet some hot nerds. Sadly, neither happened. But I did sit with Daphne, a tall, drop-dead-gorgeous brunette who may have immigrated from the Island of Themyscira. A complete sweetheart, we became friendly, helping each other understand the intricacies of star types and black holes. The more time I spent with Daphne, the more I realized just how clueless she was about her completely off-the-charts level of appearance. We'd stroll on the quad, and people's heads would snap and turn as she floated by.

"Daphne, guys are literally tripping over themselves to look at you. And some girls too."

She simply shrugged, tossed her head back—hair waving as if blown by an imaginary fan that seemed to follow her around—and giggled as if I'd said the silliest thing in the world. Olan Stone, too, appears to be blissfully unaware of precisely how hot his star is burning. It's both annoying and endearing.

Kristi attempts to focus the energy in the room. I'm grateful someone is minding the clock. Students arrive soon, and yes, Olan Stone might be incredibly handsome, but even his *punim* won't stop the school buses from delivering our cherubs.

"Mr. Stone, we're thrilled to have you and Illona here at Pelletier Elementary, and I can assure you she will be happy and successful. Mr. Block is an exemplary teacher, and he'll work to ensure her success. He would never tell you this himself, but he's been nominated for our county's Teacher of the Year," she says, and perhaps this might supersede Olan's vision of me pissing my pants.

Last October, with the utter hullabaloo of Halloween looming—with costumes and children sneaking in tempting candy for snack time—an anonymous parent nominated me for our county's Teacher of the Year. Because anxiety rules my life, the email from Dr. Knorse asking to speak to me caused my palms and pits to sweat like Niagara Falls. I racked my brain to figure out what awful thing I had done requiring her to haul me into her office on a Friday afternoon. Reading her email, I immediately felt compelled to smash my laptop against a brick wall. Why don't administrators give you an inkling or a clue about what they want to speak about? Don't they understand an email that states only, "Please come see me after school" sends teachers into a tailspin?

Tori Knorse might be our principal, but that doesn't stop most of us from seeing how downright unpredictable she can be. Some days she darts by me in the hallway without even the slightest glance, let alone a greeting. It's not uncommon to go three to four days in a row without communicating with her. Then, the next day, she treats me like a long-lost best friend from middle school, having long conversations, asking about Gonzo's favorite kitty treats (freeze-dried salmon) and what's my sauce recipe for leftover pasta (ancient Jewish secret: it's from a jar). Her moodiness confuses the hell out of me.

As I sat in her office that Friday afternoon, my leg bouncing in anticipation and her desk rattling from my leg bouncing, I wondered which Dr. Knorse I'd be presented with. On this day, she dispensed positive news, so the BFF version materialized.

"Marvin, you've been nominated for Teacher of the Year." She clapped her hands, and I swear it was the first time I'd seen her appear anything even resembling excited.

"First up, the county, so we'll focus on that. I must tell you, in addition to the honor this presents for you personally, it also creates a significant opportunity for the school."

Her brow furrowed, and she leaned forward as she spoke.

"Oh?" I asked, having no idea what she meant.

Lowering her voice, she began, "As you know, sadly, in the past few years, Pelletier Elementary hasn't received the most favorable ranking from the state. Our test scores have bruised us more than I'd like to admit, and I fear a sizeable chunk of our supplemental funding might be at stake."

She paused, and I opened my mouth to speak, but unsure what to say, nothing came out.

"If you won Teacher of the Year, even at the county level, it would shine a positive light on the important work we do here. Winning the county might help me in my bid to secure our funding, but a state win would all but guarantee it. It would be irrefutable to the powers that be. Marvin, without the funding, I'll be forced to make cuts. Cuts nobody wants. We're barely managing with the folks we have now. The school can't handle less staff. Our kids deserve it. This nomination is the golden ticket I've been praying for."

"Oh." And gulp. And holy crap. And does this make her Charlie? And me Willy Wonka? That feels completely wrong. Apparently, the knowledge of my role in securing school funding momentarily destroyed my ability to put thoughtful sentences together.

"This is good news, Marvin. Yes, there are résumés and essays to submit. A school visit and interview to schedule. Those types of things. We can figure it all out. You'll accept the nomination, correct?"

"I mean, wow. Yes, of course, I want to. I'm just concerned..."

"About what?"

"What other teachers will think. The added stress. With my anxiety and ADHD, on top of everything else. I, I, want to make sure I can handle it."

"I'll do whatever I can to help you. Marvin, the school needs you. We need this."

This wasn't simply about me winning a silly award but helping secure the school's future. If I had a lump of coal in my ass, it would be a diamond by Hanukkah.

I genuinely love teaching and consider it my passion, a calling, a reason for waking up each day. Pouring my heart and soul into my profession helped me when things fell apart with Adam. Education gives me a purpose, and the Teacher of the Year program, or TOY as we jokingly call it, could be my moment to get some recognition for all my hard work. Beyond what it would mean for the school, it may even be an opportunity to inspire and help others. Opting in was my only choice. I wanted this.

With the sharing of this news in the meeting, my face flushes crimson, and Olan Stone turns to face me. For the first time, just for a moment, he sits back and appears to settle. He rests his hand on the table only inches from mine. The closeness of our fingers sparks a small charge of energy, and instinctively I pull my hand into my lap.

"Well, congratulations, Mr. Block. You must be a stellar teacher. I appreciate you taking the time to meet with me this morning."

"Call me Marvin, please."

I attempt a feeble smile. I fear I look like a toddler learning to smile on cue for the first time. Somehow both awkward and foolish.

"Marvin, okay," he says, furrowing his eyebrows. "Illona has been through a lot of changes—the separation, the move. I'm hoping she feels welcome here."

"Mr. Stone," Dr. Knorse chimes in, "I can assure you, here at Pelletier Elementary, we will do everything in our power to ensure Illona flourishes. Mr. Block will see to it."

Oh, will I? Confession: I'll do everything in my power to ensure Illona's success, but the way Dr. Knorse guarantees the outcome rubs me the wrong way. Teachers bear the brunt of responsibility for their students, but it takes the entire school community to help students shine.

"That's fantastic to hear," Olan says as he looks from the principal to me, his eyes ping-ponging like watching a tennis match. I should probably say something now, but the peanut butter sandwich I scarfed down this morning tumbles in my belly like one of those cement-mixing trucks. This isn't the usual humming of anxiety I'm used to. This is something different, something that burns like copper and smoke and makes my insides churn.

Why am I wary? Listen, I may not be a statistician, but I know there's a direct correlation between a man's level of handsomeness and potential trouble. Personally, I am happy to be average. My dimples and the nest of dark brown curls I've learned to mostly tame and admire over the years have done me well. Experiences with devilishly attractive men have taught me the consequences of getting entangled. And gorgeous straight men are the death knell. That flag cannot be red or large enough. That scene in *Les Mis* when they're about to march to their deaths, waving a giant red flag that takes up the entire stage, that's what we're dealing with.

I begin rapidly tapping my fingernails on the underside of the table. The click-click-clicking suggests the opening bars of Dolly's "Nine to Five," but before the words rush into my head and whisk me away, Olan looks at me and cocks his head slightly like a dog hearing a strange noise. This is not Teacher of the Year behavior. Snap out of it! The image of Cher slapping me tersely flashes as sweat beads on the back of my neck.

Taking a deep breath, I collect all my resolve and attempt to gather up the energy from watching every episode of *America's Next Top Model* to smize. I want to convey to Olan that his daughter will be safe. And loved. If nothing else, I know I'll nail that. As Olan studies my face, a plump curl betrays me and jumps ship, plummeting in front of my eyes. I purse my lips together like a fish and blow a quick puff of air toward the ceiling, sending the long bouncy curl that hangs down my forehead, obscuring my right eye, swiftly back into submission. This man must think I'm the conductor of the hot mess express.

"I just met her, she's delightful, and I know she's going to acclimate nicely. I'll make sure to assign her a buddy for the next few days and give her a little extra TLC. Is there anything specific I should know about her?"

Olan Stone nods, but his furrowed brow makes me wonder if he likes what he's hearing. He faces me, lips softening, and ever so slightly, his body melts into the chair. The tiniest hint of relaxation appears to wash over him.

"Honestly, I simply want her to be happy."

"I'll do whatever I can to make that happen."

We share a small glance. The lines of concentration along his brows soften. Perhaps Olan Stone might warm up to me in time.

"I'm going to bring her down to class and get ready for the other kids to arrive," I say, glancing at my watch, hoping we can conclude this meeting of the minds.

"May I walk her down with you?"

Um, is he asking for permission? I can't imagine anyone saying no to that *punim*.

"Sure thing." I mean, a few more moments next to him won't kill me.

I stand to leave and, with all the grace of a giraffe on roller skates, trip over my chair and stumble. Thrown off balance, my arms flail for a moment, and I'm fairly certain I resemble one of those asinine inflatable tube men outside of car dealerships. As I catch myself on the table before faceplanting into his lap, my head lands inches from Olan Stone. I'm a complete klutz.

"Whoa, you all right?" He reaches for my arm, and Lord, why couldn't I have fallen a little further?

"Yup, good, totally fine, all set. Let's go!" *Oy*.

I scramble to my feet and lead us into the central area of the office. Illona spots her father, and her face lights up like a menorah on the eighth night. She leaps up and rushes over to him, slamming her forehead into his thigh and wrapping her arms around his waist.

"Daddy!"

"Mr. Block and I are going to escort you to class."

Almost arrival time, folks scramble to complete any last-minute tasks before being trapped in their rooms. Jill impatiently taps her foot at the copy machine, waiting for the out-of-date machine to finish its job. As it chugs along, making copies, Jill glances up at me and smiles. Her familiar smirk melts like a burning candle, at the sight of Olan. He's so clearly out of place in our drab school office, where everything is some awful mashup of blue and gray.

"Holy fuck," she mouths without sound.

I raise my eyebrows so high they hide behind the spirals on my forehead. I'm attempting to act natural and not like I'm less than a foot away from the most perfect specimen of a man. Not one to miss an opportunity to gawk, as the copier shakes to a stop, Jill snatches the disheveled papers, shoves them under her arm, and swiftly follows us out of the office.

As we arrive at the classroom door, I kneel down next to Illona. With her dad observing and Jill perched in her doorway staring, it feels like I'm auditioning for a role I've already been cast in.

"The other kids will be here in just a few minutes. Let's put your stuff away, and you can help me greet them. I'll introduce you to a few friends to help you settle. Sound good?"

Illona nods gently. She takes my hand and begins pulling me into the classroom.

"Well, that'll be my cue... I'll pick her up at... wait, what time?"

Oh, he's picking her up. I get to see him again. Today. My heart trips.

"Nervous dad," Olan says with a few fast blinks. "Depending on my schedule, some days it could be Cindy, our nanny. She actually lives with us. I've left her information with the office as an emergency contact."

Let's be clear, having a nanny requires a certain income level most families in our community don't have. He has a live-in nanny, and I'm having a cup of soup for lunch. And not even the top-shelf stuff, but the store-brand cup with ingredients I can't pronounce. I'm glad he can afford it. As he's a single parent, I guess Olan needs some help. Poor guy.

I turn my head to reply and get one last look at him. "Sounds good. Two forty-five is pickup. Have a wonderful day, and we'll see you later."

"Thank you," he says, extending his hand.

I put mine in his, my intent to shake, remove, and return to his child and the swarm of sprouts about to populate the classroom. Olan wraps his fingers around mine, squeezes and shakes, and my hand doesn't retract. Our eyes lock, and he finally releases my hand, a fraction longer than expected, and my face flushes, hot and airy.

Illona investigates her new classroom, grabbing a puzzle of a bumblebee riding a pony. I stand for a moment, trying to shake off the buzz from being around her father for the last twenty minutes. I'll likely be interacting with him, at least some, in the very near future. At least at pickup today. He waves and smiles at his daughter and turns to go, and my knees wobble slightly at the sight of him from behind. His dress pants grip his body as he walks, thighs and muscles flexing under the stretched fabric. That ass, so plump and perfect. Grabbable. I lick my lips and follow him closely, shaking my head. Such thoughts should not be entering my mind at this time of day. The bell rings, interrupting my daydream, and the first drips of the flood of children begin flowing down the hallways. In an attempt to escape, Olan swims upstream. Unlike the adults, none of the children are fazed by his appearance. Ah, to be five again.

Slipping over to the doorway, I plant myself, knowing I need to move, become unstuck, but also not exactly sure how to make that happen. As I glance up from my stupor, Jill still stands in her doorway, waiting to greet her minnows and staring right at me. She feverishly fans herself with both hands as if surrounded by molten lava, looks up at me, and we both cackle.

CHAPTER FOUR

Jill: Lord, that is one fine man.

Kristi: That meeting was interesting, huh?

Marvin: OMG was I horrible?

Kristi: No, I mean because we were all gobsmacked. ☺

Jill: That man can butter my biscuit any time.

Marvin: You're married.

Jill: Hey, looking is free!

Our first day back unfolds better than anticipated. Partly because I'd known my one coffee at home wouldn't suffice, and stopped for an extra cup. But also, the kids, with some reminders, remember so much. They all seem a little older, a little taller, a little more mature. A few children step up to help Illona navigate her new surroundings. In particular, Cynthia (please don't call her Cindy, thank you very much), a quiet little girl with dark brown hair that's always in elaborate braids I'm sure require enormous amounts of time and effort to achieve, takes Illona under her wing. They hold hands most of the day, and beyond the sweetness factor, Cynthia seems thrilled to have someone to show the ropes to.

At one point, I glance at the library area, and the girls are lying on the carpet reading *The Very Hungry Caterpillar*. We've read this story many times as a class. It's dear to my heart, and seeing Cynthia read every word to Illona with such verve fills me with joy. I check in with Illona numerous times, and by the time our mid-morning snack rolls around, it almost feels like she's been in our class all along.

"Teacher! Can you help open my fruit snacks?" It might take her a day or two to get my name down.

"I'm Mr. Block," I say in the kindest tone possible.

"Oh, sorry! Mr. Block, can you help me with my fruit snacks... please?"

"Of course I can. I'm going to show you how to open them yourself, so you won't need help from anyone. How's that sound?"

Her face scrunches up, and she gives me a sure-teacher-I-just-met look.

"Watch me." I take the package from her tiny hands. "To open most snacks, you can use the pinch and pull method. You pinch each side of the package." I demonstrate up close. "Pull as hard as you can." I begin to pull but stop just short of the packet ripping open. "Now you try it." I hand it back to her and begin voicing over the instructions as she tries it.

"Pinch."

She pinches.

"Now, pull."

Nothing happens.

"Pull harder, as hard as you can."

She takes a deep breath, gives it all she's got, and as if by magic, it pops open. Illona's eyes light up as if I've just shown her one of the great secrets of the universe.

"Want one?" She offers me a yellow fruit snack.

"Sure, thank you!" I pop it in my mouth as she watches me. "Oh, banana, not my favorite," I say with a rumpled face.

She lets out a genuine laugh, and hearing her giggle from her core, for the first time, only a couple of hours into our first day together, I'm reminded of the complete joy of kindergarteners. She has her father's smile, and it illuminates the room. Soon the other children join in, creating a chorus of laughter.

"Mr. Block isn't a banana fan, but I am!" Ricky shouts, making his banana into a phone and eliciting more chuckles from the room. It's my goal to model at least an openness to trying new foods and not proclaiming hate for any food in front of my students, but bananas are the one food I can't stomach. Something about the smell makes me nauseous; if I get too close to one, my gag reflex kicks in. I had taken the risk, eating the fruit snack for Illona, hoping it was lemon or pineapple, but also knowing I could stomach artificial banana flavor much easier than real ones.

In the afternoon, Illona joins Cynthia and a few others at the crafting table during Choice Time. Today, they've landed on cutting scrap construction paper and creating collages. Glancing over, I notice Illona struggling.

"Can you pass me the scissors?" I ask.

She glances at me curiously.

"The scissors. I want to help you."

Illona twists the tiny scissors in her hand, her chubby fingers wrap around the closed blade, and the handle faces out.

"Now, watch me. The key is to move the paper, not your scissors," I begin.

I wrangle my adult fingers into the child-sized scissors and slowly start cutting into the paper. As I cut, I move the paper, keeping my hand stationary to create a circle.

"See how much easier this is? Now you try."

I return the scissors to Illona. She looks up at me, confused.

"Remember, your thumb goes in the smaller hole. Here. There you go. And your other fingers in here. Now thumb up!"

Illona follows my directions methodically, and I wait for her after each step. As she cuts an irregular circle, more of a lopsided oval, her tongue pokes out of the right side of her mouth. Finishing, she proudly holds up her creation.

"Nice work." I pat her on the shoulder, and she leans her head back and grins.

Small steps. Small shifts. Patience. Building relationships with children happens in small moments.

By the time our day begins to wind down, Illona has held my hand and hugged me multiple times. It's time for her to pick a book to take home for the week, and she holds up the well-worn cover of *The Very Hungry Caterpillar*, her face beaming.

"This one."

"Oh, you've picked one of my favorites."

She simply nods and dips her smiling face into her shoulder.

Another part of the pure magic of kindergarten. Children learn very quickly. My main goal is for them to feel welcome, safe, and loved. The learning that takes place is merely icing on the cake. Relationships come first. Only then can I begin to teach them.

As we sit on the rug, I read them a silly story about dust bunnies, and we all giggle until we're interrupted by Jean reading the dismissal announcements over the intercom. Once the children taking buses depart, I line up and bring those being picked up by a family member to the back entrance. Approaching the pickup area, I spot Olan Stone immediately, standing near the back doors, waiting. His hair now hides under a Sea Dogs baseball hat, and he looks like he'd rather be getting a root canal than waiting with all these curious moms. If he's trying to distract from his looks by wearing a cap, he's failing miserably. I wonder what the pickup mothers think of him. Sure, they aren't mobbing him with platitudes, but they're definitely staring. More than a few appear to be huddled together, chattering. Illona still holds my hand as we walk, but upon seeing her father, she sprints over and wraps herself around his thick thighs. I can't say I blame her.

"Princess, did you have a good day?" The moment Olan sees his daughter, a shift takes place. He lifts her up and gathers her in his arms, and she wraps her legs around his waist, causing his burgundy fleece to ride up just enough to show a sliver of skin. Damn. There I go wanting to lick him again.

"I had so much fun! We went to Art, and I made a sculpture with clay, and we played games inside for recess because it was too cold, and I played Candy Land, and I won, and I made a new friend, and she held my hand and read me a story, and I have the book in my backpack, and everyone was so nice, especially Mr. Block."

"Wow, sounds like you had a busy day."

"She's probably going to be exhausted tonight. I know I will be." I chuckle at my own joke. Olan glances my way and gives a little grin. That *punim*. And that smile. Can I bottle it up and keep it for times I'm anxious or sad or just need a pick-me-up?

"Illona, can you share the book with your dad tonight?"

She nods quickly.

"I'll see you in the morning." I throw her a wave.

"Hey, thank you. For everything." Olan puts his hand out for a shake.

And there it is. Another chance for skin-to-skin contact. Clumsily, I wipe my hand on my pants and reach out. Our hands touch, and he wraps his long, strong fingers around my palm and squeezes just hard enough to show me he's a master at the art of the handshake.

"I truly appreciate it."

His eyes home in on mine, and I feel a warmth coming from his hand and entire body. He holds on a second or two longer than I expect, and my insides take a little tumble. I'm keenly aware of the gaggle of moms watching us, and I pull my hand away a little more abruptly than I want to.

"Okay, I will see *you* tomorrow, Illona," I interrupt, hoping he'll be back again too. "There's some paperwork in her blue folder for you." I glance up at him quickly, stealing one more look. "Some nitty-gritty information for you, all my contact info, email, and cell phone, so if you have any questions, don't hesitate to reach out. I'm here for you. The blue folder goes back and forth daily. Please check it, and I'll do the same."

Not every teacher gives out their cell number, but honestly, it avoids more problems than it causes. A simple question, concern, or issue can be addressed more quickly and easily through text than email or returning a phone call the next day. It's meant for emergencies, although what each family defines as an emergency varies. Will I heat up your child's ravioli in the teacher's room microwave at lunch? Not an emergency. In all my years doing this, I've never had anyone abuse it, but with how he's looking at me with his dark umber eyes, I almost wish he would.

"Got it, thanks again," and I swear, by all that is mighty and good in this world, Olan Stone gives me a little blink-and-you'd-miss-it wink. My pulse quickens, and I close my eyes to steady myself. How can a simple wink from this man make my insides turn to complete mush?

CHAPTER FIVE

Jill: Branch Brew after school.

Marvin: I'm exhausted. Toast.
I have TOY stuff to work on.

Jill: TOY can wait. No is not an option. 🫖

"Tell me everything. Do not leave out a single detail. I want a breath-by-breath account," Jill commands in a pointed fashion I've become accustomed to from her.

My gut wonders if she may be slightly jealous she doesn't get the opportunity to flirt with Olan herself, but she's attempting to be a good sport.

We sit in Branch Brew, a local kombucha brewery and our favorite spot because I can sip a relatively non-alcoholic kombucha while Jill gets the hard variety. I never became a steady drinker. Watching my mom struggle with her own healing and all those Al-Anon meetings as a teen quickly put a bad taste in my mouth for alcohol. When I tried a few sips in college, likening the taste to drinking warm piss, I decided right there to be sober. I've learned which local places sell kombucha, and in a pinch, at a bar, I'll grab a seltzer with lime or a local soda and be quite content. Branch Brew crafts its own kombucha and carries flavors with and without alcohol.

A cozy spot with old leather sofas and soft patchwork chairs meant to foster conversation and games, we love coming here to decompress and scrutinize men. Jill might be married to an incredibly handsome man, but, as my personal Vietnamese Yenta, one of her favorite hobbies comprises scouting guys and playing matchmaker for me. Branch Brew, a magnet for earthy Portland types we both love, proves a wonderful locale for eye candy. Today, alternative rock scorches through the speakers, and though not typically what's playing in my headphones, it attracts the right crowd and sets the mood. The whole place smells like a strange mix of vinegar and lavender, and small droplights provide an industrial atmosphere. It feels more like hanging out in a large den than a typical bar, and most importantly, it's spitting distance from the school.

"Um. Okay. And how was your day?" I say.

"Awful. Amazing. Everything in between. Molly asked when the next vacation was and made me feel like the world's most boring teacher, but then Stuart asked if he could sit in my lap during story time after lunch, so I guess it all evened out."

"You are not boring. And you do have a cuddly lap."

"Um, sure. Now tell me about Illona's dad. Now."

"He picked his daughter up, thanked me for her good first day with us, and left. Story over."

Jill's eyes squint, giving me an annoyed expression she's mastered so well. Not remotely satisfied with my CliffsNotes version of events, she pines for gory details. She slams her glass down on the low walnut table in front of us, causing a loud crack and slight spillage.

"Marvin, what did he say? How did he look? The man is a snack. Can I give a toast at your wedding? Spill it!"

"He confessed that he left his supermodel wife, moved his daughter across the country, and requested me, Marvin Block, candidate for Teacher of the Year, be her teacher because the moment he laid eyes on me, he realized he's gay and uprooting his family and moving across the country was all for me. We're engaged and the wedding's next summer. Lady Gaga is officiating. There, happy?" I give a little shrug, smile, and from my seat, take a bow.

Jill may be used to my dripping sarcasm, but she's not having any of it today.

"Marvin. I'm not fucking around here. It's not every day a man that delicious has a child in our school. Please. Tell. Me. What. Happened." Her teeth are smashed together and showing.

"He was fine. Nice. Illona had a wonderful first day, and he thanked me. He shook my hand and..." This next part, I blurt out quickly, like a confession, "I think he might have winked at me. Might have. It could have been a piece of dust in his eye, honestly. You know how filthy the school gets."

Jill doesn't speak. This is unusual. Inconceivable. For a moment, I worry she may be choking on her Beach Break hard booch. I raise my eyebrows at her in a way that means "so there" and take a sip of my pineapple kombucha.

"Okay, stop, rewind. He winked at you? What kind of wink?"

"What kind of wink? What kind of winks are there? He winked." I give her a little wink.

"Marvin, people don't wink at other people they've just met for nothing. Have you ever winked at anyone you just met if you didn't think they were at least minimally attractive? And even then, who does that? Who winks at people if you're not, I don't know, an eighty-five-year-old Jewish man making a joke? And what is he doing in Portland? And alone? What do you know about him?"

She's asking me questions in rapid-fire succession but, in her typical fashion, doesn't allow me to answer until she's truly done. The nuttiness of our first day back prevented us from eating lunch together today, and she is clearly not happy about having to wait the entire day to interrogate me. I keep nursing my drink, which is already three-quarters gone, and try to ignore her mounting energy. Sometimes Jill getting revved up triggers my anxiety, and right now, I'm about to tip.

I wait for her to pause long enough and speak. "I don't know. He's gorgeous. Stunning, for fuck's sake. You saw him. Maybe he winks at everyone. It's probably his thing. Why do we care? I'm not interested. In him. Or anyone. He's eye candy and that's it. And I'm not sure why they moved here. He mentioned vacationing here and hearing about the supportive community. I don't know. I didn't Google him." I push my hair out of my eyes and continue the motion to give a little shrug, punctuating my point.

"Wait, we're Googling him. Now."

Lord, help me.

"Jill, no, please stop."

Googling parents isn't unprecedented, but it always feels like a supreme invasion of privacy. To be fair, I know for a fact parents Google us. One year, a mom told me my entire life story, where I grew up and went to college. She knew my most-listened-to-artist on Spotify was Jennifer Lopez. It was creepy. Her knowledge of my life, that is. Not my affinity for the flawless Ms. Lopez.

"Listen, why don't we search for a guy for me on one of the apps."

Her fingers freeze on her phone, and her eyes turn up to me. My foolproof distraction works, like waving a steak in front of a hungry lion.

"Wait, really?"

"It's more, I don't know, realistic to focus on…let's say guys we know are gay and, just spitballing here, maybe don't have a child in my class."

"Marvin, you know there's no rule against dating a parent. Is it celebrated? No. Frowned upon? Perhaps."

"Dr. Knorse would...I don't even want to think about what she'd say. And with Teacher of the Year and the money the school needs... Oh, my lord. No. Just stop. Forget about it. Now find me a man," I say, dangling my phone, eager to move past this *fakakta* foolishness.

"Yes, sir," she says, clasping her hands together.

Jill smirks. She knows I detest dating apps. We simply don't see eye to eye on them. Of course, I'm the single one. I've heard enough stories, and *Dateline*'s hunky Stone Phillips should not be ignored—for his superior investigative reporting, not his chiseled jaw. If the straight-dating app-arena is a minefield, the gay-dating app-arena resembles a nuclear explosion. It simply isn't how I fancy meeting people. You can only know so much about someone from a photo and bio. No, thank you. Does this make me a unicorn in the gay community? Absolutely. But I'm happy to be branded as such. Unicorns are fabulous anyway.

Adam and I met volunteering for the local community center. He ran a queer book group. I like books and cute men who like to read. Why are nerds so damn sexy? Their glasses and big vocabulary have me babbling like a fool. At the time, I was single and more than content to live my best life alone. Being twenty-six and adorable can do that. I did, however, want the company of other queer folks. After a couple of years of rotten first dates and even worse second dates, I decided I wasn't looking for a boyfriend. In the back of my mind, I figured I'd find one when I stopped searching. And that's precisely what happened. Adam's confident energy drew me in like a moth to a flame. Or a flamer, in his case. He discussed and debated books with such ferocity, I was doomed from the start. After that first book club together, he asked for my phone number, and the rest became my personal gay soap opera.

"Give me your phone," Jill commands.

I'd rather eat an entire bunch of bananas than give her my phone.

"Give it." She puts her hand out and begins a stare down.

"Wait. Now, we're only looking. Guys on those apps only want to hook up. You know that doesn't work for me."

A combination of daddy issues, being the child of an alcoholic, and all the bad dates and attempted hookups helped me suss out that sex without a relationship isn't for me. I attempted to go out, meet guys, and have casual sex, but the quickness, the awkward morning afters, and the what was your name agains don't particularly float my boat.

Her open palm moves close to my face, and the scent of her almond hand cream reminds me I need to moisturize regularly, especially in winter.

"Phone. Now. Let's look. Looking is free!"

With the enthusiasm of a sugar addict heading to the dentist, I begrudgingly hand it over.

Quicker than me shoving a bagel and shmear into my face after fasting at Yom Kippur, Jill downloads SWISH and begins setting up my profile.

"Smile," she instructs, and before I can turn my lips into something resembling a grin, she snaps a photo.

"Wait, I wasn't ready. Take it again."

"I'll add a blurry filter. You'll look mysterious."

"I'll look like a serial killer."

"Perfect. *Dateline* can feature you. Maybe Stone will interview you."

The photo resembles a mug shot which makes me appear, at best, a criminal, if not a serial killer. Super sexy. As usual, things with Jill are moving at a breakneck speed, and I'm simply trying to keep up with her hurricane-force pace. When she sets her sights on something, an army of elephants can't stop her. I can either attempt to keep my balance and ride the wave or drown miserably.

"All right, I'm calling you Hank in case you don't want anyone knowing your personal information."

"But you just took my picture."

"It's dimly lit here, blurry, and you could have a doppelgänger."

Naturally. I shrug and nod.

"I'm putting down Pro: loves cats. Con: will snuggle his cat instead of you."

"That's scarily accurate."

"Pro: makes a mean omelet. Con: doesn't know how to make anything other than omelets."

"Hey, I can make oatmeal."

"Oatmeal isn't sexy."

"Not wrong."

"And last one... Pro: can carry a tune. Con: will burst into song in public settings."

"'Carry a tune' sounds like I'm mediocre. My voice is better than passable."

"Marvin, just because your students shower you with frivolous compliments and tell you to audition for *The Voice* doesn't mean you're amazing. They're five. They pick their noses. And eat it. Their taste is questionable at best."

"Fair."

"And we're done. Now start rating."

She returns my phone from its short hostage stint, and I start perusing candidates. Tasked with giving each one a quick thumbs-up or thumbs-down, I flick away. If the other person and I both give a thumbs-up, a match is made, and we can message and arrange a date. Supposedly, SWISH appeals to those looking to date more than quick hookups, but I'm skeptical. As I investigate the first candidate, Jill's husband, Nick, arrives, spots us, and jogs over.

A bear of a guy well over six feet tall, Nick towers over Jill. She literally has to get on her tippy-toes to kiss him. It's ridiculously cute. At their wedding, when the officiant finally said, "You may now kiss the bride," much to the delight of the guests, Jill's sister pushed a waiting chair over so Jill could hike her dress up and climb on it for the grand kiss. Even though he's huge, he manages to be gentle with her. Above all else, Nick is a complete *mensch*.

"Hey, babe." Nick sits and kisses the top of her head. "Marvin." He holds his fist out for a bump.

"What? No kiss for me?" I ask.

These dude-bro greetings aren't my cup of tea, but I know Nick's intentions come from the right place. This man asked me to cut in during the first dance at their wedding because "you dance much better than me." And he's not wrong. Of course, a duck with two left feet would dance better than poor, rhythmically challenged Nick. He may be a man of few words, but he's never been anything but warm and sweet to me.

"We're trying to find Marvin a boyfriend."

It never fails to tickle me how Nick jumps right in to join in her shenanigans, even if those shenanigans involve attempting to set up man-on-man action. Unfortunately, in my experience, most straight guys aren't as comfortable and confident as Nick in their sexuality. With Shania Twain featuring prominently on his Spotify year in review, you know he's more than okay.

"Are there any single dads you could date?" Nick asks.

"Stop!" I put my hand up, halting Jill from rehashing the preposterous idea of Olan Stone.

"Nick-Nick, we're looking on SWISH because Marvin isn't interested in any single, extremely handsome dads. Even if the dad of his new student is a total snack."

"A snack, eh? More of a snack than me?" He raises his eyebrows and looks both silly and charming.

"Buddy, you're not a snack. You're a complete meal," I say because flirting with Jill's gorgeous husband scratches my I'm-lonely-but-don't-want-the-drama-of-dating itch.

Nick's eyes go sideways. I can almost see a lightbulb pop over his head.

"Marvin, if he's so hot, you should date him."

"Yes, because hotness supersedes everything when it comes to dating potential."

I point to my phone in an attempt to distract them and divert their attention.

"Look, this guy seems nice enough?"

The guy I'm looking at, white with a shaved head and a thick chestnut beard, appears kind enough. There's no doubt he's handsome. Jill grabs the phone out of my hands.

"Let me see. Vincent M. Sexy bald head. Green eyes, wait, maybe they're hazel. Okay, let's see. Pro: can fall asleep anywhere. Con: will fall asleep anywhere."

"Sure, having a guy fall asleep on me during a date will do wonders for my self-esteem."

"Wait. Pro: loves trying new foods. Con: will eat off your plate."

"Oh no, that's a deal-breaker for me. I do not share food well. You know that."

"This is true. You slapped my hand away that one time I tried to take a crab rangoon. Just make sure you order a lot."

"Um, okay."

As I was growing up, my mom's drinking made it hard for her to keep a steady job. We weren't well off, and food was sometimes scarce. School lunches saved my scrawny ass for much of my youth. In addition to a host of other issues from my childhood, I do not fancy sharing food.

"Hold on, hold on. Last one. Pro: loves caring for fish. Con: allergic to cats and dogs."

"Gonzo." I put both hands up in my best no-way-no-how-deal-breaker shrug.

Jill knows any potential Romeo for me has to not only tolerate Gonzo but love and appreciate him for all his fluffy, silly, wonderfulness. When we adopted Gonzo four years ago, Adam was unaware he was allergic. He took allergy medicine to survive, and we kept Gonzo out of the bedroom at all times, which I detested. My baby kitty would sleep outside the bedroom door and just wait for us to emerge. Sometimes, when I got up in the middle of the night to pee, I'd sneak out and sleep the rest of the night on the couch so we could snuggle. Adam's body's disdain for Gonzo should have been a hint at our incompatibility. He also loved horror movies. And college football. The signs were everywhere if I'd only noticed them. The night Adam moved out, I opened the bedroom door so my snuggle buddy could cuddle with me and never looked back.

"One word. Claritin. Marvin, he's cute. Just give him a chance. Or, we can see what happens with Olan Stone."

"Fine, thumbs up!" I slide my finger across the screen, creating a satisfying bloop sound.

"Oh, this is kind of fun. It feels like a video game."

I stop once Vincent M. receives my approval. One potential suitor is enough. Maybe if I'm lucky, he'll give me a thumbs-down, and there will be no match, ending this charade. I know Jill and Nick are trying to help. They want me to have what they have. Do I want that? Sometimes, I think so. But Lord, men can be horrible. Adam was horrible. My dad was horrible. Focusing on work and putting my energy there fulfills me. Plus, it provides a lovely distraction. And the kids need me. Heck, the entire school needs me. Right now, flirting with Nick feels much safer, and there's no risk of rejection because, well, he's straight and married to my best friend.

"A video game? Like Mario Kart?" Nick asks.

Jill and I both look at him, look at each other, and crack up. The kind of laughter where we throw our heads back and cackle until tears stream from our eyes. Sitting here laughing with Jill, watching Nick's confused face through wet eyes, I can't help but wonder, with friends like them who fill my heart and make me feel completely adored, who needs the drama that accompanies a boyfriend?

CHAPTER SIX

Olan: Good Morning Mr. Block. This is Illona's dad. I'm so sorry to bother you before school. Illona insists on bringing her stuffed kitty Noelle to school. I told her she had to stay home but she's causing a fuss and I'm at my wit's end. Is this something that's allowed?

Marvin: Of course she can bring Noelle to school. No worries at all.

Olan: Thank you! You're a lifesaver.

Marvin: Wait. It's not a stuffed life-size tiger is it?

Olan: Ha! No, it's small and will fit in her backpack.

Marvin: Awesome. Tell her I can't wait to meet Noelle.

Olan: 😊

"This is Noelle." Illona stands in front of me, her hair pulled back into two ornate braids today, and if her dad did that, color me impressed. Her arms are outstretched, and she holds her stuffed cat. The cat isn't as small as I'd hoped, about the size of a real cat if it had been fed four times a day and slept at all times except when eating, which is pretty much how Gonzo rolls. Illona's fingers grab her cat with such force that, if Noelle were real, she would be squirming with all her might to get away.

"Oh, how lovely to meet you, Noelle. She looks a little like my cat, Gonzo. Although he's more black with some white, and she's more white with some black. Why don't you put Noelle at your seat to keep her safe? Sound good?"

Illona nods. I want to be flexible with the needs of students but also know the potential distraction a stuffy from home can cause for the class. And if letting her bring Noelle wins me a few brownie points with her father, oh well. The other children understand Illona needs time to acclimate and might need some extra attention and comfort, but a distraction is a distraction regardless.

The day turns out to be a typical Friday. A sense of needing a break, a rest, or at least the weekend off always arrives on Fridays. The children's energy soars, my tank nears empty, and I have a date with this Vincent M. fella. A few days ago, he messaged to arrange our meeting.

> Vincent M.: Hank, hello! I was hoping we could meet for dinner this weekend. How about Friday?

> Marvin: Hey there. Actually my name is Marvin. My friend thought I should use a fake name in case you're a murderer.

> Vincent M.: Smart move.

> Marvin: Wait. You're not a murderer are you?

> Vincent M.: Well if I am you've just blown your cover.

> Marvin: Crap. Well I suppose I should eat something before my demise. Do you have a place in mind for my last supper?

Vincent M.: I'm putty in your hands.

Marvin: How about The Purple Giraffe on Main at six?

Vincent M.: Awesome! Can't wait to meet you in person.

Vincent seems nice enough, but I am, to be quite honest, dreading it. I have this problem where I vacillate between wanting a healthy, loving relationship and wanting to become a professional hermit. Putting so much of myself into my work flat-out exhausts me. I love my job, but being on your feet, attending to the needs of a class of kindergarteners, and being "on" all day sucks me dry. And while fatigue plays its part, I'm fairly certain the delightful combo of childhood trauma and anxiety deserves most of the credit. What I actually want to do is go home, order a large pizza for myself, put on pajamas, and be in bed shoving pizza in my face and watching Netflix with Gonzo by seven.

At lunch, Jill and I gather around a small table in her classroom to eat. The teachers' room, one of the least inviting rooms in the school, mostly gets used for the microwave. And why people think reheating leftover fish in the public teachers' room microwave falls into the acceptable category eludes me. We typically retreat to one of our classrooms to eat, which allows some respite from the general school population and, with the classroom door shut, more adult conversations. Jill's low-calorie frozen meal appears about as appetizing as a cardboard sandwich. I poke at my dry leftover spaghetti with a fork.

"So, where's the date? What time? What are you going to wear? Tell me."

"You're clearly more excited about this date than me. Maybe you should go instead?"

Jill rolls her eyes and puts her hands out in a "so, tell me" pose.

"We're going to The Purple Giraffe for dinner at six o'clock because

I hope to be home in my pajamas by eight, and I'm wearing this." I gesture to my outfit.

"Marvin, you're wearing a T-shirt that says Book Nerd, jeans, and sneakers. Ratty sneakers. Even I know this does not qualify as a date outfit."

"Well, this is what he's getting."

My phone, which sits on the table, dings with a message alert.

> Olan: Hello Mr. Block. Illona's nanny Cindy Rodriguez will pick her up today. If you need anything else from me please let me know. Thank you!

Swallowing hard, I quickly give his message a thumbs-up and put my phone in my pocket.

"Who was that? Vincent? Excited for the date?"

"No, it was Illona's dad letting me know the nanny will pick her up today."

"Oh, of course, he has a nanny. I bet she's young, gorgeous, and they're all over each other when Illona's at school."

My chest tightens at the thought of Olan canoodling with his nanny. Why the hell do I care?

"First, you had him flirting with me, and now he's having a torrid affair with his female nanny?"

"No, you're marrying this Vincent guy. Olan can have the nanny."

"Lord help me." I scoop my plastic container up and bring it over to the classroom sink to rinse. I slosh water around the container, give it a few sturdy shakes, and use a paper towel to dry it off. My mind wanders to Olan. He's texting slightly more than I'd expect. Are we becoming friends? Being friends with an attractive single straight man is so out of my wheelhouse I'm not sure I'd know how to handle it. Literally, the only straight man I consider a friend is Nick, and that's because he's attached to Jill. Why does he keep sending me those damn winky face emojis? What's that about?

"All right, friends, we have a few minutes before the buses are called; let's share our weekend plans!"

You learn to start early when you have to wrangle twenty kindergarteners into full winter gear and backpacks and have them ready to go on time. On the flip side, sometimes, not often, miracles do happen; they actually focus and finish quicker than you anticipated and planned for, leaving you a few extra minutes. I instruct them to make a circle on our brightly colored rug so we can share a little about our weekend plans.

Here's what you need to know about asking five-year-olds to share their thoughts, ideas, or plans. You simply never know what you're going to get, but it will most likely be random, confusing, inappropriate, or some combination of the three.

To help move things along, I give a sentence stem and example.

"Who would like to go first? If you have plans, you can share that, and if you don't have any plans, you can share something you hope to do. It might sound something like this... this weekend, I hope to have fun with friends."

I nod at Ricky, sitting next to me, to begin.

"This weekend, I'm hoping the tooth fairy comes!" He whistles through his missing front tooth.

"This weekend, I'm going to the park with my cousins." Kevin lives next door to his cousins, who are often part of his outings.

"This weekend, I'm going to Disney." Jessica, a sweet girl with brunette pigtails, wants desperately to go to Disney and shares this often, sometimes telling us on Monday mornings that she'd been to Disney over the weekend. There's an unspoken understanding among the class to simply smile and nod at Jessica.

"This weekend, I'm going to play with my puppy."

"This weekend, I'm going to make a snowman."

"This weekend, Cindy is taking me shopping," Illona shares.

"Who's Cindy?" Kevin asks.

"My nanny."

"What's a nanny?" Ricky wonders.

"She lives with us and watches me and helps my dad. She's amazing."

"So, like a babysitter who lives with you?" Kevin again.

"Yes," Illona says.

I nod to Charlie to continue.

"This weekend, I'm going to blow bubbles in the bath," Charlie says.

Some giggles at the mere mention of Charlie in the bathtub gurgle up, and finally, the announcements blare, saving me from the simmering mayhem.

"Bus students, please head to the hallway!" Jean's voice booms.

Our dismissal routine begins. Children taking the bus line up to be gathered quickly by Kristi. Popping her head into the room, she gives me a quick thumbs-up, and my line follows her like she's the pied piper. It always amazes me to witness lines of children moving throughout the school. Where else in the world do we move in intricate lines, weaving in and out of places in a (somewhat) orderly fashion? Oh, wait, prison.

With the bus children gone, three children wait with me. Kevin and Sophia go to an after-school science program. Once in line, Illona pokes my stomach to get my attention.

"Mr. Block, remember I'm getting picked up by my nanny, Cindy, today."

"That's right. Your dad sent me a message earlier."

Of course I remember. Hoping to catch a glimpse of Olan at pickup and interact with him has become part of my daily routine. Instead, today I'll scope out Illona's nanny. Secretly, I'm hoping she's more of a Mary Poppins than Fran Drescher. Illona mentions "Cindy, my nanny," often but hasn't spilled any clues about her appearance.

"Teachers, please walk pickups to the back door."

"Ready?" I put my hand out, and Illona latches on.

As we stroll down the hallway together, past the book display the librarian curated with books about snow, snow animals, and snowy stories, Illona tilts her head up toward me.

"Mr. Block, do you have a wife?" My eyes bulge slightly at her question. "Or a husband?" I wasn't expecting that either, and my eyes glisten.

Being out to my students has been a journey. When I began teaching, I was petrified of anyone finding out. I'm not exactly sure what I was so afraid of, but the potential ramifications of being a queer male teaching kindergarten haunted me. As Adam and I became serious, I slowly began including him in my conversations. We weren't married, and I hate the term "boyfriend" (we weren't twelve) or "partner" (we weren't opening a law firm together). I simply just spoke about him in a matter-of-fact way. My students and their families knew I was with Adam. They knew we lived together, and he was my "person." Once that changed, unable to simply mention a significant other in passing and use him and our relationship as my proclamation, explaining I'm gay became more complicated. But I'm always honest if children ask about my personal life.

"Oh no, I'm not married. But someday, maybe."

"Do you want a wife or a husband?"

Persistence. I respect that.

"A husband."

Illona's soft smile tells me this isn't earth-shattering news to her. And that has been my experience with almost all children. They simply do not care about anything other than the happiness of their teacher. If only all society felt the same. This explains part of why I love working with littles. They truly have beautiful, open hearts.

As we corner the back hallway where pickups happen, Dr. Knorse stands at the long folding table with a binder opened for signing out children. She doesn't always help with dismissal. She is, as Jill and I liked to joke, extremely busy and important. Truthfully, she is busy and important. In my nine years of teaching, one thing I've learned, being a principal has absolutely no allure to me. It seems like Dr. Knorse spends most of her time dealing with unruly children, disgruntled parents, and problematic teachers. Even with their snotty noses, loose teeth, and questionable hygiene, I'm much happier in the classroom with my little charges.

As we get closer to the table, Dr. Knorse spots us.

"Mr. Block, Illona can wait here. You're free to go."

Um, as much as I'm ready to bolt home, there's no way I'm leaving without putting eyes on Illona's nanny because, well, I'm curious as hell and who wouldn't be? And Jill's comments have gotten to me, clearly, so here I am, on a Friday afternoon. I should be zooming out of here and thinking about my date with a guy named Vincent M. Instead, I linger to meet Illona's nanny. Does Jill unnecessarily wait with her pickups as well? Of course.

Not knowing what Cindy looks like, I wait for Illona's cue. She drops my hand and shouts, "Cindy!" and I know the eagle has landed.

How can I best describe Cindy Rodriguez?

To be blunt, she's a fucking bombshell. A total *shaineh maidel*. Cindy wears jeans and a simple beige wool coat, the type of outfit that would appear casual on most people but on her, looks like something from a catalog photo shoot. Long brown hair cascades down her back and frames her face and ample physique. As she approaches the table, the smell of apple blossoms washes over the space. As she speaks, her face simply radiates beauty. Clearly, this vision takes care of more than Illona's needs at home. Fantastic.

"Hi, I'm Cindy Rodriguez, and I'm here to pick up Illona Stone from Mr. Block's class. Her dad said he sent a message to him." Her voice comes out delicate and fragrant.

Dr. Knorse begins looking through papers for a note, which of course, Olan did not send because he texted me directly. I advance toward the table to sort this out.

"Hi, I'm Marvin Block, Illona's teacher. Yes, Illona's dad sent me a message."

"But we need a written note." Dr. Knorse, ever the rule follower.

Olan signed his permission for Cindy to pick up Illona on the first day he came in to meet with us, but the school requires a note if there's a change from the usual person. Olan's text, along with his original consent, suffices, but now I need to show Dr. Knorse the message.

I pull out my phone and rush to make sure only the message about Cindy appears on my screen. Cindy's face scrunches up in confusion at the temporary holdup. Funny thing, even with her confusion, she glows as if ready for a photo shoot. I want to hate her, but the damn aroma of apples ushers my stomach to memories of pie.

"Her dad messaged me earlier today," I say, holding my phone up.

"Oh, well, that's all we needed. Have a good weekend, Illona." Dr. Knorse studies my phone and attempts a smile. She never wants families to be out of favor with her.

I give Illona a little nod and release her grip. She joyfully skips over and grabs Cindy's hand. As they walk out, I can't help but think about all the hands Illona's held today and how in some cosmic way, she ties us all together.

CHAPTER SEVEN

> Olan: Mr. Block, thank you again for understanding about Noelle. Illona was all smiles. I truly appreciate it. And you. Have a great weekend.

Standing outside The Purple Giraffe, waiting for Vincent M., I send up a short prayer; Lord, I hope he at least resembles his profile photo. Not because I am particularly lusting after that picture, but I've read horror stories of meeting someone online only to have a completely different person show up to the actual date. Honestly, I'm uncertain how I would handle such an encounter. *Um, well, hello, you, um, look nothing like your photo. Let's have some overpriced food together.*

Of course, who am I to judge? My profile picture looks like it was taken from twenty feet away, in a dark room, with Vaseline spread on the lens. My rationale for allowing Jill to use that horrible picture—after meeting me in person, I'll present as an upgrade.

Feeling anxious and restless, I fidget with my phone. Rereading that text from Olan Stone and not replying. I'm fairly certain his text doesn't require an answer, but also not sure if ignoring it would be rude. Being impolite to a handsome man cannot be tolerated. He texts me regularly at this point, at least every few days, which isn't entirely uncommon at the beginning of the school year or for a new student's parent. I'm also starting to wonder if he has any friends locally. It's not my business to know or care, but the amount of communication makes me curious. Does he want to be my friend?

Being friends with parents of students isn't something I usually entertain, but other teachers do it all the time. Many teachers, especially those with children of their own, often socialize with families in the community outside of school. It isn't beyond the realm of possibility. But I honestly can't imagine why Olan Stone would want to be my friend. He knows nothing about me beyond my role as his daughter's kindergarten teacher.

"Marvin?"

As if on cue to save me from perseverating, Vincent M. strolls up. Thankfully, he looks exactly like his profile photo. With a shiny shaved head, Vincent gives me serious Mr. Clean vibes. It's actually quite sexy. Scrub away, sir. His green eyes sparkle when he spots me, and I could bounce a nickel off that harsh jawline. A lovely, trimmed beard adds to his handsomeness, and I'm not mad about it. He wears a long, caramel-colored wool coat, fuzzy in a way that makes me want to rub it a little. Would that be awkward? Probably. He bounces up to me with a wide grin and a few solid neck rolls.

"Vincent? Nice to meet you." I put my hand out for a shake. He takes it and pulls me into a hug. All right, he's squeezing me, which I'm not upset about either. He smells like a mixture of wood and oil, so come on, baby, light my fire. He's slightly larger than me, probably just over six feet tall, and being wrapped up in the woolly arms of his coat almost melts my icy heart. As I pull away, our faces get close enough for me to catch a whiff of the wintergreen mint he's sucking on. A slight omen, as wintergreen, much like banana, makes me nauseous.

It may sound strange, but if I were stranded on a desert island and the only way off was to suck on a wintergreen mint, I'd have to consider spending my life alone on the island. Maybe a hunky merman would wash up and rescue me. Or at least sing to be part of my world. Something about the smell, the lilting taste of wintergreen, does not jibe with the olfactory neurons in my brain. If Vincent M. hopes for any kissing action, we'll need to discuss his propensity for wintergreen.

"I'm so sorry about the fake name thing. My friend thought it would be funny," I say.

"No worries, I get it. It's a circus out here. Shall we?" He opens the door, and we head in.

A simple place, The Purple Giraffe fuses two of my favorite cuisines: Asian and Mexican. Walking in, I'm hit with a mix of spices I can't quite put my finger on, but it's like the best of both cuisines mixing and swirling in the air until they hit your nostrils with a tease of what's to come. People chat, and a low murmuring permeates, punctuated by clinking silverware. I'm not sure where the name came from. As far as I know, there are no purple giraffes in the wild, but it makes for an interesting logo design. The inside of the restaurant is ample, if not large. There are probably three too many tables smooshed into the space to make room for as many customers as possible, and everything has tones of brown and tan, with purple accents on everything from seat cushions to palm tree wall decals. Vincent chats with the hostess, a woman with jet-black hair and purple highlights (naturally), and I find myself drawn to peek at my phone and the message from Olan Stone. Again.

"Right this way." She motions us toward a small table near the window. I fumble quickly to pocket my phone, gently wrapping my fingers around the warm screen in my pants. Vincent hangs his coat on the back of his chair and sits across from me, looking up, hope in his eyes, as I touch my phone. I remove my hand from my pocket, take my jacket off, place it on the back of my chair, and sit. Deep breaths, focus.

"Have you been here? The food is amazing. This is one of my favorite places to get takeout. They have this burrito with bibimbap sauce that I order without fail." My stomach growls in anticipation.

"This is my first time, but I love trying new foods."

"Right, you had that listed on your profile."

"Oh yeah, those are silly, but you know, we can't all only rely on our cute profile pic to sell us," he teases. Okay, Vincent, I see you.

I offer him a small smile as my ears turn pink behind my mop of hair. So far, this isn't a horrible disaster. Vincent is attractive and sweet enough, and my red flag radar isn't wildly beeping. Wintergreen mints aside, Vincent presents as a lovely man. Of course, the night is young, and there's a reason I stopped dating. I'll be friendly but cautious.

The server approaches. She's young, perhaps a college student, with a crisp white shirt and long purple apron. She's pulled her hair back into a tight, high ponytail and has a patient face. Can she tell we're on a first date?

"Hello, welcome. I'm Val. Can I get you any drinks?"

Vincent nods at me to order.

"Thanks, I'd love a ginger ale, please."

She looks at Vincent.

"Sure, let's see, I'll have a glass of the Merlot. That okay?" He looks at me, eyebrows raised.

"Sure." I smile.

"I'll grab those and come back for your food order in a minute," Val says and turns to leave.

"Oh, excuse me," Vincent says to her. "Would you mind bringing some extra napkins?"

"Oh, sure thing." She looks confused. We literally haven't ordered anything to eat yet. We each have a cloth napkin wrapping our table service. Vincent places his on his lap, and well, why more napkins?

"Tell me about yourself. You're a teacher, right?"

Here we go. Whenever I report I teach kindergarten, reactions usually vacillate somewhere between "that's so cute" and "I could never do that." For the record, yes, the children are extremely precious, but teaching kindergarten is anything but cute. It's challenging and exhausting. There are days I wonder why I keep coming back. But I also find it extremely rewarding, and the idea of inspiring other teachers with the Teacher of the Year program excites me. My stomach pinches, remembering how much Dr. Knorse and the entire school community need this.

"Yeah, I teach kindergarten." I brace for his reply.

"Oh wow, that must be rewarding."

Not cute? I'm almost disappointed.

"Yeah, it is," I start. Val returns to our table with our drinks and two extra napkins. She places our drinks on the table and hands the napkins to Vincent. He stacks them neatly near the edge of the table. What order requires three napkins? I glance at the menu, not to figure out what I want because I will always order the bibimbap burrito forever and ever amen, but to try and discern what might require such a plethora of napkins.

"What about you? What do you do?" Safe conversation ahead.

"I work for a statistical software company," he says, and my mind races to find a connection.

"I took a statistics class in college. It was education stats, but, well, it was incredibly hard. It was actually the one class I struggled with."

"You probably could've used our software to help," he says, his lips curling up slightly. I give him a little chuckle for his effort. He's cute.

"So, how did you land in kindergarten?"

"When I did my student teaching in college, I was placed in a kindergarten class. At first, I was petrified. They were so tiny! But I had a phenomenal mentor teacher who showed me how much fun they can be. When I graduated, it was my first job offer, and well, nine years later, this is a little embarrassing, but I've been nominated for the county's Teacher of the Year, so I must be doing something right."

"Oh, Marvin, wow, that's amazing! Congratulations, you must be incredibly proud."

"Yeah, it was a surprise. The nomination came from a parent, which means a lot to me. I'll find out about the county results at the end of the month, so just a few more weeks."

"That's amazing. I bet your students adore you." He smiles in a flirty way, and well, Vincent M. is ticking some boxes for me. I've avoided dating for so long, and since "pathetic hermit" is not a title I aspire to, at some point I need to dip my toe back into the germ-filled dating pool.

Val comes back to take our order. I order the bibimbap burrito because, if nothing else, I'm reliable, and Vincent orders a bulgogi taco salad…and more napkins. I start to worry about the number of napkins he's hoarding. Val makes a face like she's having the same fear and goes to put our order in and presumably jokes with the rest of the staff about the guy stockpiling every napkin in the restaurant.

The temptation to ask him about the extra napkins festers, and I spy my first clue. At the conclusion of each sip of his wine, Vincent takes the napkin from the top of his fresh pile, wipes his face with it, folds it neatly, and discards it to a new stack he's started on the opposite side of the table. He takes another sip a few moments later and uses a fresh napkin to wipe his mouth and discards the napkin to the "used" pile. He's very organized, I'll give him that.

"Well, yes, I like to think they enjoy having me as their teacher."

"And what about your family?" he asks. My job discussed, it was either going to be family or past relationships, and honestly, I'm not sure which I'd prefer.

"Well, it's really just my mom. She's in Phoenix, so we don't see each other too often, which I'm okay with. Our relationship falls into the complicated category." I lift my ginger ale to toast.

Picture the stereotypical overbearing Jewish mother. Falling over herself to spoil and dote on her children. My mother threw that idea out with her sobriety when my father left. Twenty minutes after meeting him, I'm not ready to out her as a recovering alcoholic to Vincent.

"Are you okay if I order another?" Vincent raises his empty glass.

"Oh yeah, it's fine. I mean, as long as you don't get hammered."

"No worries there." He picks his glass up, finishes the remnants, sets it down, and, for god's sake, takes a fresh napkin to wipe his mouth. At this point, it's clear that Vincent will not reuse a napkin once it's touched his face, and I can't fathom why. The napkins are large and soft, and I'm confident the single napkin lying in my lap will get me through a rather messy bibimbap burrito.

"I'll take another." He lifts his empty glass.

On cue, my phone begins to vibrate. I didn't ask Jill to call and bail me out with an intricate lie about some horrible tragic emergency demanding my immediate attention, so I quickly yank my phone out.

"Everything okay?"

I glance at the screen and see my mother's face staring up at me.

"Yeah, just my mom. I'll call her back later. She gets confused with the time difference and tends to call late."

Val delivers Vincent's drink and our food, and anticipating Vincent's request, she places a stack of napkins on the table before he can ask. At this point, he must have seven or eight on his clean pile, which, if his one sip or bite per wipe holds, will probably not be enough for the meal. Watching him take the first sips of his new glass of wine, a whirling sensation kicks up in my stomach. My mother's drink of choice was red wine. Any red wine. The deep smell of fermented grapes sneaks into my nose, making my head dizzy. As Vincent manages his napkins, the precision and clarity with which he uses, folds, and stacks them might provide some curious entertainment for some but sparks my already festering anxiety. I'm sensing the acceleration of my heart rate and slight lightheadedness coming on. Dismissing myself to regroup seems like my best course of action.

"Excuse me, I need to hit the restroom," I say and quickly make a beeline for the bathroom, leaving Vincent to straighten his clean pile of napkins.

Once I lock the bathroom door, I sit on the closed toilet seat and put my head between my legs to get the blood flowing to my brain. Investigating the cleanliness of the bathroom floor, I close my eyes and begin taking deep breaths. This almost always works within a few minutes. As I'm parked on the toilet, trying to center myself, the Caribbean beats of Rihanna's early bop "SOS" blare in my head, and I nod slowly between my knees. The music carries me away to the islands, swaying palm trees, white sandy beaches, cool salty breezes, and, oh look, a shirtless cabana boy bringing me chips and guacamole.

A few moments of Rihanna's rich, unique voice soothing me and I'm almost ready to return. How long have I been sitting here? It could have been two minutes or twenty, I'm not certain. Surely, Vincent M. has used every available napkin in the place by now. He also probably thinks I have explosive diarrhea. Lovely.

With that thought, I shake my head to halt Rihanna, splash some cool water on my face, and glance at the last text from Olan.

Trying not to overthink, I tap out a reply.

> Marvin: You're welcome. Honestly, it's my pleasure. Illona is a complete delight. And please call me Marvin. 😊

His text was unnecessary. Sure, it was nice to let me know Illona was happy, but I could have surmised that. And he appreciates me. No, *truly* appreciates me. Olan's face. His smile. That gap between his two front teeth. His low, rich voice. It all floods into my mind. Why am I allowing Olan Stone to hijack my date with Mr. Extra Napkins?

I tuck my phone into my pants and swiftly head back to the table.

"Everything okay?" Vincent asks as I sit. He's clearly asked for and received more napkins in my absence. Val must be mortified but having just dealt with my own struggle in the bathroom, I see Vincent and his growing pile of napkins in a new light.

"When my mom called earlier, she was having a crisis. And by crisis, she couldn't figure out how to record a show. I was trying to help her. I'm sorry," I fib.

"No worries." He smiles, but I'm not sure he means it. He finishes his bite and, yup, another napkin.

"So, I hope you don't mind me asking, but I've gotta know, why all the extra napkins?" At this point, my curiosity gnaws at me like a bunny going to town on a carrot. Clearly, I have my own mental health issues, but I'm curious about how his brain works. Maybe we have more in common than I thought.

"I was wondering when you were going to ask me about that. Honestly, I just like to be clean, and well, fresh napkins help," he explains like it makes perfect sense for him to stockpile napkins like a squirrel saving nuts for winter. His honesty endears me.

"Oh, got it, cleanliness is next to godliness after all."

He smiles and it prompts me to confess.

"You know, just now, in the bathroom, I didn't need to go and wasn't talking to my mother. I just, well, sometimes I get anxious. Really anxious. I needed a second to catch my breath."

"Anxious? Because of me?" His eyes widen, and I rush to ameliorate his feelings.

"Gosh, no, not you. More this…" I motion to him, the table, the restaurant. "Being on a date. I haven't really dated much lately, and our date, combined with my anxiety and ADHD, started to overwhelm me."

"Wait, you thought this was a date? Kidding. No, I get that. Dating is hard on its own. Guys are, well, confusing. But hey, I appreciate you telling me."

He offers a sweet smile.

"You know, we're all dealing with our own stuff, and sometimes I think we try to push it down and hide it."

Vincent wipes his face, seemingly at nothing, and even with his sexy bald head, angular face and jaw, and that beard, right now he feels more like a friend than a prospective romantic partner. I realize we're definitely not going to have a repeat date, but he's a nice guy. He's been nothing but kind. Maybe the combination of his issues and mine feels like too many damn issues. Doesn't one of us need to be issue-free or at least with minimal relationship-impacting issues? I'm ready to go home to my sweet Gonzo.

As Val grabs our empty plates and Vincent's enormous pile of napkins, she asks, "Would you like to see the dessert menu?"

"No, I think we're all set," I say.

"Just the check, please," Vincent adds.

Val brings the check, and before we can discuss it, Vincent grabs the bill.

"Please, my treat, I insist."

"You're a sweet man, Vincent. Why don't you let me get the tip?"

He slides the tray over to me and I leave Val 30 percent because she's spent the last hour scouring the place for every clean napkin.

Standing outside the restaurant, I'm fairly certain Vincent starts to agree with my better-off-as-friends assessment.

"Well, it was great meeting you. And this place, I'm definitely coming back. Did you drive? Where'd you park?" he asks.

"No, I actually walked. It's just a ten-minute walk to my place."

"Can I give you a ride?"

"Oh, thanks, but I actually prefer walking after a meal, but thank you again. It really was nice meeting you."

"Are you okay with walking alone?"

"Vincent, you are a gentleman. Thank you, but yeah, I'm good. Let's keep in touch. I can always use a thoughtful friend."

I lean in for a hug, and there's an awkward moment when our faces get close, and it confirms—what I think we both feel—there's just no heat. Down there. A peck on the cheek feels right because even if Vincent isn't the right guy for me, I'm sure someone will appreciate him. All of him. Even the extra napkins.

"Good night," I say and give him a little wave and turn to walk away.

As I begin my stroll home, I pull my phone out. My heart skips a beat seeing Olan has replied to my text.

> Olan: Okay. Marvin. I hope your weekend is off to a good start.

> Marvin: Yes, heading home from dinner now. And you too. Hopefully I'll see you at pickup Monday. 😌

CHAPTER EIGHT

Olan: Illona told me "Mr. Block did his best with my hair" and man you gave it your best shot. 😊

Marvin: OMG I'm sorry. You might think teaching kindergarten I'd have learned how to braid and do ponytails. You'd be wrong. 😫

Olan: Don't be so hard on yourself. Braids and ponytails are next level tricky.

By the middle of January, Illona has been at school for a couple of weeks and the kids have bounced back to pre-December levels of routine. Illona has seamlessly become an integral member of our community. It warms my heart how she and Cynthia have become fast friends. The rest of the class welcomed her quickly and fiercely too. It reminds me of what a loving and empathetic group of children they are. Sure, there are moments I feel like I'm about to lose my shit, like when Sophia threw up all over her entire table during Writing Time. The aftermath was devastating enough I had to throw away four writing folders and all the work inside. Her table mates were not amused, but nobody wants vomit-covered stories. Even though bodily fluids are par for the course in kindergarten, it was not cute.

Besides Sophia's puking incident, the days churn on in typical kindergarten crazy fashion. Adding the Teacher of the Year requirements and deadlines into the mix only intensifies the mayhem. My essays and peer reviews were turned in last week and the county winner will be announced on the thirty-first, which is next Monday. Yikes. Having no clue what my chances are, I try my best not to overthink it, but knowing the school's staffing hangs in the balance makes it difficult.

Olan's frequent messages are a welcome distraction. The texts have gradually increased in volume, and at this point, I'm fairly confident we are more than acquaintances, if slightly less than actual friends. We may not chat on the phone or get together outside of school, but he texts daily, and I've even messaged him a few times unprompted. The cool demeanor from our first meeting has melted away to reveal a caring, thoughtful man. He's almost charming and definitely harmless.

Is having a straight, single, gorgeous man as a friend new for me? Sure, but maybe I'm evolving? Do I read too much into his messages? Duh. Being unattached and almost thirty, sometimes you have to create your own entertainment. Illona mostly centers our conversations, and I'm not worried our kinship would be viewed as inappropriate. I've checked the employee handbook. Four times. There are no rules against fraternizing with parents, let alone dating one. I'm not sure I'd even classify us as friends. Yet.

Mondays are always arduous for me to get my ass up and out the door. Today, feeling recharged from a weekend cuddling with Gonzo on the couch, I've come in ready to tackle the day with a positive attitude. The children arrive, and their sweet faces bring such joy...even on a Monday. We go through our typical routine, sharing about our weekends at Morning Meeting (Ricky made slime), and by mid-morning, we're ready for a break outside—Maine winters be damned.

Jill and I huddle on the blacktop, trying to stay toasty in the direct sun, flanked by packs of children yelling as they zoom by us. The rhythmic swoop of the swings swaying back and forth draws my attention, and I wave to Cynthia.

"The sun feels nice. It's almost warm," I say.

"Yeah, the snot in my nose isn't completely frozen solid today."

"Gross. But also, same."

"Nick and I painted our bedroom this weekend. I was getting tired of staring at the bright red accent wall he thought was a good idea."

"I told you not to let him binge *Queer Eye*. Poor guy. How did you get him to relent?"

"I told him red makes me angry and asked why he'd want me angry in the bedroom and he caved."

"Smart man."

My phone vibrates in my pants. Slipping my mitten off, I take it out to see who's texting me in the middle of the school day. Seeing Olan's name pop up prompts my heart to gallop in my chest, creating a surge of warmth against the crisp air.

> Olan: According to a little bird, your coffee is usually cold by snack time. I'm out for a meeting and dropping you off a hot refill in the office. How do you take it?

> Marvin: Thank you, that is beyond nice and also totally unnecessary.

> Olan: I insist. How do you take it?

> Marvin: Just one sugar. I'm sweet enough on my own.

> Olan: ☺

"Who was that?"

"Nobody. I mean, it's nothing."

"Does this nobody's name rhyme with Rollin'?"

Jill's face breaks into the widest grin, her eyes glistening in the direct sun.

"Maybe. Okay, yes. He's dropping a coffee off for me in the office."

"Are you kidding me? That is beyond sweet. Wait, I want one too. Text him back."

"No way. It's done. I'll share mine with you."

"A hot coffee. You realize he likes you, right?"

"Of course he likes me. I'm his daughter's teacher, and his daughter loves school. Even I can do that math."

"I think he might like you a little more than in a my-daughter's-teacher-is-fantastic way, but what do I know."

Jill's words make my stomach flip. Part of me wants her to be right, but the thought of Olan having more than friendly feelings for me also makes me incredibly anxious. I don't need to be catching feelings for anyone right now. And a parent? *Oy.* Rationally, I know there's nothing imprudent with romantic sparks between a teacher and parent, but I'm conflicted about how others might view it. Other teachers, Dr. Knorse, the TOY folks—what would they think?

"We're friends. Or becoming friends. Or friendly. Friends do nice things for each other. Like, bring each other coffee."

"Okay, Marvin. Sure. Whatever you say."

Crash! Olivia, Martha, and Taylor zipping around roaring like lions, or tigers, or maybe bears, come crashing into me with the force of three stampeding baby hippos.

"Mr. Block, we're playing tigers!" Martha yells.

Ah, so that's what tigers sound like.

"Well, tigers, it's time to line up, I'm about to blow the whistle."

My hand grabs the keys in my coat pocket and yanks them out, and I blow the whistle as the children sprint to the line. We head inside, taking the long way past the front office, so I can grab the coffee Olan's left with Jean. Spotting the familiar white cup with Olan written on it, my lips curl up thinking of him waiting in the coffee shop for it. Along with the steamy sweetness, his thoughtfulness warms my entire body to the core.

CHAPTER NINE

Olan: Illona can't stop talking about the sledding field trip. Are chaperones allowed to sled too?

Marvin: Allowed? Required. I'll be barreling down the hill myself. That's part of the fun for the kids.

Olan: Wonderful. Can't wait.

The days leading up to our field trip, the children bubble with anticipation. Tomorrow we are leaving school. On a bus. Together. There's something magical about exploring the world with your teacher and friends, and as the school day draws to an end, the anticipation of our day of fun boils to the surface.

I walk Illona down to dismissal, and a cheery, all smiles Olan appears. This gleeful version of him invites butterflies to my stomach, swirly and soaring, causing my breath to catch, but I do my best to appear unfazed.

Under his long coat, unzipped to his waist, he's wearing a color-block sweater. The fabric, shades of blue and white, clings to his chest, and for a moment I think he catches me staring. To distract myself, I avert my eyes to his hair, thankfully not hidden by a hat today.

"Princess, another good day?" Illona never fails to leap into his strong arms. She hugs him, and he squeezes her tight, the fabric on his coat stretching around his biceps.

"Mr. Block." We agreed he'll call me Marvin privately, but for now, in front of Illona, it should be Mr. Block, and it's rather adorable how he snaps the consonants. "I'll see you in the morning for the field trip." He smiles that smile, with that barely-there groove between his two front teeth behind lips so soft and plump they demand I stare, and a stunning straight male friend may be the end of me. *Oy.*

"You will. Make sure you dress for sledding," I remind him, knowing he'll look ridiculously handsome decked out in snow gear.

"Can't wait," he says, and damn him, he winks, sending my insides into melt mode. Am I supposed to wink back? I simply let out a feeble "heh."

Our annual sledding trip to Chickadee Farm brings a much-needed jolt of post-holiday-season enthusiasm. Jill's brainchild from three years ago, when she attempted to pull me out of my post-Adam breakup funk with some school-based adventure, it quickly became a winter kindergarten tradition.

"Let's take the kids sledding," she said at lunch one day.

"But we can sled on the playground."

At the time, I had no idea where this sudden urge to sled came from.

"Marvin, that's barely sledding. If we take the kids to a farm with giant, rolling hills, they can sled for an entire afternoon. Plus, there'll be hot chocolate."

"Are you using chocolate to persuade me?"

Jill opened her mouth and smiled, showing every single tooth, raised her shoulders, and squeaked, "Who me?"

Field trips present an interesting dichotomy. On the one hand, you don't have to plan or prep for the time away from school. On the other hand, the kids bring a level of energy and excitement requiring extra supervision. Losing a student is never cute. Depending on the outing and number of chaperones, groups need to be created and monitored. My favorite trip, the sledding excursion, simply involves our two classes repeatedly climbing up an enormous hill on the farm and sledding down. Mr. and Mrs. Shelton, the farm owners, serve us hot chocolate for the last twenty minutes. Easy, peasy.

Because we don't board the bus until after lunch, the morning consists of a series of vignettes where I attempt to contain the erupting exhilaration the entire class arrives with. I try to keep our routine as close to typical as possible, and during Morning Meeting, we put Sledding Field Trip on our schedule to have a concrete visual reminder of when we're actually leaving the school. The children buzz with eagerness.

Finally, Jill and I, dressed head to toe in our finest snow gear, go to the cafeteria to fetch our classes. In her pink and purple snowsuit, Jill resembles a cotton-candy-covered astronaut.

"That outfit is...a choice," I say.

"Hey, when you're barely five feet, the children's section calls. It's cheaper, and the styles are way more playful." She does a quick spin for me.

We pick the children up and they practically burst out of their snow gear, knowing we're heading for the bus. Kindergarten thrills most children on a typical day but leaving the school building with your new friends and teachers takes it to the next level of elation. We trudge outside to the purring school bus, along with the family members joining us. My eyes spot Olan right away.

Huddled with the other adults joining us, he appears to be conversing politely with three mothers—two from Jill's class I haven't met yet, and Mrs. Schroeder, Teddy's mom. He's wearing a bright blue parka, black snow pants, and heavy boots. His hair hides under a black fur-lined cap with flaps, which currently are up but can fall down to keep his ears toasty. Even though he's covered head to toe in winter gear, seeing Olan melts my frozen butter heart.

We head over to the bus, and the smell of burning diesel welcomes us as Ms. Darlene, the driver, pops open the door and perches on the entry steps, ready to squawk. Wearing what appears to be four thick flannel shirts instead of a coat, Darlene's auburn mane pokes out from a Bruins baseball cap. I've never seen her with a cigarette, but Darlene's raspy voice makes me wonder if she smokes an entire pack daily.

"All right, with the number of children and adults and the size of our bus"—she bangs the side of the bus, causing a few of the children and Teddy's mom to jump—"I need three kids or two adults to each seat," she barks.

"Kids on first. Adults, wait here for just a minute," Jill shouts.

I love it when she takes charge because it allows me to hang back for a bit. The two of us bring the children aboard and mostly let them sit wherever they like, three to a seat, as Darlene instructed. We leave three empty seats for the grown-ups, one in the back, one in the middle, and one in the front.

"Do you want the front or back?" I ask Jill as we seat the last children. We need to be on either end of the bus to monitor any issues.

"Front. I don't want to get carsick."

"Okay, fine, you grab the chaperones," I reply and take my spot in the seat closest to the back.

Entering the bus, it's clear Mrs. Schroeder, Teddy's mom, and one of the moms from Jill's class know each other from outside of school and plop down in the middle seat. The other mother from Jill's class joins her in the front of the bus, leaving Olan to trot toward the back to ride with me. The mushy pit in my stomach gurgles with anticipation as he advances.

The drive to the farm only takes fifteen minutes but being smooshed with Olan Stone into a seat meant for children seems like a mischievous turn of events from the universe. As he approaches, I do my best to make room, plastering myself against the cold metal frame of the bus, my neck inches from the frosty window.

"I guess we're bus buddies." Olan flashes a smile that doesn't quite reach his eyes.

He plops down, sending me up momentarily as I huddle near the ice-crystal-covered window. Illona, in the seat directly ahead of us, pops her head up to see her father.

"Daddy! Hi!" Her face beams.

"Hey, princess," he says softly. His deep voice is only inches from my ear, and the hair on the nape of my neck stands up.

"All right, everyone, hands inside the bus, bottoms on seats, facing forward!" Darlene's voice booms over the bus speakers, prompting Illona to spin herself back round to face the front. Olan leans forward and pats her on the back. Why is being such an attentive father so damn sexy?

The engine spits and pops, and we begin to roll toward the farm. Cocooned in our seat, Olan and I have a tiny semblance of privacy in the crowded school bus. Deep breaths.

"This your first time on a school bus in a while?" I ask.

"Probably since high school. It certainly seems more compact than I remember."

"They're not made for comfort, that's for sure."

"No, I think they're designed to transport the largest number of occupants in the safest, most cost-effective manner." He nods and scans the inside of the bus.

Olan Stone is a complete dork. A dashing dork. I'm doomed.

"I think you're right."

We drive over the bridge leading off the peninsula, taking us out of

Portland and into more rural surrounding towns. Strip malls, full of pet and cell phone stores, gradually morph into a mixture of wooded areas and farms. Eventually, nature completely takes over with only the occasional gas station and convenience store. Being a smaller city, Portland never overwhelms me, but serenity and peacefulness wash over me whenever I'm somewhere you can see all the stars in the night sky.

"You mentioned you sold your business. What exactly do you do?"

With all the pleasantries Olan and I have exchanged, I know very little about him outside of his daughter. Welcome to the getting-to-know-you portion of our adventure.

"Well, I sold my aerospace company last year."

"Aerospace, that's like…outer space?" My cheeks rise, and I give a little shrug because I have no clue.

His face bunches up, then relaxes, and he chortles. He laughs so loud that Jill, sitting in the front, stops chatting with the parent from her room and whips her head around, eyes wide.

"Not exactly. More aircraft. Turbo engine technology. Although some spacecraft utilize the same tech. So, technically it could encompass outer space. It all depends on the application and classification of travel."

As Olan speaks, my mouth becomes agape. Only slightly, but I rush to close it.

"That sounds, um, complicated."

"Let me try to clarify it. Jet engines require air. Typically, a turbine powers an air compressor. The compressor rotates, and any leftover power supplies the thrust through a propelling nozzle. It's called the Brayton thermodynamic cycle. It's how jets can fly long distances and it's the core principle behind proposed inter-solar-system space travel."

My head makes small circles, trying to catch some understanding, but I am completely lost. Little Red Riding hood in the woods lost. But make her kosher for the wolf. I grab at the base of my neck and struggle for a reply and finally say, "Olan, please don't take this the wrong way, but you are a complete nerd."

He blinks a few times and bites his lower lip. Crap, did I insult him? I jump back to rambling.

"Nerds are cool. Very cool. Everyone loves nerds. They're, they're very in. I, myself, adore nerds."

His face softens and, dear Lord help me, he puts his right arm around my shoulder and gives me some sort of macho side hug, yanking me to him. I turn toward him, and he stares back at me with bright eyes.

"Cool. I'm perfectly content being a nerd." His breath reaches mine, and his cherry ChapStick taunts me as I gape at his mouth. I want to lean over and lick his juicy lips. Get it together, Marvin.

I pull back from him and ask, "So, you sold your company. What's the plan now?"

"Well, I have funds from the acquisition. I'm pondering my next move, but I have meetings and commitments that keep me occupied. Having Cindy's help is immeasurable, but I'm trying to be more involved with Illona, too."

"That sounds smart. I mean, duh, clearly, you're smart." And I sound like a *meshugganah*.

"I've been told I'm intelligent. But thank you." Olan reaches over and pats my knee. My hand rests there, and with my mittens in my coat pocket, his hand grazes mine and there's a tiny spark of static. The bus begins to feel like a sauna. Does he understand how touching me might not be judicious?

"And clearly, I'm thrilled you put Illona at Pelletier Elementary, but do you mind if I ask, with your, um, means, why not a private school?"

"Well, the decision really was about diversity. About having her somewhere with children from all different backgrounds and cultures. I know I can't shelter her forever, but for now, it's important that she's not the only Black child in her class or school. I'm a product of public school. I know the finest educators work at public schools. Present company included."

The heat rises to my face, and I feel my ears flush hot.

"What about you? Tell me about your life outside the classroom."

"Well, there's Gonzo, my cat. I have a slightly unhealthy affection for him."

"Yes, animal relationships can provide necessary companionship. Is there anyone besides Gonzo?"

Does Olan Stone want to know my relationship status? Okay, friend.

"Oh, I'm single. Completely. Free and open," I blurt out with a grin and jazz hands.

Kevin, sitting in the seat in front of us next to Illona, pops his head up.

"Mr. Block is single. Single means one. Alone. He doesn't have a boyfriend."

My face flushes. Again.

"Yes, Kevin, single means one. Now turn around and sit, please."

Olan snickers and takes this information in, nods, and manages to wrangle his lush lips into a thin line. Should I return the question? Maybe find out more about Illona's mother. It seems like the perfectly reasonable thing to do. I take a deep breath, amping myself up.

"Two minutes away! Everyone, please make sure you collect your belongings, all of them, and stay seated until we come to a complete stop and I open the door." Darlene's blaring voice interrupts us and halts our conversation, and I'm disappointed to be leaving the bubble of the back seat.

We file out of the bus like ants heading to a picnic. The snowpack creates a dampening effect, absorbing all the sound in the area. The farm animals are all stabled because of the weather, but the smell of manure and hay wafts from the barn.

The children spend the next hour and a half traipsing up the snow-covered hill that provides the backdrop of Chickadee Farm. A narrow path created from shoveling and continued stomping helps the process of ascending the hill go smoothly. For the first half hour or so, I remain at the bottom, and the complete joy on the kids' faces as they shoot down the hill makes me bend over with laughter. The magic of winter in Maine bursts inside my torso. The small mounds of snow we fashion on our playground simply can't compete.

Among the sea of tiny faces, there's Olan, molded into his plastic sled, his solid frame allowing him to fly down with incredible momentum. I wonder if he's thinking about velocity and speed as he zips toward the bottom. I mean, it's probably a solid bet.

Jill grabs me and shouts, "Teachers' turn!" and I'm more than ready.

She slaps her sled down next to mine, and we push off simultaneously, hamming up a mock rivalry for the children.

"Okay, Mr. Block, my turn to smoke you," she snarls.

I beat Jill every year simply because I outweigh her by at least fifty pounds, but I let her make a show of it for the kids.

When everyone's hats are damp and sprinting up the hill slows to more of a saunter, Mr. and Mrs. Shelton call, "Who wants hot chocolate?"

The kids scream and scramble over to the wooden shed cleared out for this purpose and line up, waiting for their warm, sugary refreshments. They remember to hold their cardboard cups with two hands and blow gently on their cocoa before sipping, as we'd discussed that morning.

In the hubbub of toasty chocolaty delight, Zoe trips over a chunk of ice, falls into me, and my hot chocolate cascades down the front of my jacket (because, of course it would), once again leaving me looking like a complete klutz. As I stammer for assistance, Olan materializes with paper towels from the shed.

"Mr. Block, let me help you," he says, wiping the sugary mess from my jacket, and I'm simultaneously embarrassed at my clumsiness and charmed by his thoughtfulness. Even through his gloves and my thick coat and sweater, the pressure of his hands on my body sends a jolt of heat into my stomach.

"I can be so clumsy sometimes, and there's no air dryer here." I let out a feeble laugh.

"Accidents happen. Nobody's hurt. There." He takes a final swipe. "You'll want to launder this when you get home," he says, crumpling the wet paper up in his gloved hands.

"Thank you." I place a hand on my chest and confirm he's achieved the best possible result for now.

He takes a step toward me to inspect his work, brushing his hand over my chest, and it feels like a full vat of hot chocolate rushing over me, this time on purpose.

"Looks excellent," he says.

I look up to meet his gaze. Our eyes lock, holding a few moments longer than they should, especially on a field trip, and I turn to gather the children.

"Everyone, line up for the bus!" I shout, shattering the moment.

I shake my head, dismissing the thought that having Olan close to me makes my entire body weak and tingly. Clearly, my flesh and brain haven't come to an agreement about my feelings. I tell myself that having a gorgeous straight male friend is fine, but whenever he looks at me, smiles at me, or touches me, my stomach turns to mush. Remaining solely friends with Olan Stone may be a bigger challenge than I can handle.

CHAPTER TEN

The bus ride home chugs along with a new quietness. I don't cram myself toward the window, and when the bus hits a pothole, and our knees brush up against each other, a jolt of energy surges to my groin. I don't pull away, and neither does he.

"That was quite an amusement-filled afternoon," Olan says, facing forward.

"Yeah, it was fun."

"I haven't had that much merriment in a long time," he says. Who talks like this?

"I'm glad you came."

I turn to him. He faces me, pulls his lips in slightly, and nods.

"For Illona, I mean, I know she was thrilled to have you here," I say and pray he believes me.

Back at school, with only a few minutes until dismissal, Jill and I scramble to get all the children back inside, packed, and ready to go. Both Mrs. Schroeder and Olan come back to the classroom. Teddy grabs his backpack and lunchbox, his mom waves, thanks me, and takes him to the office to sign out. Olan plants himself on the rug, helping children with zipping and attempting to fit various items not designed to fit inside tiny backpacks by shoving with all his might. Watching him surrounded by children, playing whack-a-mole, trying to help each of them, I'm overtaken with a sense of affection. For my friend. We're friends. Just friends. But if he's trying to receive a good grade from me, he's exceeding the standard.

The intercom spits to life, Jean's voice announces pickups, and Kristi pokes her head in. I dispatch most of the class with her, leaving only Illona and Ricky.

"Ricky, I'll walk you down in just a minute."

I look at Olan. "You can take her and sign her out whenever you're ready. Or you can walk down with us."

"Actually, I wanted to ask you something. Would you mind if I wait here for you?"

Gulp. So, there's a reason for his lingering. As if on cue, Jill strolls by with her pickups.

"Mr. Block, I'll gladly take Ricky down for you. Come on!" she belts, putting her hand out for Ricky and smirking at me.

And it's just the three of us.

"So, my question for you..." Olan resumes.

"Shoot." I mime shooting him with my right hand in an attempt at humor, but he only stares at my hand and tilts his head.

"I'm not sure if you're available or if this is acceptable, but would you consider watching Illona Friday evening? I've kind of found myself in a pickle?"

Oh. He wants me to babysit. Visions of me lying on my stomach in a bedroom with three tween girls as the fourth and gayest member of the *Baby-Sitters Club* flash in my head. Teachers do this all the time. Sandra, the preschool teacher, works with a family regularly, and three years ago, I watched two little boys, one of whom was my student, a few times so the parents could have some date nights. But what about Cindy? Isn't the whole point of having a nanny not to need a babysitter?

"Um, sure. I mean, I think I'm free Friday night. Yeah, I could do that," I stumble out.

"Are you sure? No pressure, but you'd be a lifesaver. I wasn't sure who else to ask."

"No, really. I'd love to."

"I'll text you the address."

"Oh, I have it in her file. I mean, I can look it up," I reply, not wanting to let on how I already curiously mapped his address on my phone.

"Perfect. How about six? Does that work?"

"Yeah, I can do six."

Olan asking me to babysit confuses me. On the one hand, I'll get to explore their house and maybe scope out his bedroom once Illona goes to sleep. Not in a creepy way, in an oh-this-is-where-you-sleep way, which sounds a tad sketchy, now that I think of it. Maybe I'll skip Olan's bedroom.

I relish Illona. Yes, she's sweet and funny, but she also has a tenacity I always admire in children. She's in a new city and school, surrounded by new people, and yet each morning she skips in with a smile ready to have the best day ever. Spending a little time with her outside of school would be wonderful, but, as Illona's babysitter, I'd officially be paid for my services by Olan, and friends don't pay each other for helping each other out. I could make up an excuse and cancel, but he's clearly pressed and wouldn't ask if he didn't have to. I'll just refuse if he tries to pay me. Doing this for Olan isn't a big deal, so why should I make it one?

Checking my phone for the address, I ensure I'm in the right place and ring the bell. The house overlooks the ocean and rests in one of the most scenic spots in the city. Three stories, to take advantage of the view, there's an abundance of glass, with no shades drawn. On the top floor, what appears to be a bedroom and sitting room has the best view in the entire house. It's hard for me to imagine how much a house like this costs because I can barely pay the rent on my minuscule apartment, but I'm clearly entering a place that doesn't come cheap. These are the homes you walk by and think "how can anyone afford to live here?" And yet people do. Olan does.

"Mr. Block, come in, welcome. I'll go get Illona."

Cindy, not Olan or Illona, greets me at the door. She wears a long periwinkle dress and taupe high-heel shoes, with her hair swooped up into a messy bun that looks anything but unkempt on her. The exquisite makeup on her face is another clue about why I'm here, and my ribs grow tight with the clarity of the situation.

I step inside to wait. It's one of many houses I passed on my walk over that made me wonder who would need all this space. There must be multiple bedrooms and bathrooms upstairs. The entire downstairs is open, with a modern kitchen as the centerpiece and a living room, dining room, and den (with a large television) combined. You could fit four of my one-bedroom apartments in this downstairs space alone. Suddenly, I regret not letting Jill Google him. Between the full-time nanny and this house, I can't help but think that was no lemonade stand he sold.

Olan glides down the long stairway that's off the side of the living room. Tonight, he wears a navy cable-knit sweater, gray slacks, and deep brown loafers. His hair stands up in all the right places, and he wouldn't be out of place in any men's catalog or one of my fantasies, and oh crap, I'm staring.

"Marvin, welcome. Thank you again for doing this. I can't tell you how much we appreciate your assistance."

We. And there it is. I feel like a complete dolt. It's not like me to take friendliness for flirting, and yet here I am.

"Illona is upstairs putting her pajamas on." He approaches me with an outstretched hand. I put mine out to shake it, but he grabs it and pulls me into a handshake/bro-hug combo I have no idea how to carry out, so I let him lead. Continuing to grasp my right hand, his left wraps around my shoulder, and he pulls me in for the embrace portion of the greeting. I squirm and attempt to mirror him but end up patting his back like I'm petting a stray dog on the street. In such close proximity, all his smells, the coconut, the cherry, his skin, electrify me. Even with the awkward start, my chest expands with comfort being this close to Olan.

As I fidget away, Cindy reappears at the top of the stairs, now with Illona clasping her hand. They trot down the stairs together, never dropping hands and humming a song together until they approach the bottom and Illona spots me.

"Mr. Block! You're here!"

Before I can speak, Olan interjects, "Yes, princess, remember, Mr. Block is going to stay with you while Cindy and I go out for a few hours."

As the overplayed hip-hop duo Tag Team sing, "Whomp There It Is." With that one sentence, my fantasy of Olan sweeping me off my feet, stealing me away to a Mexican resort—where a gorgeous young waiter brings us frozen drinks but Olan comforts me with "Oh, Marvin, you're way more my type"—and we lounge by the ocean all day while I put sunscreen on his rippling back are dashed. In stereotypical fashion, the ridiculously handsome single straight dad is dating his equally stunning, on the younger side, nanny. I'm slightly embarrassed I ever thought this exact outcome wasn't inevitable, but here I am. Deep breath. Moving on.

Plucking my backpack from my shoulder and unzipping it, I reveal the goodies I smuggled in for my time with Illona.

"Illona, look what I've brought." I procure each item from my bag with a flourish as I announce it. "Popcorn...Swedish Fish...Shrinky

Dinks...and *The Very Hungry Caterpillar*. For your bedtime story! When is bedtime?" I ask Olan.

"We usually do a story at eight and then lights out," he replies.

See, I can do this. I can spend the evening with Illona while Olan and his sultry nanny go out for a romantic evening together. No problem.

As I'm bent over chatting with Illona, Cindy and Olan are watching and, honestly, looking rather chummy. The two of them are dressed to the nines, like they could be going to a concert or trendy awards show. And then there's me in a comfy hoodie, joggers, and backpack. I'm the teenager coming to babysit for the hot parents heading out for a date night. Except double the age. And the dad in this set of parents makes my insides jiggle like jelly. This is my version of hell. *Feh!*

"Well, Illona's had dinner, and it appears you've brought provisions. That was kind, Marvin. You didn't have to do that. Illona, listen to Mr. Block, have fun, and I'll see you in the morning." He lifts Illona into his arms, and I swear the fabric on his sweater lets out a little scream as he flexes to raise her. He gives her a goodnight kiss and gently puts her down while Cindy grabs their coats.

"We should be home by ten. If you need anything, just text."

"Got it." I smile and nod, trying my best to hide my awkwardness.

As they glide out the door I entered through only a few minutes ago, Olan gently puts his hand on the small of Cindy's back, turns to give me a small wave, and pulls the door shut. A consummate professional, the click of the door reminds me to focus on Illona.

"Have you ever made Shrinky Dinks?"

"Um, I don't even know what those are."

"You are in for some wild fun tonight, my friend."

Illona and I head to the kitchen for some Shrinky Dink shenanigans. I'm unsure if I can fully explain the gorgeous fanciness of this kitchen. Where the kitchen in my apartment is beyond basic, and the dishwasher doesn't work and probably never will, this looks more like a place a cooking show might film. The number of buttons and lights overwhelms me. The stove has eight burners. Eight. Who needs eight burners? I barely use one on my small compact stove. What army does Olan prepare food for? Two stove doors confuse me as one appears smaller than the other, and I can't understand why. Then again, why two stoves? Eight burners and two stoves. Does he cater events on weekends? My brain insists on torturing me because now I'm picturing Olan whipping up a feast for me wearing a crisp white apron and nothing else.

Turning our attention to the Shrinky Dinks, Illona and I set up shop on the enormous granite kitchen island. I've brought a collection of animals, and Illona chooses a unicorn, horse, and cat. Not to be left out on the fun, I work on a lovely butterfly. To complement our story, I attempt to match the colors of the illustrations. Our treasures baking in the oven, we feast on popcorn and candy. Filled with anticipation, Illona twirls in front of the oven as I click the light on so she can watch our creations shrivel up.

"They're shrinking!"

Illona watches gleefully as the colored plastic animals wrinkle and writhe in the oven. Much like my heart when Olan left with Cindy. Even though seeing the two of them together felt like a punch in the stomach, spending a little one-on-one time with Illona is a wonderful consolation prize.

At eight, we head upstairs so she can brush her teeth.

"I don't need any help," she instructs, so I sit on her bed with the book and wait.

Illona's bathroom is attached to her bedroom and has a large tub, way bigger than a small child would ever need. The wallpaper has purple and pink peonies and somehow appears both juvenile and sophisticated. Her room, about three times the size of my bedroom, is a lighter shade of purple, and multiple unicorn, horse, and kitty stuffies join Noelle on her queen-sized bed. Small twinkle lights are tacked onto the ceiling, and it's not hard to imagine any small child loving this space. Heck, I'd move in and never leave.

On her bedside table, a framed photo of Illona with both her parents rests. I've never seen her mother, and naturally, I'm curious. The woman in the picture has long sandy blonde hair pulled away from her face and hazel eyes that sparkle, just like Illona's. She's stunning, which given Olan, doesn't surprise me. In the photo, Illona appears to be about three, and everyone smiles and appears connected when this moment was captured.

"Ready!" She sprints into the room, jumps onto the bed, and scurries under her pink pastel comforter.

One of my all-time favorites, Illona knows *The Very Hungry Caterpillar* well from class. I hoped she would read it with me, and as soon as I begin, she joins in. We giggle at the caterpillar eating all the junk food, and she nestles into the space between my arm and chest as we finish the story.

I close the book and Illona instinctively scoots down and lays her head on the pillow. I'm still in my spot and Illona says, "Mr. Block, can I ask you a question?"

"You know, outside school, you can call me Marvin if you want." I should have offered this earlier, but given our evening together, it's a no-brainer. Her eyes open wide, and she lifts her shoulders, and I know she's fond of the idea.

"Now, what's your question?"

"Okay. Do you think the butterfly misses being a caterpillar?"

"Hmmm. You know, I never really thought about it. I bet he misses eating all the yummy snacks."

"I'd miss the cupcake and the ice cream."

"Well, I'd miss all the fruit. And the chocolate cake. Okay, mostly the chocolate cake," I add. "But, no, I don't think he misses being a caterpillar."

"Why not?"

"Well, even after he changes into a beautiful butterfly, he's still the same on the inside. He's been the butterfly all along, he just wasn't ready to grow yet."

"Yeah, that makes sense," she says, and I'm not sure if I've gotten too philosophical. "Thanks for watching me, Marvin," she says with a yawn.

"Thanks for letting me. Good night, Illona."

"Good night, Marvin," she whispers.

Illona snuggles Noelle and, witnessing how ferociously she loves her stuffed kitty, I think of Gonzo asleep in my apartment, waiting for his dad to return. I know having a cat isn't the same as having a child, but being here with Illona, spending some quality time with her, and putting her to bed, I understand the fuss over being a dad. Nothing would make my mother happier than having a grandchild, and sometimes I think I want that, but I'm not sure I'd enjoy doing it alone. Being a single parent seems incredibly difficult. Maybe I need to cut my mother a little slack.

I turn the lights off, leaving Illona illuminated only by the sparkly lights above. As I close her door, leaving it open a few inches, I contemplate what to do with myself for the next couple of hours. At least a modicum of snooping is expected. Jill directed me to investigate. Not wanting to be a total creeper, I'm going to look in rooms but refuse to open any drawers or medicine cabinets. That feels fair. Getting a vibe for the space works for me but looking at Olan's personal items crosses a line.

There are many doors up here, but there's one room I'm most curious about. I head down the hallway, and doors have been left open, making it easy to glance inside. The first door next to Illona's bedroom appears to be an office. A large white desk wraps around the entire corner of the room, filled with computers, printers, and other technology I'm unable to identify but that appears as if it belongs in a home office.

At the end of the hallway, I poke my head into a room, and if I were a betting man, Olan's bedroom lies in front of me. Why a single person needs or wants a king-sized bed is beyond me, but Olan's bed, covered with a deep brown blanket with orange and red accents, invites me. I carefully sit on the edge of the bed and take it all in. A deep cedar dresser rests opposite the bed, with a large television on it. Photos of people I don't know, but I'm assuming are friends and family, decorate his bedside tables. One looks like it might be his parents and brothers, based on the resemblance. The size of this house and high-end furnishings has piqued my curiosity. I need a distraction because my mind begins to wander off to a foolish place where I might belong in this bedroom.

I lounge on the bed, fish out my phone, and shoot Jill an SOS text.

> Marvin: Guess where I am? Lying on Olan's bed. Call me.

CHAPTER ELEVEN

That should get her attention. I set my phone down and spread my arms out like I'm making a gay snow angel on Olan's bed. The bathroom door lies across the room, and I can make out some of the details even with the light off. In addition to a shower large enough for at least two people, there's a giant stand-alone soaking tub, waiting for someone to relax in it. I think of him taking a bath and snuggling under these covers and taking up the space I'm in, and blood rushes to my dick like a mighty wind.

My phone jolts me from my daydream with a buzz, and the picture of Jill's face wearing cat ears and painted-on whiskers from last Halloween pops up on the lock screen. There's not much you can count on in this world anymore, but the gay man's female best friend responding to his bat signal is one of them.

"Hello?" I answer as if I don't know the caller, mostly to tease her.

"Tell. Me. Everything."

"Well, I'm pretty sure he's sleeping with the gorgeous nanny. I mean, why wouldn't he be? He's an insanely handsome man, and she's, well, gorgeous. Why else would he need this enormous bed?" I slide my arm over the comforter. "Anyway, they went out together, hence why

I'm here, and the house, Jill, it's next level extravagant. I'm pretty certain you could fit four of my apartments downstairs alone, and there are three bathrooms that I've seen, but I'd bet there are more. Illona was sweet as I expected, and now it's eight-thirty, and I have at least an hour and a half until they get back, and I don't want to snoop, but well, I'm lying on his bed, but I'm not riffling through drawers, so don't even ask."

Thankfully Jill is used to my rapid-fire verbal onslaught. It takes an understanding friend to be patient with my ADHD.

"Marvin, first, breathe."

I follow her orders and take audible breaths so she can hear.

"You know the bedside table drawer would offer some excellent evidence, but I respect your ethics."

"Thank you."

"Okay, we know he's an engineer who recently sold his business. I'm Googling him."

This time, there's no protesting from me. I attempt to relax while Jill works her private-detective magic. When she wants information, Jill has a way of scoping it out. Google may be her jumping-off point, but she careens down side streets and back alleys on the internet I never knew existed. This isn't novel. Secretly stalking parents to find out more information is a hobby for Jill. She's a pro. Jill could find out someone's weight, eye color, favorite flavor of ice cream, and social security number.

Once, she discovered a mother of a student in her class was running a pyramid scheme, and she anonymously alerted the authorities. I know she'll get the goods on Olan.

"Oh my god. Are you sitting down?"

"No."

"Well, sit down."

"I'm lying down. But I can sit up." I smooth the pillow, imagining Olan's face against the ridiculously high thread count.

"Okay, this is interesting."

"What the hell does that mean?"

"Hmmm. This explains the money." She sighs, and my hand travels through my hair in frustration.

"Jill, if you don't tell me what you're reading, I will reach into this phone and tickle you until you beg me to stop."

"All right, chill. Listen to this. Olan Stone, thirty-three, began his company, Stone Aerospace, his senior year at Stanford."

"Oh, he's thirty-three. Damn, he has flawless skin."

"Thirty-four. This is from last year. May I continue?" Another sigh. Clearly, I'm trying her patience.

"Sorry."

"Based on his capstone research project on a new turbofan engine, Stone's company created the technology that led to the IR-1 supersonic jet engine prototype, thought to revolutionize supersonic travel; Stone's work as a student at Stanford propelled him to be one of the country's top engineers specializing in air and space travel."

Jill stops and waits for my direction. My eyes widen, and I prompt her, "I have no idea what most of those words mean but go on."

"Stone recently sold Stone Aerospace to Boeing for an undisclosed amount. While the exact amount of the sale was not revealed, leading industry experts believe it to be a multi-million-dollar deal."

"Millions?" I say, sitting up and catching a glimpse of myself in the mirror on his dresser.

"No. *Multi* millions."

"Fuck. So, he's got money. That explains the oceanfront home. And he's, like, smart."

"Marvin, that's not money. That's outrageous money. He's filthy rich. And Einstein-level smart. And why is his daughter in public school?"

"Diversity. He told me he doesn't want her in some elite private school." My chest warms, sharing the source of his decision.

"Well, good for him. And you. Marvin, this guy is a catch. Like, a big one. If you were fishing, and I realize you'd never go fishing, but if you did, this would be like bagging Moby Dick."

"Okay, first of all, ew. Second, Moby Dick was a whale. Whales are mammals, not fish. Third, he's clearly straight and literally on a date with his hot nanny as we speak. Fourth, he's newly separated from his wife. And fifth, I'm his daughter's teacher." Even though Jill can't see me, I put a finger up with each point I make. Olan and I have become friends, and though I know crushes on straight men are hopeless and maybe even a little embarrassing, I don't need Jill egging me on and making it worse.

Jill begins her cross.

"First, he may be incredibly handsome and wealthy, but he's a human being. Second, he may have been married to a woman and had a child with that woman, but you have no idea if he's totally straight. I saw the way he looked at you on the sledding trip."

"What? How?" I pull my legs under me and attempt to get comfortable.

"Like he was wandering the desert dehydrated, and you were a tall glass of water. And anyway, bisexual people exist. Don't be biphobic. Third, he may be reeling from his separation and looking for comfort. Comfort you could give him. Fourth, there's no rule that says you can't be friends with a parent, and if that friendship developed into something else, well, there are no rules against that either. I've seen the two of you at pickup. That's chemistry, baby."

"We're kindergarten teachers. We don't teach chemistry. Sure, he's sweet, and we're getting to know each other, but this is foolishness. Even if he were plausible for me, he's so, I don't know, out of my league, and…"

"Stop. Stop right there. You're adorable. Those unruly curls and that nose, if you were straight and I weren't married, I'd be all over you. We'd make gorgeous children."

"Ew," I say again. My face pinches up at the thought.

"Do you think giant, blond guys are my only type?"

"I mean, no. But I wouldn't kick Nick out of my bed for eating crackers."

"No, you'd ask him to share the crackers."

"With a lovely soft cheese."

"Okay, enough lusting after my husband. Why do you think Olan winked at you? Can you at least be open to the idea of someone thinking you're attractive?"

"I'm open to a Destiny's Child reunion but not much else."

"Deflecting."

"Fine. I know there are people who don't find me hideous. Occasionally, random baristas smile at me. That cute bank teller gave me two lollipops instead of one. So much sucking that day. There, happy?" I can hear the sound of her feet on tiles. She's pacing, most likely in her kitchen.

"Euphoric. Marvin, you are a catch. And even though I'm your friend and you think I have to say that, I don't. I need you to hear me on this."

"All right, I'm a catch. But he's on a date. With his nanny. Who happens to be a woman. I'm going to eat more candy and work on my TOY interview prep."

"When do you hear?"

"Next week for the county, but if I move on, there's so much to do, so I'm being optimistic and keeping busy by starting. What are you up to anyway?"

"Besides attempting to fix your life? I'm about to run a bath. Nick's watching football, and, well, I'd rather not be in the room when he screams because his team loses. Or wins. There's screaming regardless."

"Tell him I hope his team hits lots of home runs."

"Okay, night, homo."

"Night, shorty."

And with that, I'm back to waiting in this ostentatious home. I push myself up and off Olan's bed and head back to Illona's door. Peeking in, she's sound asleep, her breathing low and slow. I head downstairs to wait on Olan and Cindy's return.

Sitting on the deep brown leather couch, the day catches up to me. I immediately pop off my sneakers, swing my legs up, and look at the artwork on the walls. I'm no expert, and I couldn't tell you details about the artists or pieces, but these are clearly not the cheap framed prints from Target hanging in my apartment.

One of them appears to be metallic. Geometric shapes have been painted onto the metal with shades of bright orange and blue. There's a piece partially hanging off the bottom that might be a magnet. It's a person or creature, it's too abstract to tell, but the way it dangles off the main frame intrigues me. Almost a part of the universe of the work, but not quite. I lie there and imagine what else might exist in the world the artist created. Maybe a partner for me.

CHAPTER TWELVE

"Marvin...buddy..." I crack my tired eyes open and Olan rests on the sofa's edge, gently nudging my shoulder.

"What, what time?" I grumble.

"It's after eleven. I'm sorry we're later than I thought. I texted you, but you..."

"Fell asleep," I say. Oops.

I push myself up and touch my hair, trying to assess the level of bedhead on display. The brown curls on my head feel askew and matted, and my hoodie twists around my torso from my nap.

"Let me drive you home."

"I'm good. I can walk. It's only fifteen minutes," I lie. My humble, barely one-bedroom apartment is closer to thirty minutes away by foot but dozing off on the job isn't cute. I don't want to push my luck.

"Marvin, get your bag. I'm driving you home."

Olan's car reminds me of something from a sci-fi movie. Although I know it must be some sort of metal, the black exterior sparkles like glass. This car fills the odd request to be incredibly high-tech and expensive but also practical for a family, with a hatchback and large back seat. Illona's booster seat, a necessary accessory, looks out of place in a car James

Bond might drive. Wait, does that make me a Bond girl? Clearly costing more than the combined yearly salary of the entire staff at my school, there are buttons, screens, and switches everywhere. All I can think is "Don't touch anything," but also "I want to touch all the things."

"What does this do?" I ask, pointing to a silvery, woodsy button right of center. My gut tells me this is a passenger seat button, so I should be privy to its use.

Olan glances at where my finger points and grins.

"That calls for assistance."

"Calls who?"

"The service that assists in an emergency."

"The police?" I ask, trying not to sound ignorant.

"No, Aston Martin has a service. It calls them. They call for help."

"Who's Aston Martin?"

"Aston Martin's not a person. It's the company that manufactures the car."

"Oh, got it. So Aston Martin calls the police for help."

Olan looks over at me and smiles, and the expression on his face confuses me. But I'm keeping my mouth shut. For now. I don't push the button or ask about any of the others. I suddenly feel quite content with my old car. Even with all its coffee stains and its trash-filled back seat, I prefer simplicity. Thankfully, we approach my apartment. Olan will now observe the relative squalor I live in compared to him, but he knows my occupation and I can't imagine he'd expect much more. The car pulls to a stop, and as I feared, he reaches for his wallet.

"Olan, I'm not taking money from you, no way."

"Of course, I have to pay you, I insist," he says, opening his wallet. There are bills. Paper money. So many bills. Bills I've only read about or seen in books but never had in my possession. Who's on the fifty-dollar bill, anyway? Elton John?

I turn to him and say, "Look, we're friends, right?"

"Yes."

He considers me a friend. That's lovely. Mushiness expanding.

"Friends help each other out."

"Yes, but. Well, I'll have to do something to repay the favor."

"Olan, that's not how it works. Friendship isn't transactional."

"Well, I'll take you out."

Out? What kind of out?

"Sure, I love going out with friends. But we're *friends*, we're hanging out because we're *friends*, not because you owe me."

"As friends. Sure. I mean, we've been chatting, and I find you charming"—he blinks quickly and slowly leans in my direction—"and I was hoping, kind of…" His voice fades out.

He reaches over, across the console, his arm lurches toward me, thick and sturdy, and he places his hand on the soft spot right between my thigh and knee. My heart was already racing, but now churns up to full throttle as I feel the air leaving the cabin of this brash car. I genuinely don't fancy a panic attack sitting in this car with Olan, so I close my eyes and take a cavernous breath into the core of my belly. The opening bars, flute, handclaps, and the glorious Four Tops voices sing "Reach Out I'll Be There" to me, and Levi Stubbs's voice sounds like butter if butter could sing, and I move my tongue in my mouth trying to taste the soft creaminess. Breathe. Reach out.

"Marvin, are you okay?" Olan's fingers now squeeze my leg, and I attempt to return to reality. I'm unsure what Olan's doing, but I'm genuinely perplexed.

"Oh, yeah, I'm fine. Sorry, I needed a moment to, um, yeah, we can hang out sometime if you want, but Olan, honestly, well, I'm a little confused." With my chest lightly trembling, I turn to face him. "I think I've missed a beat. You were out with Cindy tonight. What happened? Did it not go well?"

Olan smiles, not the hesitant one I've become accustomed to, but the cosmic, beautifully luminous one he seems to only let out of the cage occasionally. He actually chuckles. His low, deep laugh reverberates inside the car's cabin.

"Oh boy. You thought Cindy and I were on a date together?"

The tart lilt in his voice hints he may be mocking me.

"Well, since you asked me to babysit and literally went out together. Yeah."

He takes a deep breath.

"Marvin. Cindy has a boyfriend. Plus, she's like family. She's been with us since Illona was two. She's dating the sous chef at a new restaurant and tonight was their opening. She asked me to escort her. That's why I asked you to watch Illona."

"Oh."

Never in my twenty-nine years have I been at such a loss for words. Somehow, I have become the prince of misunderstanding. My cheeks flush, and I feel drops of sweat beginning to bead on my forehead. I suddenly wish I could melt into the car seat and disappear.

"Marvin, why do you think I text you all the time?"

With all my obsessing about Olan, you'd think I'd have an answer, but I don't.

"Because you're new here and don't know many folks, and maybe you're bored?"

He gives a small rich laugh.

"Marvin, you're adorable."

He's not wrong. Wait, did he just call me adorable?

"You're not wrong, but I'm confused. You like men?" I ask because my brain can't keep up.

"I like you."

Hearing this from his lips makes my chest feel tight. The air feels thin and distant. All the texts, the coffee, the school bus closeness, and the glances at pickup take on new meaning. Olan begins to shift, leaning over the center console, no small feat in this luxury vehicle. As his face passes over and moves closer to mine, I smell his cherry Chap-Stick, see it glisten on his full lips, and do the only sensible thing for a neurotic Jew to do—fling the door open, jump out of the car, and sprint away like the biggest *shlemiel* in the universe.

"Thanks for the ride, bye!" I yell in his general direction over my shoulder, but also to anyone in my building awake and listening.

"Marvin, wait!"

Wanting to vanish into the night, I dash up to the front door of my building, fumbling for my keys. I crash my key into the lock, shove the door open, and fly up the stairs like a gaggle of gays racing for Gaga tickets. As I approach my front door, my phone vibrates in my pocket. Because I can use all the help from above possible, I quickly touch my mezuzah and kiss my finger. I throw the door open and Gonzo lingers inches from the entryway, purring. Startled by how his human exploded into his apartment, he darts away.

My phone wobbles in my pocket again, and I swear by all that is holy, if my mother is calling me at almost midnight on a Friday night, I will run, okay, walk very fast, to the coastline and hurl my phone into the ocean. For some reason, ringing her adult son past his bedtime has become acceptable behavior in the last few years. The first time it happened, I bolted up in bed and imagined someone was in the hospital, or worse, only to have her profess her love for me and ask if I remembered the website for the kugel recipe she loves. I worried she had relapsed and was drinking again, but there was no slurring or telltale noises of pouring or clinking glasses. The second time she explained she was confused by the time difference. Beyond discussing the three-hour gap multiple times, I even made and shipped a time zone chart to help her visualize the difference, and she systematically disregarded it. After that, I simply ignored any late calls.

I pull my phone out to cancel her call, but it's not her. Olan's number flashes on the screen. Not a text, the man is calling me. Does he not understand cell phones are only meant for texting, social media, and Candy Crush? Even though my head feels like a popcorn popper busting with kernels, making an ass once a night feels like my reasonable limit, so I pick up.

"Hello, this is Marvin." Of course, it's me, and I know it's him, but I don't know how else to answer.

"Marvin, it's Olan." His voice, deep and sure, sounds like he's making a business call. Why are nerds so hot?

"Oh, hi."

"You left your bag in the car."

Naturally.

"I'm at your front door. May I bring it up?"

"Oh, sure, I'll buzz you up. I'm on the second floor. 201."

And with that, I hang up, press the black entry button by the door and wait. Typically, I'd open the front door for my guest, but nothing feels typical about this moment, so I leave the door closed, a barrier between us, and take deep breaths, counting the moments until Olan Stone knocks on my door. After whatever just happened in his car. And what did happen? The sweat on my brow becomes palpable, and I use my sleeve to wipe it away because even when panic overtakes me, I'd prefer not to look like a hot mess. He's coming up. To my apartment. Now. In most situations where I'm required to be cool, I fail miserably. I close my eyes and offer a quick prayer that, this time, I remain calm. I dip into my bathroom, grateful the poor placement by the front entrance facilitates my current needs, and splash cold water on my face. The coolness sparkles on my skin and soothes the rising heat in my body. As I grab a towel to dry myself, the soothing smell of bleach and cleanliness takes over until Olan's soft rap on the door startles me.

As I open the door, Olan stands, his coat buttoned up, looking out of place in the hallway of my rent-controlled building, with its tan paint peeling from the walls and ratty avocado-green carpeting underfoot.

Coming from his home, so elaborate, so pristine, so expensive, embarrassment begins to trickle in. But Olan knows I'm a teacher, and well, America, your teachers are poor. He's holding my bag in his arms like an infant and wearing a sheepish grin that makes my mouth feel like the Sahara.

"Your bag?"

"Thanks." I take it, and my fingers brush his. We stand silently for a moment.

"May I come in for a minute? Please."

"Of course, sorry," I say, and he pierces my space, and even though I know embarrassment makes no sense, I wonder what he thinks about my apartment. The entire space, except my small bedroom, can be seen from where we stand near the entrance. The bathroom door lingers a few feet from us, and the main room a few feet away contains a small kitchen needing an update but unlikely to get one. My sofa sits across from an old buffet I found at a resale shop. There's a small two-person table, but with all my papers and forms for Teacher of the Year strewn about, eating only takes place on the couch. My bedroom door on the furthest wall feels far away and unattainable.

"I freaked out. It's my anxiety, it's not you, I don't always manage it well, sometimes it overwhelms me and, I was starting to panic, I'm, I'm..." I'm not sure what more to say.

"Listen, maybe I've read things incorrectly, but we've been texting, and when I see you, something's there. For me. And you've been so sweet, not only to Illona but to me. I thought we had a connection."

He stops. We stand a foot apart. The aroma of his soap, fresh, clean, and earthy, swirls to me, and I attempt to ignore my quickening pulse.

"I have wanted to kiss you," he continues. "For a while. Since the field trip, for sure. Perhaps sooner." He pinches his eyebrows like he's calculating. "Maybe I've misconstrued signals. I, I do that sometimes." His face falls slightly, and Olan Stone appears dejected.

I'm surprised by the shift in his tone, and my left foot moves a few inches in reverse. I stumble into the wall with a loud thump and Gonzo leaps from his perch on the counter. Smooth. Apparently, I'm so out of practice I don't even know when a gorgeous man makes advances. The sweat slowly begins to start up again under the curtain of curls covering my forehead. He's standing in front of me, waiting for me to speak, and once again, I've got zilch.

"I should probably go. I'm not entirely sure I'm parked legally."

This would be the time to speak, to say something, anything, but what?

"Olan," I stammer.

His eyes are waiting, wondering. I reach out and take his hand. His fingers fold into mine and the intimacy of our skin, palms warm and damp, makes my chest blossom. I tug him forward and wrap my arms around his broad shoulders, pulling him into an embrace. He melts into me and links his arms around my torso. As we stand there squeezing each other, my eyes close, and I take a deep breath, centering myself, allowing myself to be in this moment. Olan's heart thumps against my chest. Or is that mine? I'm unable to distinguish his heartbeat from mine, and the room swirls around me as I'm smelling his scent—not soap or cologne, but the slightly sweet smell of skin as my face lands right on his neck. He's warm and solid, his muscles strong against my chest, even through his coat. At this juncture, all I can wonder is why don't people hug more. Enfold yourself in another person's essence and hold there for more than a nanosecond while the world stops spinning and give yourself over. I want him to know that I've heard him and am here for him, even if only as a friend. Because we are friends. But friends don't hope for more. Right now, gathering Olan up in my arms cracks me open and carefully, as we stand so close, begins to piece me back together.

We begin to move apart, our faces again passing like ships in the night, his scent making it difficult to separate.

At the moment our faces are closest, Olan pauses.

"Hello," he says. The vibrations from his throat reverberate against my chest.

"Hey."

His breath, warm and sweet, gives me a jolt of confidence. We stand there dangerously close, and for once in my life, I don't overthink the situation. Instead, I blurt, "Do you still feel like that kiss?"

"Marvin, I'm not leaving your apartment until you kiss me."

His gaze falls to my lips and his pupils dilate, an electric tension quivering between us. He extends a hand to my face, my breath hitching from his touch. I close my eyes as his thumb traces my jaw to my chin and north to my lower lip, and what the fuck is happening? My heart, already racing, revs to overdrive, and I take it as a sign to move forward, closing the small gap between us. My lips graze his cheek, and finally having them on his skin, the urge to lick him from head to toe surges in my core. He carefully turns, our mouths meet, and it takes every ounce of restraint to pace myself. At first, he's slow, cautious, and curious. A gentle brushing of his lips on mine. But as space and time disappear, I can feel Olan relax and press himself into me simultaneously. There's an urgency and eagerness to him now. Our mouths coming together opens a new gateway between us and sends a shockwave through my entire body.

And his lips. His fucking magnificent lips. Plump and soft and coated with cherry ChapStick making me want to nibble every bit of them. He cups my face with his hands, leaving one on my cheek and sliding the other up to my hair. His fingers become entwined in curls, and his hand moves with conviction. Holding my face and my hair as our mouths take these first steps together makes me feel so damn cherished, I'm not sure I can bear it. I move my hands toward his head and rest them on the back of his neck, just below his hairline.

"You okay?" I ask.

"Absolutely," he mutters into my mouth.

My hands begin returning the motions he's made in my own hair, becoming entwined in his soft coils. He lets out gentle moans and whispers. They're low, and I'm not positive, but I think he whimpers, "Fuck," which sends a jolt of blood right to my groin. I want to keep exploring and get lost in him. All of him.

Rationally, I know the kissing must stop eventually, but I don't want it to. I stopped searching, hoping for this feeling of connection, and now, our lips locked and his tongue beginning to explore my mouth, I feel brainless for thinking I didn't want this.

Olan's kiss secures me: warm and wet, steady and sound, and everything a kiss should be. I'm sure the kissing will come to an end, but it doesn't. His hands have migrated, one on the small of my back and the other on my neck. He massages my back with his hand, forcing my body to succumb. My hands still entangle his hair, thick and springy to my touch, and I use it to pull him closer. We kiss like horny teenagers in the back seat of a car, and his energy radiates. My entire body flushes. The continued stirring in my groin becomes palpable. Our hips rest against each other, and Olan Stone resembles, well, an actual stone. Down there. He presses against me, and my excitement becomes more evident against his. Overcome by the moment and needing a breather, I pull away.

"What are you doing?" I murmur.

"I'm kissing you."

"Oh."

With that, his lips move on mine again, and this time, I clutch him, and I don't care if the stiffness in our pants creates more friction. Grinding his stiff cock against mine through our pants tosses gasoline onto the fire raging in our mouths. He bends to kiss my neck and begins to move toward my earlobe, and heaven help me, he takes it in his mouth, sucking it gently at first, exploring my ear, and honestly, I'm unsure if

I can remain upright. The sensitive nerves in my ear and neck explode with bliss. For a fleeting moment, my body forgets to be anxious. There's no music. No singing. Only Olan's hot, damp breath in my ear, deep and forceful. I'm so fucking aroused, lustful noises rampantly escape my mouth. Olan replies with a deep moan as his teeth bite at my ear.

"Holy crap," I whisper.

How did I fail to notice this fervor in him?

"Mmmh. Good, Mr. Block?" he growls into my ear, and my insides simmer over.

He thrusts his midsection on me in a way that's making it harder to keep this to a neck-up-only activity. The kissing, the biting, and the licking need to be enough. For now. The man hasn't even bought me dinner. Keep it in your pants, Marvin. But my dick disagrees and strains against my briefs and pants. He keeps going back and forth between my ear, neck, and lips, and I'm not sure I can take it anymore. I can feel the precum on my underwear from the grinding, and my dick aches from the pressure. More noises escape my mouth, and I struggle to stay silent because I don't want to appear foolish. Right now, words feel unnecessary, but because I'm me, I speak anyway.

"Should we...couch?" I whisper and attempt to nod toward it as he mouths my neck in a manner I truly hope doesn't leave a mark. He's seemingly in a trance, as my words interrupt and startle him, snapping him back to reality.

"I, I should probably go." His face pulls away, but our arms stay jumbled, so his lips are still only inches from mine. The rational part of my brain takes over.

"You definitely should."

Olan is a parent of a student in my class. Until about fifteen minutes ago, I was certain Olan was straight. If he's not straight, then what? Bisexual? Something else? Does it matter?

Because we never moved from the front door, Olan simply detangles himself from my limbs and turns to leave. I take a single step toward the door to see him out, and he turns and kisses me one more time, quick and earnest, and I'm desperate for him to stay.

"I'll text you. Please don't be anxious about this."

Laughing, I say, "I'll try."

The door closes. I shut my eyes and take deep breaths. My heart thumps with such ferocity my entire chest is heaving. What in heaven and earth just happened? I close my eyes, and immediately a bass slaps, strings swell, and a sultry rhythm guitar welcomes Luther Vandross's silky voice as he begins to sing the first lines of his sultry classic "Never Too Much." My head sways with the music and Luther. Ah, Luther. My body shudders with pleasure at his voice combined with the lingering taste of Olan on my buzzing lips.

I finally open my eyes and Gonzo, perched on the counter, stares at me with a judging glare only he can get away with.

"Listen, buddy, maybe if you weren't neutered, you'd understand."

He stretches, yawns, and heads toward his food bowl.

CHAPTER THIRTEEN

As happens more often than it should, I wake up on the sofa instead of my bed. I probably should consider a studio and save a few hundred dollars a month. Settled on my chest, Gonzo watches me, patiently waiting to be fed. I reach to pet him, and he leaps to the floor, bolting over to the lower cabinet, meowing toward his food.

"Okay, buddy, I can take a hint."

As I sit up, in a flash, last night rushes back to me. I slowly touch my lips, still numb from our intense make-out session, the faint smell of cherry lingering. A swirl of conflicting emotions overtakes my head. Clearly, necking with the father of a student will not win me Teacher of the Year. Oh, my lord. Teacher of the Year. Dr. Knorse. The funding. My heart drops to my stomach, and I'm elated to be seated as the blood rushes from my head. But the way Olan touched me, his hot breath on my neck, my body reacted to his in a new and incredible way. I grab my phone from the coffee table and thumb a text to Jill.

> Marvin: Morning, slag. Olan drove me home and kissed me. How was your night?

Grabbing a small plate, I shake the can of wet cat food out as Gonzo looks on, purring in anticipation. He begins scarfing down his breakfast, and I head to the bathroom where the faint smell of Olan lingers. Whatever soap, cologne, or deodorant he uses, the hints of lavender and sage dance on my nose. With a full inhale, he's back here, nibbling on my earlobe and making me weak.

My phone dings from the coffee table, interrupting my daydream.

> Jill: Who's a slag now? I'm coming over. Stopping for nourishment and coffee.

> Marvin: I have coffee.

> Jill: Do you have real cream and Splenda?

> Marvin: Stop for coffee.

My propensity for milk alternatives and real sugar never flies with Jill. I really should stock her necessities, but I mostly survive on frozen foods and seltzer and, much like putting gas in my car, only go food shopping when the cupboards are empty. Nick plays intramural hockey on Saturday mornings, so Jill and I often get together. It helps to have time as friends outside of school, away from the children and the overall circus of teaching. Usually, we meet up at a small local coffee shop equal distance between our places. Drinking coffee, gossiping, looking at catalogs before recycling them, and of course, peeping and dishing about men in the coffee shop are our favorite ways to spend Saturday mornings together.

Occasionally, we'll just go to one another's place because getting out of our pajamas feels too complicated. The time Jill had her wisdom teeth out, and her reaction to the anesthesia made her resemble a chipmunk for a week, I drove over and made us milkshakes. Of course, she could barely drink with her swollen cheeks, but I only laughed a little while cleaning up her mess because I'm a caring friend.

Awaiting her arrival, I sit at my small table—pushing aside random papers, bills, and lists I make to help me remember the minutiae of life—and pull my laptop open. I surf the web for pop news and take a minute to check my email. Among the spam from the most random senders (no, I'm not interested in an over-fifty Christian dating service, thank you very much), I spot a message from the Teacher of the Year committee. I wasn't expecting to hear anything until Monday, so I'm intrigued. Gonzo pounces on my lap and butts his head against my arm for attention. I stroke him with one hand, which elicits immediate purrs, and click to open the message.

To: mblock@pelletierelementary.org
CC: tknorse@pelletierelementary.org
From: AngelaH@METOY.org
Subject: Cumberland County Teacher of the Year Selection

Dear Mr. Block,

Hello! We know the excitement a nomination for Teacher of the Year brings to educators and schools. The selection process for Teacher of the Year takes months of hard work and dedication from our board.

We understand the time and commitment nominees put into the process, and we do not take our jobs on the committee to designate our county's representative teacher lightly.

We are thrilled to inform you the committee has selected you as Cumberland County's Teacher of the Year, 2022.

Next week you will receive additional instructions on the next steps to help you prepare for the state selection process. We will be in touch to schedule your interview and school visit for March.

Respectfully,
Dr. Angela Hayes
Cumberland County Division Director
Maine Teacher of the Year

Hot damn! I won. Sure, it's only the county, but I won. I've never won anything. There was that couples dance-off in PE with a girl named Olivia in second grade. We made up a quick routine to "Rockin' Robin" and slayed it. But the only prize was a round of applause. Which was lovely. But still. This is huge. Even the county win. I wonder if the state title comes with a crown and scepter.

As much as I hoped to be chosen, I knew the competition was stiff, and I'd tried to manage my expectations. Dr. Knorse will be elated. This should give her some ammunition to fight for our school. I'm almost tempted to call her, but on a Saturday? No way. Winning feels odd to me. As a child, I wasn't competitive. The fear of losing overtook my urge to even participate in common rites of passage like spelling bees or board games, and with my clumsiness, sports were never an option. My athleticism only pertains to walking, maybe quickly, only if the right music blares in my ears. And now I'm thinking about my ears and Olan nibbling on them like he was tasting the sweetest ear of summer corn. My stomach does a little flippy-de-do until the roar of the buzzer brings it to a halt.

Jill enters, cloaked in her winter coat, a scarf wrapped around her neck and covering the bottom half of her face. She's holding a box of Rockstar Donuts, and the sugary aroma hints at least one of the confections inside is my absolute favorite, usually sold out, sinfully delicious, frosted strawberry topped with freeze-dried strawberries and rainbow sprinkles. I grab the box from her mitten-covered hands, and we head to the kitchen as she peels off her winter gear.

"That was the last strawberry, I had to lie to a German tourist to get it. She ordered it and I poked my head in and told her the cinnamon ganache put Rockstar on the map as a donut destination shop."

"You did not. Cinnamon ganache?"

"I did. Because this calls for a celebratory donut, and you require strawberry. I would have wrested it out of her strong arms if necessary. She's German, and I needed it for a nice Jewish boy. The universe will call it even."

"Jill, I love you."

"I know you do. Now tell me everything."

"Well, I got it."

"Wait, what? You got what? Olan?"

"Oh my god, no. Teacher of the Year, for the county anyway, I was selected, the email came last night, but with watching Illona and getting home so late and, well, the kissing, I didn't see it until this morning."

This is what happens when you take school email off your phone, which, honestly, I'm happy I did. Getting emails on the weekend about the second-grade team looking for books about mammals is not part of my self-care plan.

"Wait, stop. You got it? Teacher of the Year? Marvin, that's amazing!"

Jill drops her Mexican chocolate donut and squeezes me with all her might, and because she possesses the strength of a tiny rhinoceros, I let out a little "uhhhh."

As we pull apart, she beams. "I am thrilled for you, for the kids, for our school, and for me because if you end up going to D.C., I'm so going with you."

"Slow down. This is for the county, there are big hurdles to jump through for the state. Let's not put the cart before the horse. And anyway, they aren't going to select a *chazer* for Teacher of the Year."

"You tart. FYI, Nick called it. You and Olan. He told me there's no way this 'hot dad' would be able to ignore your charms. I told him to go crash into other men on the ice. Now, tell me everything that happened, and don't leave out any of the gory details."

"Nick thinks I'm charming?" My voice lilts up higher than usual and Jill smirks.

"Yes, but he also thinks cargo pants are high fashion so take it with a grain of salt."

"Noted. So, we thought Olan was going out with the nanny, but nope. He took her to the opening of Bangladesh, that new place on State Street. Cindy's boyfriend is the sous chef. It wasn't a date. Well, not a date-date."

"That tracks. She's not his type."

"Jill, she's everyone's type. She's *my* type."

"True. I'd probably hook up with her myself. Anyway, not dating the nanny." She scoops her hand, urging me on.

"He drove me home, and we're sitting there in his James Bond car, and he started to lean over and got really close, and when I realized he was making a pass, I panicked. I jumped out of the car and bolted upstairs."

"Wait, you didn't kiss?"

"Not then, no."

"And you ran away? From that hot specimen?"

I dip my head, curl my lip up and give Jill my listen-don't-try-me look. She knows it well.

"Wait, why did you panic? He's, well, gorgeous. Lord, I'd like to make out with him."

"I know, I know. Clearly, not a shining moment for me. I think even though I'd been wanting this, secretly hoping for it, when it actually happened, my inner saboteur screamed, 'Alert! Alert! Horrible idea ahead, Marvin Block. And why would a man like Olan want you?' and I bolted."

"Oh, sweetie, I'm sorry. You should've texted me. I would've given you a pep talk."

"I love you, but in the moment, pulling out my phone to text you didn't really cross my mind. Anyway, I left my bag in the car because, well, I'd lose my head if it weren't attached. He brought it up, and after a few minutes of blabbing, he kissed me."

"What kind of kiss? Are we talking 'haven't seen your aunt since last Thanksgiving' kiss or 'the love of your life returns from being away for a year and you spot them in the airport, and they dash and leap into your arms' kiss?"

"More like the latter."

"How was it?"

I take a full breath. My belly expands, and I blow air out through my circled lips.

"Holy fuck. That good? Show me."

"Ew. No."

"Fine. How long was he here?"

"Honestly, I'm not exactly sure. More than five minutes, but less than twenty-ish."

The kissing, the way my insides thawed when he went to town on my neck and ear, time seemed to slow down, and by the time we stopped, and he was gone, I'm not sure I could say, with any accuracy, how long our tongues tangled.

"And how much of that time was kissing?" Jill can be relentless for details.

"Most of it. All but maybe two minutes. Three tops."

She's almost rendered speechless but squeaks out, "Damn."

"My anxiety began bubbling, and I think he sensed it. The last thing he told me was not to freak out, and I'm trying extremely hard to stay calm about it."

"Wait, so does this mean he's bi?"

"I have no idea. My guess would be yes, but we didn't talk about it. We didn't talk much."

"Damn. What happens now?"

"I'm going to finish this donut, which, thank you very much, tastes like supreme strawberry heaven, and hang out with my friend until she heads home to her incredibly sweet and attractive bear of a husband."

"No, you dunce, with Olan. And you. What happens next?"

"No clue."

"No texts?"

"Nothing. Thank you for the reminder."

Did I expect Olan to call me? Text? Send a carrier pigeon? Hire a skywriter? Something, anything, yes. Am I wildly disappointed it's been radio silence since he left? Utterly.

"You. Text. Him. Doofus." She pokes my phone on the counter.

Kissing Olan already feels like walking on a high wire. Even though there aren't explicit rules against it, I'm fairly certain Dr. Knorse would not be thrilled to learn I've made out with the parent of a student in my class. My head feels light, imagining the stern talking to I would receive from her. Letting Olan take the lead makes the most sense. He's the parent, not the employee of his daughter's school.

"He's the parent. I'm leaving the ball in his court."

"The way I see it, collectively, you have four balls. There could easily be at least one ball in everyone's court."

I wake from my sugar-crash-induced nap and grab my phone to check if Olan has made any overtures. Nothing. Tragically, a missed call from my mother taunts me. We haven't spoken in over three weeks, and my guilt usually begins to creep in at the month checkpoint. Seeking a reprieve from brooding about Olan, I unlock my phone, find Sarah's blurry photo at the bottom of my favorites, and huff as I press it.

"Hey, how are you?" Her chipper tone makes me unsteady.

"Pretty good. I saw you called."

"We haven't talked in a few weeks, so I figured I'd try you. Were you out?"

"No, not out, Jill was over earlier, and then I took a little snooze with Gonzo."

"How is my grand-kitty?"

Every single conversation, at least once, if not twice, I'm passive-aggressively reminded about my mother's lack of grandchildren.

"He's fine, lying right next to me now."

"Well, give him a kiss from his grandmother." And I do because loving on Gonzo never gets old.

"How's work?"

Our conversations have a familiar trajectory, which I appreciate. It helps avoid landmines. We start with pleasantries, move on to work, and typically end with reporting and kvetching about the weather.

"Fine, the kids are doing well, I have a few starting to read, and that always makes me proud."

I want to tell her about the Teacher of the Year, but also don't want to overexcite her. My mother looks for places to focus her frenzied energy. When Adam and I got engaged, she became laser-focused on trying to help. From Arizona. Calling flower shops in a city she has no familiarity with and demanding they hand dip roses did not go over well. A part of me knows it's her fucked up way of attempting to make amends, but it still annoys me.

"What about that award? When do you find out about that?"

"Well, I actually got it." I wince.

"And when were you going to tell your mother?"

"Mom, I literally just found out this morning."

"Well, you could've called me."

Sarah refers to herself as my "mother" whenever she wants to make sure I don't forget she carried me for nine months, endured long, painful labor, and, even with all her faults, did her best to turn me into the man I am today. If guilt were an Olympic sport, she would be a multiple gold medal holder.

"I'm calling you now."

"Calling me *back*."

I let out a loud sigh I'm certain she hears, but also, there's no stopping it.

"Anyway, they selected me. I'm the county Teacher of the Year. Pretty cool, right?"

"Oh, Marvy, I'm so proud of you. What do you win? Is there money? A trophy or engraved pen?"

"Well, nothing, actually. I now get to submit and run at the state level, so I guess I win more work. That's what I win." I give a defensive chuckle, hoping she doesn't chastise me.

"More work? Are they paying you for all this?"

"No, Mom, they don't pay me. It's an honor, I made the choice to do this."

I haven't told her about how this could impact the school too. It feels too heavy.

"Okay, I just don't understand why you'd want more unpaid work. That seems foolish to me, but what do I know? I'm just your mother."

Just my mother. In case I've forgotten. I'm never sure if she means to remind me she gave birth to me or that she raised me by herself. My parents' marriage was over before I took my first steps. They were high school sweethearts. I was a surprise and not the "hey, kids, we're going to Disney" kind. My mother swears she loved being a young parent, but the strain it put on them evidently broke their brief marriage. My father dropped out of high school to work and support his new family. Working as a janitor at the local library sounds charming enough, but not when you fall for one of the librarians. My mother didn't find out until after my birth when he ran off to Texas with Lady Librarian. The details from my mother are vague, but she thinks they moved to Dallas at the time. Almost thirty years later, he could be anywhere now. Who knows? He could be dead. He could have a new family. I could have siblings. Somewhere out there, my father is shacking up with Lady Librarian. I only hope he's at least well-read. My mom's drinking started to rev up soon after, and well, the rest is drunk history.

"Mom, I'm good with it. I chose this."

"Fine, fine, I hope you get it. There can't be anyone better than you in the entire state. In the entire country!"

"Thanks, Mom."

"Now, have you met anyone? Please tell me you're dating."

When I came out to my mother in middle school, her biggest fear was I would end up alone. After Adam and I called off our engagement and split, my love life dried up like a stale raisin bagel, and her distress went into overdrive. I could mention Olan, but there's not much to tell.

"No, Mother, not dating. I have no time. Anyway, how's the weather?"

Subject-change-game on point.

"You need to make time. And it's January in Arizona, sixty degrees feels downright chilly. I still don't know how you manage all that frigid cold and mountains of snow. I'll never understand why anyone would choose to live there."

"Well, for one thing, I enjoy living where I get to witness the change of seasons."

My mother and I paint our conversations with broad snide strokes. She resents me for living so far away, but I wouldn't have it any other way. Distance provides the ultimate buffer for our dysfunctional relationship. I resent her for littering my childhood with traumatic episodes, and she would like nothing more than to forget all about it. My heart tells me she did her best at the time, but my head remembers too much. On good days I can get lost enough in my daily routines to momentarily forget, but true forgiveness eludes me.

"I know, I know, it's beautiful in summer. Leaf peepers come by the busload in the fall. Vacationland and all that jazz," she says.

"I mean, you're not wrong."

The shift to weather kvetching signals me to wrap up our chat.

"Well, I should go eat something. It's way past lunch," I fib. Full from the donuts I gobbled down this morning, my stomach wants for nothing, but the idea of sustenance for her child never fails to motivate Sarah Block.

"Go. Eat. Call me next weekend. Love you."

"Love you, too."

I toss my phone on the sofa like a hot potato.

The chances of me calling her next weekend rival turning my head to the heavens and spotting a drift of pigs fluttering through the air. Ain't gonna happen. But she says it every time, and I concur. We go through the motions because lying is easier. It's our bit.

On Sunday, I waffle between the bed and couch, following Gonzo like a lost lamb. If he stirs to eat or use his litter box, I rouse to replenish snacks and pee, waiting to see where he settles down to shadow him. By mid-afternoon, it's been almost forty-eight hours since Olan and I snogged like the world was ending, and there's still no word from him. Gonzo may give me a few dirty looks, but once I begin petting him with enough pressure, his purring takes over, and we return to snuggling. I vacillate between scrolling on my phone for distractions and watching old episodes of early two thousand sitcoms I've seen more times than I'll ever admit in public.

As I finish an episode where the female lead finally connects with her love interest after he does a sexy striptease for her, my frustration refuses to abate. I bite the bullet and shoot Olan a brief text.

Marvin: Hey. Hope you're having a good weekend. Sunday scaries on deck for me.

I hit send and regret the message immediately. Why can't I ever play it cool? Because I'm decidedly uncool. It's my lot in life.

By bedtime, with no reply from him, I wonder if what happened with Olan was part of some imagined fever dream or if I'm losing my mind. I almost text him again about seven times but stop after the first word each time. Do I have reservations about what happened? Of course. Then why does thinking he might also sting? The rest of the school year will be more uncomfortable than an ill-fitting corset on a drag queen. We have four and a half months left, and parent conferences are two weeks away. Fan-fucking-tastic.

CHAPTER FOURTEEN

I jolt up from my slumber, heart racing and breath heavy. For a few seconds, I'm positive I'm being chased by someone faceless or in a battle in some unfamiliar place, or the world is simply crushing to an end on top of me. It takes me snatching Gonzo from the foot of my bed, pulling him up to my chest, holding him like an infant, and kissing his sweet head and face ten times to calm and center myself. Peeking at my phone through tired eyes, I realize it's three in the morning. And zero notifications await me. My alarm won't go off for almost three more hours, and there's only about a 50 percent chance I can actually fall back to sleep.

As I love on Gonzo, my motor begins to downshift, and slowly, the brakes are engaged, and my pulse slows. Looking at his round softball head, damp from my slobber, I'm buoyed by the unique bond we share. I only became a Cat Dad as an adult. My mother could barely take care of me, let alone an animal. I remember years when I'd begged for a cuddly pet, though she never relented. For my tenth birthday, in a fit of guilt, she bought me a goldfish. I learned quickly I'm not a fish person because, well, you can't do much with fish but feed them, and if you're ten and want to love on your pet, you stuff it with fish pellets until it dies before you can settle on a name for it.

Gonzo's eyes are closed, and he purrs like a motor. I've read stories about people needing emotional support animals on airplanes. Random creatures like turkeys and peacocks taking up entire rows and causing a commotion, but if they give their owners a smidge of the comfort Gonzo brings me, I say let them fly.

I try to envision how Gonzo would have consoled me in my youth. There were days I'd get off the school bus, nobody waiting for me, walk into our apartment, and my mother was passed out on the kitchen floor from an afternoon bender. The first few times, I was alarmed and tried to rouse her, only to realize she'd blacked out from the booze, and there was nothing I could do but wait it out. Eventually, I learned to check for breathing, step over her, and slink to my bedroom to watch television. Unconditional love from a small, soft, domesticated animal would have been more than appreciated.

I stop petting him for a nanosecond, and Gonzo chirps like a gremlin, letting me know he objects to the pause. At some point, thinking about this furball and the fellowship we share soothes me enough, and I doze off.

You are going to be known as the school harlot. This thought repeats in my brain while I ping around the classroom setting up for Monday with my students. With no word from Olan, my anxiety takes on a life of its own. In a short matter of time, I'm able to convince myself I will be disgraced, fired, and the Teacher of the Year folks will chortle at the idea of my nomination. The embarrassment I'll bring upon the school will thwart Dr. Knorse's attempt to secure our funding, and the blame will be squarely on me. I'll be forced to resign and spend my days searching for menial work in an unemployment office that plays *Fox News* on blast. I've perfected with precision the skill of winding myself up in seconds.

I stand at the easel, a fresh sheet of lined paper mocking me. The date and greeting are simple, standard, and routine.

February 2

Dear Friends,
Taylor is First.
Martha is the calendar helper.
We have Music.

Love,
Mr. Block

Right now, attempting to come up with a share, something for the children to write on the message, to engage with, feels impossible. My mind feels empty and distracted. On cue, Jill pops her head into my room. I brace for her sass, knowing she'll provide a simple share.

"Anything?" No joke from Jill on a Monday morning articulates everything about the situation. Her tone tells me she's trying to be optimistic but also realistic.

"Nothing."

She enters my room and, clutching her bag, plops herself down on the table closest to the door. Knowing she came to check on me, bypassing her own room, comforts me. Putting my marker down on the easel's tray, I walk over and sit next to her, brushing my shoulder against hers.

"It doesn't mean anything," she offers.

I raise my eyebrows and give her my *oh really?* look.

"It feels like him not replying to my text means something," I say.

"The kids will distract you," she offers, and deep in my gut, I know she's correct.

Being present, truly present, is a requirement of working with small children. You can't wander off in your mind, or on your phone for that matter. They need something from me at every moment and keeping them safe requires all my focus. Add teaching to the mix, and alertness is critical.

When Adam and I broke up, I took a day off because complete sobbing in front of my class felt wrong. Once I returned, the attention, affection, and dependence helped. The children gave me a much-needed diversion, and anyway, writing sub plans could be considered a low-level form of torture in some countries. Did I cry in the back closet when my class was at lunch? Absolutely. But for the most part, they provided an indispensable distraction. I know today, those sweet cherubs marching into the classroom will divert my attention from Olan. From the kissing. The hot, sweaty, sweet kissing. I'm eager for their arrival.

"Can you give me a good share?" I ask.

"How about something about love?"

"Love? Really? Are you trying to torment me?"

"It's February. Valentine's Day is looming."

I jot *Write someone you love* at the bottom of the message and scribble Gonzo as my example.

"Perfect," she says and stands to leave.

"Thank you," I tell her, not only for the share, but for Saturday, and for when Adam left, and for being someone I can truly count on. I don't say all that, but I don't need to.

With my message complete, I check my notes for any other prep needed before the children arrive. We'll need some brown craft paper for a display I've planned for us to make together for Groundhog Day. I head down to the closet in the hallway that stores supplies. Every school has one filled with paper, pencils, paper clips, thumbtacks, and cartons of white chalk wondering why it's been forgotten. As I unroll a long swath of brown paper from the rack holding giant spools in basic colors, Kristi and Dr. Knorse walk by and spot me. I adore Kristi, but with my anxiety on edge about Olan, pleasantries feel harder to fake, and Dr. Knorse often sucks my energy dry.

"Marvin, good weekend?" Kristi asks.

"Not bad," I say as I touch the spot on my neck Olan nibbled.

"We are so proud of your Teacher of the Year progress. I've researched the other nominees and had a good feeling you'd win the county. Everyone loves a male teacher. A male kindergarten teacher? Absolute gold. If we can nab the state win, we'll be a lock for the funding," Dr. Knorse strategizes.

Although nothing new, it still rubs me the wrong way to hear my success in early education accredited simply to my gender. Are men in primary grades rarer than a unicorn swimming through Atlantis? Of course. Dr. Knorse assuming being male is the main reason for my selection as county Teacher of the Year smacks of contempt, but hearing her actually say it cuts even deeper.

"Well, I'd like to think I wasn't only nominated or selected because I'm male."

"Of course not," Kristi says. The wince on her face tells me she knew what I was thinking.

"We need to focus on image now. Appearances matter. We've walked the hallways to document what repairs, cleaning, and paint touch-ups need to happen before the school visit in March. We'll have to spend a little, but you've got to spend money to make money," Dr. Knorse says.

Our school, which never seems to have funds for anything teachers actually ask for and need, oh, say, like books, has somehow found money to shine our veneer. Of course, the school could use some help. Everywhere you look, chipped paint, loose boards, and weird unidentifiable splotches on the ceiling scream for attention. Now, in addition to feeling like the school tramp, I get to be the reason monies are irrationally spent. Complete *mishigas*!

"It's not until the last week of March, so we have about six weeks to get it all done," she continues. Kristi and I give each other this-is-slightly-out-of-hand-and-foolish looks.

"Sounds good," I say through clenched teeth and squeeze my way past them into the hallway. The children will be here any moment, and if I'm not in the classroom when they come bounding down the hallway, it will not be pretty.

I do a fast-walk-slow-jog-trot back to the room and plop the brown paper on a table as the bell buzzes, signaling our day's official start. I quickly wash my hands in the small combination sink and water fountain, and the lovely chatter of kindergarten arrival approaches outside the door. I close my eyes and take a deep breath, today a little extra grateful for their presence. Kevin bolts up to me, baring his teeth.

"Mr. Block, look!" He points to his mouth, and I begin to investigate.

"Kevin, you lost another tooth. How on earth will you eat solid food?"

"I have to use the teeth on the sides," he says, yanking his cheek to the side with a finger and pointing to the side teeth in question.

"Well, I'm pleased to know you won't starve," I say as he hands me his blue folder.

Children file in and greet me with a variety of fist bumps, waves, and hugs, as they hand me their folders and enter the classroom. I chat with them and ask questions about siblings, pets, lunches, and every random subject under the sun while peeking in folders and retrieving the odd note about a change in dismissal or an impending vacation.

I take a little extra breath with Illona's arrival because simply the sight of her reminds me of her father and Friday night, even though she clearly knows nothing.

"Good morning, Mr. Block. I went to the movies yesterday!"

My mind immediately pictures Olan in the dark theater, watching the latest animated film with her, and a tiny sharpness prickles my chest, wondering why he didn't reach out.

"Fun! That would be a perfect share for Morning Meeting."

"Oh, good idea!" She hands me her blue folder and skips inside the classroom.

I peel back the cover of her folder and a small envelope with "Mr. Block" written on it peeks up. I slowly pull it out and drop her folder in the basket. For about five seconds, I contemplate waiting to open it until I'm alone because a room full of small children bubbles around me, and I'm not sure how the contents will impact me. Not being a patient person, I carefully slip my finger under the end of the envelope and rip it open, pulling out a small, folded note.

Marvin,

Can we please talk after school?

Olan.

That's it. Can. We. Talk. Can we snog on each other? Please? And now I have to endure the entire school day awaiting this conversation, but he wants to speak to me, which is much preferred to never communicating again. A wave of relief washes over me, and I inhale the deepest breath I've taken since Olan left my apartment Friday night. I move to tuck the note into my pocket and Jill appears in the doorway. Sure, I've been telling myself I'm not looking for romance, but when a man like Olan comes into your viewfinder, he's really hard to ignore.

"I saw Illona and asked Brenda to watch my class…anything?"

I hold the note out like it's both a treasure and burning my hand and hope she'll grab it quickly. Which she does.

"This is good. He wants to talk. In person."

The air entering and exiting my nostrils makes a loud whooshing noise.

"It's going to be okay. I promise," Jill assures me and spins to head back to her own brood.

Thankfully, the bedlam of kindergarten fills my day, and I don't have much time to perseverate about Olan. Teddy has a terrible nose-bleed, a gusher, and the adrenaline pumping through me to stop the surge of blood and help him calm down carries me through most of the morning. By the time we're packing up to go home, I'm more than ready for the child-filled portion of my day to be over.

An empty feeling lingers in the pit of my stomach as Illona and I walk hand in hand to meet her dad by the dismissal table. This is what I've been waiting for, but I'm fearful. What if Olan tells me he's made a horrible mistake? Can we still be friends? Could I handle that after what happened? It was only a kiss. But Lord, what a kiss. My head feels light and dizzy.

"Are you ready to go home?" I ask Illona, trying to calm myself with conversation.

"Yeah, I'm hungry. Daddy told me I'm going to have a snack and play on the playground for a little bit with Cindy. He said he needs to chat with you."

"Did he?"

"Yup."

A pause.

"Am I in trouble, Mr. Block?"

My legs come to a halt, and I tilt over so my face comes closer to hers because I need her to understand what I'm about to say comes from my soul.

"Illona, no, you're most definitely not in trouble. Sometimes grown-ups need to chat about, well, grown-up things, but please, please listen to me. You have not done a single thing wrong."

She sighs and turns her lips up, pulling me toward the table, her worry now assuaged. Olan and Cindy stand by the table waiting, and as much as I look, Olan's face gives nothing away. He spots his daughter and lights up like a streetlight at dusk. They do their ritual where she leaps into his arms, and she squeezes his neck like a python. Cindy stands behind them smiling, and I can't help but wonder what she may know about why Olan wants to chat with me. He clearly asked her to come and be with Illona, and they're also definitely friendly since he escorted her to the restaurant opening. Cindy's poker face reveals nothing.

Finally pulling back from their hug, Olan says, "Princess, remember I need to chat with Mr. Block for a few minutes. Cindy has a snack for you and will take you to the playground."

On cue, Cindy unzips her oversized bag and pulls out a small package of cheese crackers that I would gladly gobble down right now because stress eating is one of my favorite pastimes. Olan pops Illona down, and she takes Cindy's well-manicured hand, and they head outside. I'm keenly aware of the other adults. In addition to Dr. Knorse, Kristi is helping today. Various parents, grandparents, and other adults dot the hallway, awaiting their children.

"Mr. Stone, good afternoon," Dr. Knorse greets him.

"Hello," he replies.

Olan smiles at me, and my stomach does a little summersault as I swallow, unsure what to say. I'm fairly certain Dr. Knorse watches our interaction with curiosity.

"Can we chat outside? The path across the street, maybe?"

I expected he'd want to go back to the class and chat but being outside in the fresh cool air might assist my head and breathing.

"Oh, sure, let me run and grab my coat. Why don't I meet you on the playground?"

I bolt from curious eyes, and five minutes later, wrapped in my warmest down coat, mittens, and sock cap, I'm strolling up to Olan by the edge of the playground. Noticing me, he laughs a little, which makes me worry because I literally haven't said a word, and if simply the sight of me strikes him as funny, this probably isn't going to go well for me.

"You. In that hat," he says.

"What? It's winter in Maine. I have recess duty. I like to stay toasty."

"No. It's adorable. You're adorable."

Oh.

He nods toward the entrance to the path, and we stroll over.

The trail begins across the street from the school building and follows the coastline, snaking in and out of view of the street and ocean. In warmer months, the trees, lush with blossoms and leafy cover, are bursting with wildlife, and attempting it without bug spray means coming out covered in tasty nibbles. But in February, only the evergreens provide cover and snow blankets everything in sight. This path provides such solace, a buffer from the reality of life with the sanctity of the sea thrown in as a bonus. I walk it often, more in summer when time feels unlimited and less rushed. On frigid days, like today, there's an extra sense of tranquility.

We cross the street in silence, and my head blows up like a balloon. I haven't eaten since lunchtime, and my stomach growls in protest. The combination of hunger and anxiety threatens my blood sugar, and since I do not fancy passing out in front of Olan, I pull a bag of walnuts out of my pocket and pop a few in my mouth.

"Walnut?" I offer, and he puts a hand up and shakes his head.

We enter the path, snow packed down by walkers. The trees provide a blanket of privacy, but Olan still hasn't truly spoken, and the quietness is killing me, so I hurry to fill the empty air.

"Listen, I'm sorry about the kissing. I was out of line. Way out of line. You're a parent, and you've just moved, and I shouldn't have let it go that far. It seemed like we were becoming friends, and I like you. As a friend, I mean. I like you as a friend. The last thing I want is to ruin any chance of that continuing. Please, I hope you can forgive me because..."

Interrupting my rambling, he grabs my shoulders and pushes me up against a thick tree. Our lips collide, and the rough bark rubs my back through my coat. Caught between Olan and the tree, both solid and real, I feel enveloped. The familiarity from the other night reminds me of remembering how to ride a bicycle—easy, natural, and uninhibited. The freezing air is no match for the warmth of his face on mine. He starts slowly but quickly intensifies, and his tongue dances into my mouth, exploring, tangling with mine, the nuttiness of the walnuts adding some unusual texture, but he clearly doesn't mind. My tongue enters his mouth and lands right on the small space between his two front teeth, and I'm suddenly overtaken with heat. Ablaze with passion, my tongue grazes the gap and slides back and forth over it. His arms wrap around me entirely, and this must be what heaven feels like because I'd be very content to stand here in the freezing cold, kissing this man forever.

But he pulls away.

"Marvin, I'm so sorry I didn't text you back or call you. I needed to process what happened. And I wanted to converse in person, not over the phone. In my mind, even though I initiated it, I did not expect what happened Friday to happen. It wasn't planned. I've wanted to kiss you but had no idea if it was appropriate. Or if you even wanted me to kiss you. We were sitting in the car. So close. And you looked so adorable and well, I surprised myself as much as you. I'm a tad disoriented, but I don't regret it."

"So, you, um . . . like me?"

"Isn't that obvious?"

Once again, I feel like a dolt. Even with the kissing, I questioned his feelings because why would anyone amazing like Olan like me?

"Does this"—I use my hand to gesture between us—"mean you're bi?"

"Honestly, I don't know. I think that's what's confusing me. The only relationship I've had was with Illona's mom, and right now, I really shouldn't even be dating. I didn't expect these feelings, but we were hitting it off, and I just, I don't know, when I was younger, I knew something about me was different."

"Go on," I say.

"There was this time, I think I was about four, I remember going

127

to the park with my family. My mother packed a picnic, and I rested on the blanket as she unpacked the sandwiches. My two older brothers, Liam and Gabe, tossed a football on the field near the playground. Liam shouted for me to join them, and I remember feeling a pit in my stomach. They threw the ball so hard and fast that I knew I would never catch it and most likely get hurt trying. My mother handed me a book from the library I loved. It was filled with cars, trains, boats, and airplanes. I studied the pages, the photos, and the diagrams, tracing them with my finger. 'Leave Olan alone. He's reading with me,' she shouted, and they finally stopped hounding me. But I knew. Something deep and frightening in my stomach screamed I was different. Different than my brothers. Different from other boys. And not in a simple way."

Olan takes my hand and leads me a little further into the shelter of trees. Even through his glove and my mitten, the pressure of his fingers around mine feels tingly and toasty.

"Wait, so you've never kissed a...a..." I stammer.

"A teacher?"

I laugh because he's so ridiculously literal and hilarious and then say, "No, silly. A man."

"Nope. I've never kissed anyone except Isabella."

"Oh."

"Growing up a boy who was more into math and science than sports was tough in my family. I think questioning my sexuality felt like it would tip the scale. Pushing the idea out of my brain just sort of happened. When Isabella and I met, I suppose it was easier. And I did love her."

My ears are listening to him, but my head's ability to keep up is struggling. I heard he shouldn't be dating. He might be bi, but he's not sure. But there's a confidence in the way he kisses me. Olan Stone may be confused, but there's no doubt in my mind, he's a good man. No, a *wonderful* man. Catching feelings for a parent is brainless, and the

Teacher of the Year contest should be my focus. Dr. Knorse is counting on me. Damn, the entire Pelletier Elementary community is counting on me. And handing my heart over never works out. Stopping this nonsense would be the right course of action. Yes. No more kissing Olan Stone. Put those lips out of my mind.

"Listen, I like you. Maybe we can slow it down a little and hang out," he says.

"I can hang out. I like hanging out. I'm an expert hanger outer."

"See, you have to stop being so adorable." He leans forward and kisses me, gently this time, short, like dotting an i or crossing a t.

"Let's head back. I'll send you a text to make some plans to..."

"Hang out," I finish for him.

He takes my hand, stuffed into a mitten like a packed dumpling, and squeezes it. And even though it feels like the brakes have been slammed on our train, it's still chugging along, and considering I expected the worst, I'm not entirely disappointed. Being friends with Olan makes perfect sense. No more kissing. I can do this.

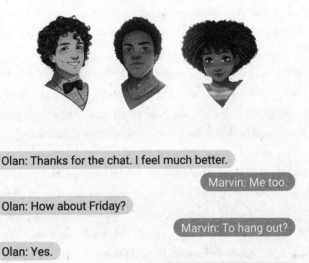

CHAPTER FIFTEEN

Olan: Thanks for the chat. I feel much better.

Marvin: Me too.

Olan: How about Friday?

Marvin: To hang out?

Olan: Yes.

Marvin: Sounds awesome.

With our heart-to-heart chat on Monday behind us, my expectations plummet to a fairly low level. Think when any former member of Destiny's Child (besides Beyoncé) releases music. The problem lies in that I don't typically neck with friends. I haven't kissed anyone in a long time. Truthfully, I've never kissed anyone that way.

Part of me wonders if simply being out of practice, with the kissing stuff, made it all supercharged with Olan. There's no denying the heat between us was palpable, but with so many reasons not to get involved, maybe being stuck in the friend zone wouldn't be so terrible.

"Having a friend that hot isn't necessarily a bad thing," Jill says, always knowing how to comfort me. We sit collating and stapling papers for a project.

"Thank you for that."

"Hear me out. Hot people attract other hot people. It's simple physics."

"What the hell do you know about physics?"

"I read a book about this. Seriously. If you hang out with him, even as a friend, he'll attract other hot people and increase your chances of meeting a hot person who wants to date you. It's one of the laws of attraction. Like attracts like. Hot attracts hot."

Her logic, while ridiculous, comes from a place of caring, and I'm unable to be upset with her.

"Well, bring on the hot people!" I shout.

To be clear, Olan's irrefutable hotness might be part of what drew me to him, but it's his awkward nerdiness, his tenderness with Illona, the uncomplicated way we communicate—those are what truly thrill me. I need to work on dampening that flame, not fanning it.

As is often the case, the week keeps me focused and busy, while the remoteness of Friday annoys me. I throw myself into teaching and being present for the children. Their sweet faces and random antics distract and entertain me. On Wednesday, at snack time, Zoe puts a raspberry on the tip of each of her fingers and tries to open her milk with "raspberry fingers." The ensuing mess is worth the hilarity of the entire class cheering her on. These small moments balance the stress of school. Sure, the teaching part matters, but the silliness, the affection, and the time together matter a whole lot more.

Friday finally arrives and I'm more than ready for some rest. One positive about Olan and me being planted firmly in the friend zone, there's less pressure surrounding our hanging out, and I'm actually pleased about that. The sight of Olan at pickup still causes a flip in my stomach, but it feels smaller, more manageable.

"Princess!" I wonder how long it will be until she'll be too big to leap into his strong arms.

With Illona's arms around her father, Olan looks at me and asks, "What time are you thinking?"

We'd already agreed I'd come over to his place as Cindy has the weekend off, and he wasn't keen on leaving his five-year-old alone for the evening.

"I'm totally flexible."

"If you want to share a meal with Illona and me, you could come at six? If you would prefer to wait until she goes to bed, maybe eight-ish? I totally get if you want a night off from children."

While thoughtful of him, more time with both him and Illona sounds way better than going home, eating a frozen meal, and waiting until eight to leave my place. I'd probably pass out on the sofa, drool spooling on my chin, and miss the entire evening.

"Well, I'm always hungry, so how about six? What can I bring?" My stomach's already rumbling.

"Just yourself," he says with a wink. Damnit. Apparently, friends wink now.

Illona pulls herself back. She's still in her father's arms.

"Mr. Block is coming over for dinner?"

"Is that all right?" Olan asks.

She nods and smiles with such zeal my heart gives a little flutter as I take them both in, and if I had ovaries, they'd be exploding right now. Boom.

"Okay, I'll see you both soon," I say.

As I walk to Olan's, the cold February air bites my lungs, but I enjoy the jolt of energy it provides. My view morphs as crowded apartments and small homes with nearly impossible street parking transform into single-family homes with yards, driveways, and garages increasing in size the closer I get to the coastline. Even though Jill uncovered why Olan uprooted his and Illona's worlds and relocated, I'm still clueless about what happened with his ex-wife. Clearly, Olan's more than comfortable financially, but we haven't spoken about money because nothing kills the mood faster than talking about finances. But now, as friends, maybe I'll learn more about him. He's upstairs. I'm downstairs. But if it doesn't bother him, I'm not going to worry about it.

Opening the door, Olan wears a red and tan flannel (how very New England of you, sir) and dark green joggers. The combo makes him resemble a lumberjack, and I'm not upset about it. He gazes at me and lets out a little laugh. This man clearly finds me hilarious, and although it's harmless, having him always examine me and snicker puts my self-confidence on edge.

"What did I do now, John Henry?"

He chuckles again and says, "You didn't do anything. Come inside, it's freezing. Why didn't you drive?"

"I prefer to walk whenever possible. It's the only exercise I get besides teaching, which, let's be real, is the ultimate cardio. Plus, the last time I was here, I needed a ride home, and look how that turned out."

We haven't established if we're pretending the kissing never happened or if we're even allowed to talk about it, so I'm unsure if that was out of line. Olan's eyes dart down, and I think I might have embarrassed him.

"Did I make you blush?"

He looks up, takes my hand, and places the back of it against his cheek. Heat radiates from his skin, instantly warming my hand and sending my belly into a tumble.

"You might not always see it, but yes, I blush."

"Now, who's being adorable?" I say because playfully teasing him makes my heart happy.

He takes my coat and hangs it up in a hallway closet. Illona comes charging down the hallway, barrels into my leg, and her arms encircle my waist, much as she does at school.

"Hey you," I gush. It truly feels wonderful to spend time with her outside of school and know our closeness translates. For this friendship between Olan and me to work, Illona must be a part of it. I sneak a glance at Olan's face. He lights up watching Illona and me, and Lord, his fatherly joy ignites something inside me.

"Marvin's going to prepare pizza with us," Olan says.

At this, in one motion, Illona breaks free from my waist, grabs my hand, and pulls me toward the elaborate kitchen.

"Just boss me around," I tease.

"Don't worry, we will." Olan nudges Illona, and she giggles in agreement.

The three of us fall into an easy rhythm making pizzas. With a Motown station playing through a hi-tech audio system, we begin. Thankfully, Olan bought premade dough. We roll it out, with Illona taking the pin as her dad stands behind her, pushing her small hands with his strong ones. She periodically directs me to sprinkle the dough with "flour, please." I'm also working on chopping an onion, red pepper, and mushrooms and am thankful for the gum secured in my pocket. Kissing may not be featured on the dessert menu, but I'd rather have fresh breath, even for chatting.

"Where's Cindy?" I ask.

"She's over at Sam's for the weekend. I'm home, she has a boyfriend, and we're pretty flexible with each other."

"She seems wonderful."

Illona grabs some shredded cheese from a bag and sprinkles it on the pizzas. Her tongue pokes out like when she uses scissors.

"Cindy relocated with us from California. With so much change, she's been a consistent presence for us."

"She moved with you? That's amazing."

"Well, her boyfriend was part of the restaurant launch here, contributing to her verdict."

With the meal in the oven, Olan grabs a small remote and turns the music louder. Just as "My Mistake" begins and the voices of Marvin Gaye and Diana Ross infuse the space, Illona grabs her dad's hands, and he begins to twirl her. I sit on one of the stools that were tucked under the lip of the island and crack up as Olan sways his hips to the beat. For a self-proclaimed nerd, Olan's got moves. Illona hears my laughter, lets go of one of her dad's hands, reaches out, grabs one of mine, and pulls me over to them. She's between us, swinging her arms to the music, and Olan reaches his free hand over to mine, and we become a circle of rhythm. I try not to let his fingers wrapping around mine shake me, and having Illona here, smiling, head back, lost in the music helps.

"Drink?" Olan asks me, opening the fridge. It's covered in the same dark gray as the rest of the cabinets, camouflaging it.

"Water is great."

"Tap or fizzy?"

"Oh, fancy! Fizzy, please."

"Juice for me, please," Illona says.

Olan pours Illona a glass of apple juice, takes out a large blue bottle that sizzles upon opening, and pours bubbly water for us.

Shrieking through the kitchen, the timer sounds more like an alarm, and Illona and I both jump. The three of us sit on tall stools flanking the island, eager to gobble up our pizza.

"It's hot!" Illona warns us.

"Give it a blow to help it cool off," I say, showing her how to blow gently on her bubbling toppings.

I blow on my own piece, take a bite, and the cheese stretches into long strings. As I pull the piece away from my mouth, Olan reaches over, grabs a small stray strand stuck to my chin, and pops it into my mouth, and I giggle because it's ridiculously cute.

"Adorable," he declares, making my face blush, matching the sauce. He probably should stop calling me adorable.

Once we've eaten, cleaned up, and played two rounds of Candy Land, which Illona wins, Olan declares, "Bedtime."

"But, Daddy, can't I stay up just a little later?" she implores with puppy dog eyes.

"Sorry, Princess, you know the rules."

"How about I read you a story tonight since I'm here?"

She bolts upstairs to brush her teeth.

"That was sneaky," Olan says.

I give a little shrug. "What's the point of having your teacher over for dinner if he can't read you a bedtime story?"

"Good point," he says and we head upstairs to join her.

She insists on not one, not two, but three books (because they were "too short"), but finally Illona's eyelids start looking rather heavy.

"Good night, Illona. Thanks for letting me make pizza with you and your dad."

"I'm glad you came. Daddy smiles a lot around you. Good night, Marvin," she murmurs.

Olan winks at me, and I leave them to their bedtime ritual. Heading downstairs, I pop a piece of gum in my mouth and steady myself for the "just us" portion of the evening. You know those candy shops in airports where they sell every sweet known to humankind in bulk? One time, I walked by one of those and didn't stop to buy anything. I can do this.

CHAPTER SIXTEEN

Sitting on the sofa, staring at this massive home, I remind myself that I don't require excess. My small one-bedroom often feels too much for just Gonzo and me. If I had money like Olan, would I want to live in a home like this? I'm not entirely sure. I think I'd feel lost. And who wants to clean all this? Wait, he probably has someone who cleans for him.

"Sorry about that. I think she was pushing her bedtime with extra stories. Probably because she figured you'd be a sucker," Olan says as he lands on the other end of the couch.

"Oh, no doubt she was, and no doubt I was."

"Do you want to watch a movie? Chat? You're the guest."

"How about if we watch something we've both seen so we don't have to pay too close attention?"

"Deal."

Sitting on the sofa with Olan, I'm starting to understand why friendship might be enough. He's been through many changes in the last few months, and I'm still unsure how he identifies. Bi? Curious? It doesn't matter. Two friends. Hanging out.

"So, you don't drink?" Olan asks.

"No."

"Not at all?"

I shake my head.

"Mind if I ask why not?"

We're having such a lovely time. I don't want to be a Debbie Downer, so I simply say, "There's a family history of…" I mime taking a swig from a bottle. "It's easier. What about you?"

"Same," he says.

That explains the lack of booze in the house and provides one less thing I need to worry about. Sober friends are always a plus.

We land on a rom-com from the early 2000s we both admit to seeing (maybe I've seen it more than once, but Olan doesn't need to know that).

"So, you're an engineer or something."

"Yes, I'm an engineer or something."

"What got you into that?"

"I guess I've always been curious. My dad had this old dead Dodge in the garage. He was always tinkering with it, determined to make it useful. We'd spend hours each weekend on the engine, dismantling it, cleaning it, and reassembling it. I was fascinated with how engines worked and read every book I could find. I think my dad thought I'd be a mechanic. For a time, I did too, but what I truly wondered about was how to make these engines superior, more robust, more efficient."

As he talks, his eyes light up and sparkle as his hands move more than I've ever witnessed. Enthusiasm vibrates off him. He's so passionate about this and getting him to chat about it appears to have opened something in him.

"I worked extremely hard. Pushed myself. Took as many AP math and science classes as I could. Once Stanford became a reality and not just a fantasy, I knew this was something I could build a life around."

"Is that how you got to California?"

"Yup. College and my friends in the engineering program became

138

my life. It's where I discovered who I am. I'm a nerd who loves jet propulsion technology."

I chuckle and say, "Um, most nerds don't look like you."

Warning, friend zone diversion.

"Marvin, I'll have you know, I'm what's known as a hot nerd."

"Excuse me. Did you actually just call yourself hot?"

His eyes dart down, and I recognize this as his tell. He's blushing. His skin shines, and bashful Olan feels like the sweetest tiny gift.

I begin to recline and move my feet out a little. With the entire couch between us, it feels like a football field separates us. Probably a good thing.

"Do you mind?"

"Of course not. Make yourself comfortable."

We turn toward each other, me sprawled out and him with his legs up under him, making him appear slightly taller than he truly is.

"Can I ask you something?" he asks.

"Shoot."

"If this is too personal, please tell me, and I'll cease the subject, but you're young, handsome, and a terrific guy. Why are you single?"

"What I heard is you think I'm handsome?" His eyes dart down again, and this time, I know he's blushing, and the mischievous part of me relishes it. "What makes you assume I'm single? Maybe I've just got myself a new boyfriend."

Olan's eyes go wide, and he looks like he's just seen a ghost.

"I'm kidding. My last boyfriend kind of broke my heart, so I've been, I don't know, recovering, taking it easy."

"Oh, Marvin. Do you mind if I ask what happened?"

"The short version, he cheated."

"On you? I'm so sorry," he says, and leans over and rubs my calf.

"Yeah, not ideal. I walked in on them in our laundry room. Which probably explains my contempt for washing clothes. I gave my heart to

Adam and he squashed it, so that was a colossal mistake. Anyway, I'm focusing on teaching. Which, by the way, can consume you if you let it. And it's not like I meet throngs of men, teaching kindergarten."

"This data tracks. And you clearly put everything into your job. I know a little about that."

He pulls his hand away, and my calf yearns for him to return his powerful fingers.

"I guess after Adam I just didn't know if a relationship was in the cards for me. I tried loving someone, building a life, and it bit me in the ass."

"It's probably not fair for me to speak about someone I don't know, but he must be a fool to have been unfaithful."

"That's sweet. And thank you. When he told me, it was less about asking for forgiveness and more about him asking if we could have an open relationship."

"An open relationship? Like dating other people?"

"Well, for Adam, more like fucking other people, but yes."

"Wow."

"Yeah, an open relationship doesn't fit into my framework."

"Well, coming from someone who literally has only been with one person, me neither."

My heart flutters, knowing our relationship rudders work similarly.

"My heart broke so quickly, my head couldn't keep up. It hit me like a punch to the stomach. So, it's just me. And Gonzo. He's hoping to keep me all to himself for the foreseeable future. He's a fantastic cuddle buddy and only requires minimal feeding and scooping of litter, so I'm not kicking him out anytime soon."

Olan grins, and damn, his lips curl up enough to allow the tiny gap between his two front teeth to peek out at me, making my stomach wobble. Being friends with a hot man you've made out with feels like going to a gourmet ice-cream shop and only ordering water.

"What about you? What happened with Illona's mom?" I'd had no intention of asking him this, but since he brought up my relationship status, why not?

"Oh, it's complicated. Isabella and I are more...convoluted. We're still friends. Illona talks to her every few days. We just, well, working together became an issue. For me, not her."

"Oh. Is that why you sold your company?"

"Partly. I needed...a break. But we can talk about that another time. I'm enjoying myself. Let's not ruin it."

He reaches out and pats my foot. Even with my sock blocking direct skin-to-skin connection, I welcome the contact. Jill and I are affectionate all the time. Being friends with Olan might not be as hard as I thought.

The long week catches up to me, and much like my teenage infatuation for NSYNC, I begin to fade. Friday nights are tough, and I slowly close my eyes, relishing Olan's hand resting on my foot. Olan grabs a blanket draped over the back of the couch and gingerly covers me. The blanket's warmth, the crackling fire across the room, the lingering smell of pizza in the air, and Olan's hand resting on my foot all comfort and lull me out.

My eyes struggle to open. Olan lies before me, his feet up on the chaise portion of the sofa, head tilted back, softly breathing, the right portion of his body tucked under the blanket with me. Apparently, once I dozed off, he followed suit. Netflix mocks us with the damn "are you still watching" message. Clearly, no. Peeking at my watch, I see it's close to midnight. I should be home by now. Carefully, I attempt to get up without disturbing Olan, but he stirs, and one eye, followed by the other, cracks.

"What time is it?" he grumbles.

"Late. Stay put. I'm going to head home. I had a nice time tonight." I swing my legs off the couch and prepare to stand.

"Stay. We have two guest rooms. Seriously, it's late."

"No, I should go."

Do I want to walk home? Not particularly. I could call for a car. Would I rather spend the night here with him? Duh. But being Olan's friend needs to happen in baby steps. Hanging out tonight has been lovely, and though I've enjoyed myself, I need to limit my exposure to him because, friend zone or not, chemistry gurgles under the surface.

"At least let me call you a car."

"You're sweet, but it's not necessary."

"Just stay, please."

His voice shakes when he says "please," and he moves closer and under the blanket's cover, gingerly resting his hand on that spot between my thigh and knee he seems so fond of. A jolt of electricity rushes up to my chest, and I worry we're teetering into dangerous waters. Doesn't he know the thigh area lies in the erogenous zone? Friends aren't allowed to put their hands on their friend's thigh area when said friends are trying to remain in the friend zone.

He's peering at me now, and I swear, by all that's good and mighty, I know I'm rusty, and maybe I'm reading him wrong, but I swear there's an eagerness and urgency, and um, I'm fairly certain he's eye fucking me. His fingers crawl up my leg, and he takes my hand. The feel of his warm skin on mine leaves me paralyzed with uncertainty. My head tells me to stop. I'm frozen in motion. My heart tells me to carry on.

"I thought we were slowing things down?" I ask.

"Slowing down, yes. Stopping, no." Have I missed a step? "Marvin, I want to kiss you so fucking bad."

Apparently, I've missed more than a step. I've missed an entire flight of stairs. My breath catches, but I manage to murmur, "Oh. Um, okay."

"Come here," he says, his voice low and raspy, and I eagerly scoot over.

And his soft lips are on my face. On my cheek, yes, but so close to my mouth. A question, an invitation. At this juncture, I have a choice to make. Push him away and bolt home or succumb. I give a little sigh. If I died tonight, what a shame it would be to abandon this opportunity.

"Are you sure?"

He nods twice and mumbles, "Uh, huh."

With permission granted, I adjust my face a few inches, and our lips connect, and though we've done this a few times now, the fire between us still makes my stomach do an entire gymnastics floor routine. We're talking flips and somersaults and long sparkly ribbons waving in the air. A perfect ten. I'm not sure I've ever felt this aroused from simply kissing someone. With Adam, there were sparks but no sizzle. His bravado always left me feeling inadequate, like I wasn't quite enough. Olan makes me feel like I'm the entire universe waiting to be discovered, explored, and adored.

Being this close to him urges my soul to crawl out of its hiding place. Olan makes me feel protected from all my worries and fears. The act of kissing does something to him, too, clearly. His tongue dances with mine, and he slowly begins to push me down, my back to the sofa, and crawls on top of me.

"Is this okay?" he asks.

Okay? I give you the understatement of the year, and Olan asking me, wanting consent turns me on even more, which I didn't think possible.

"Omigod, fuck yes. Come here."

I put my arms around his torso, drawing him to me, urging his lips to stop speaking and get back to kissing. His tongue brushes my teeth, exploring my mouth. He shifts to my ear again, and there's no hiding how much he excites me. Having Olan on me, all his weight, the pressure of his body, my dick comes to life, blood rushing to it, aching as he gently thrusts against me. I know I shouldn't push him off me, but— overwhelmed by the sensations, the emotions, and the moment—I do.

Shoving him up, he's now between my legs, on his knees, staring at me. My spit dotting the corners of his lips, he gives me a *what now?* look.

"Is something wrong?" he asks. The concern in his voice warms my chest.

"God, no. Nothing's wrong. But, are you sure?" I ask, nodding toward my pants, unable to hide my rock-hard erection.

"Affirmative." His voice trembles and he points to his own tented pants.

"Sit," I command.

With his permission, Mr. Block takes over. Olan swings his legs off the couch, and as soon as his feet hit the ground, I'm up, straddling him. On top, my view shifts. I'm now almost a whole foot elevated above him, and he squirms for a second. Taking charge feels necessary, and being in control makes my skin crackle with pleasure.

"Okay?" I ask.

"Uh, yes. Yes. More than okay."

His hands land on my hips, and mine explore his neck and back. Grabbing at his glorious hair, my fingers knead like a baker working through dough. The noises he's producing increase in volume as my lips investigate his neck and ear. I continue using my tongue to paint the inside of his ear with affection. He whimpers louder and I suddenly worry about Illona upstairs, hearing her teacher going to town with her dad.

"Illona, I don't..."

"Hold, please." He puts a finger up, wiggles out from under me, and shoots up the stairs like a roadrunner zipping through the desert. He flies back to his spot and I give a little laugh at his eagerness and speed.

"She's out cold. I shut her door. We're good."

With this welcome news, I grab his hand and drag him back to a seated position so I can climb back on top and go back to work. He resumes the low moans, and whimpers vibrate through his throat into my mouth, turning me the fuck on. As I work on his ear and neck, I raise my hands in a "put 'em up" position, cupping each of his firm pecs. With his groaning and occasional lick to my neck, I'm confident this is turning Olan the fuck on too.

"Are you sure? I don't want to pressure you." I've paused because, based on his earlier comment, this might be the first time Olan's been with a man, and it's important he wants this. I've not only stopped the kissing, but my bottom has come to rest on his lap and based on what pokes my ass from his pants, he's more than into this.

To answer, he takes my right hand off his chest and moves it to the rigidness in his pants. Lord, that's one way to reply. He's rock hard, his poor joggers stretched to their limit. This was most definitely not on my agenda for the evening. The surprise in Olan's pants sends a shock of bliss up my arm, straight to my heart, up to my head, and zips directly to my groin.

"You're so fucking hard," I say with glee.

He replies by licking and sucking my neck. I begin to apply pressure, slowly at first, pausing from kissing and shifting my attention to teasing the head of his cock through his pants. Lower noises rumble out of him.

"Olan?"

He lets out a sound that resembles "unh," and I take it as verification.

"Um, the thing is, well, this will be more challenging with your pants on."

He angles his head up and replies, "Well, if you're adept with your hands, you can always make magic happen."

"Are you being naughty?" I let out a little chuckle.

He grabs my hips and gently lifts me up, not entirely off him, just enough so in one sweeping motion, he can pull his pants and underwear down around his ankles. He gently pushes me back down and places my hand back where it was, now unrestricted by fabric. He's solid, firm, and the heat from his dick makes my palm sweat. To continue properly, I need to move down to the ground, so I begin to kiss Olan's chin, progressing slowly down, caressing his entire neck as I lift up his sweatshirt. He lifts his arms to assist, and I pull the damn garment off entirely. I pause for a breath, numb for a moment, taking him in.

"Is something wrong?" he asks.

"No. You're just fucking beautiful."

I put my hands back on his chest, my fingers now touching his deep ebony skin, and secretly wish I could keep my hands here forever. As I continue my descent, kissing his neck and moving lower, my fingers play with his chest. Finding new ways to titillate him thrills me. My mouth moves to assist my hands. I lick my thumb and slowly tease his left pec. My tongue mirrors the motions on his right nipple, and they promptly respond to my touch, sensitive and alert, eager for attention. He writhes under me and grabs the back of my head, massaging my scalp as I taste the sweet saltiness of his skin.

"Holy fuck, Marvin," he breathes out.

"Do you like that?"

"No, I love it."

By his reaction, I'm almost positive no one has ever paid attention to Olan's chest this way, and I make a mental note about his fondness for it. I continue down, sampling his stomach and licking the small patch of hair surrounding his belly button. The nearness almost overwhelms me. He twitches under the heat and wetness of my mouth.

"Am I tickling you?"

"Um, a little. But please don't stop."

He finally settles, all the jumpiness and worries thawing from him as his abs melt into my mouth. Feeling mischievous, I give him a quick zerbert on his stomach, and he releases a low laugh that makes my insides soften.

Finally, I'm on the floor, the area rug beneath me, all of him in front of me. All of him. He's completely vulnerable, and I feel beyond lucky knowing I may be the first man to witness him in this way. From my new vantage point, I inspect Olan's cock, and it's, well, stunning. The perfect Goldi-cock—not too big, not too small, but just right.

He bows his back, his hand on my head raveled in my shaggy mop of curls, as I begin to stroke him. Slowly at first, until he acclimates. The gentle tugs at my hair signal me to open the throttle. I look up, catch his eye, and spit, adding a slickness as his eyes widen.

"Damn," he moans.

"Okay?"

"Uh-huh. Yup. Definitely, okay."

I press on, and Olan begins a continual low growl. I peek at his face and he's watching me, intrigued. He takes his free hand and caresses my cheek. I turn my head slightly and take his thumb in my mouth, sucking on his finger as my hand continues working his slick shaft. Keeping my eyes locked on his face, I watch him bite his lower lip. His hand, now a fist in my hair, latches onto my head. I move closer to spit on his cock again and bump up the speed.

He leans his head back and sways his head a little.

"Marvin, fuck. Oh god, don't stop."

I give him a grin, and he slowly starts thrusting his hips up. Yes, sir, I can take a hint. Accepting his invitation, I lick the tip slowly, teasing him as his thighs shudder, and put the head in my mouth. He tastes salty, delicious, and heavenly. Swallowing him slowly, working all of him in, I begin matching his thrusts. This feeling. I've never felt this uninhibited. This freedom from worry and self-doubt drives me wild.

"God, I love it," he purrs.

"Love what?" I say, pausing, wanting him to name it.

"Watching your lips around my dick."

Feeling his body in the throes of pleasure sends zings of hunger down my chest to my own cock. Right now, gratifying Olan becomes my sole focus. I use my right hand to create a tunnel of flesh, his unyielding cock sliding in and out. He's still pumping up into my mouth, but he can only do so much from his seated position.

"Do you mind standing?" I ask.

"Oh, um sure. Am I doing something wrong?"

"Hell no. I want you to fuck my face."

Olan's eyes go wide. I fear Mr. Block has shocked him.

"I mean, only if you want."

"Uh, yeah. Yeah. I want."

With that, he stands, the pants around his ankles causing him to wobble. I tug at his left cuff, trying to get it off to afford him more balance. "Lift, please."

And he does. With his one leg free from the pants, I kneel in front of him and place my hands on his ass. It's firm, slightly fuzzy, and my fingers delight in grabbing it.

"You good?" I ask.

"Yeah. Oh yeah. I don't want to hurt you."

"Olan, you're not going to hurt me, but thank you. If it's too much, I'll let you know. Now," I say.

He slides his glorious cock into my mouth, and I move my hands to his hips. Feeling his hesitation, I give him nonverbal direction by pulling and pushing him with increased speed. Once he realizes where I'm leading and that I'm actually requesting this, he takes over, and I move my hands away. His sturdy hands on my head, massaging my curls, occasionally grip fistfuls of hair. My left hand moves to cup his balls, and I gently begin rubbing and applying a small amount of pressure underneath.

"Oh. Damn. You are so beautiful."

I peek up, and his eyes are fixed on me. Watching me worship his magnificent dick.

"Your cock is beautiful."

He laughs and says, "Nobody's ever told me that."

"Well, take it from me. It's beautiful. Gorgeous. And delicious, by the way."

I resume sucking, slurping, and making a sloppy mess of it all. I'm not exactly sure what's happened or who I am right now, but something about Olan causes me to let go. Unhinge. Go wild. A huge urgency drives me on, reveling in bringing him to the edge. He begins to breathe faster, thighs shaking, hands gripping my hair hard and tight.

"I'm close," he says, perhaps as a warning, and I switch back to using my hand, his shaft all slick from both my mouth and his own precum, tangy and sharp.

"Fuck, yes, come for me," I say.

Olan lets out a sudden sound, a deep moan from his throat, full of air and grit, and the sudden punch in his breath as he comes delights me beyond measure. I do my best to catch it all with my hands, but a few drops land on my cheek, tickling my skin as it drips down, eliciting a giggle.

"You're fucking adorable. And amazing," he says, joining me with a laugh.

He sits down, his breathing beginning to slow, my head now resting on his thigh, and because I'm slightly mischievous, I grab his dick and pop it in my mouth to make sure I've squeezed every ounce out of him. He shudders and begins to shimmy away, so I relent.

"You're a mess," he says, nodding toward my hands and face.

"I'm fucking perfect."

"Yes, you most certainly are."

Returning from the bathroom, where I've cleaned myself up, I drop down next to Olan, who reaches out for the washcloth in my hand. Holding the fabric hostage behind my back, I tease him. "Not yet."

Leaning forward, I start at his forehead with a soft kiss, repeat it on his nose, lips, and chin and move my lips on the soft spot just below his neck, tasting his saltiness.

"Let me," I say and take the powder-blue rag and clean him up judiciously, paying careful attention to make sure he's spotless.

"That was unexpected."

"You're telling me," I say with a sigh.

"What about you?" He reaches up and playfully tugs at the waistband of my pants.

"Just tasting you was enough. Truly. Plus, it's late, and I'm exhausted," I say, letting out a big sigh. Between teaching all week and savoring Olan's cock, I'm spent.

Olan remains reclined, naked, in front of me, and with the frenzy over, I drink in his gloriousness. He's got one of those bodies I understand exist from magazines and movies. But sitting here with him, I'm not sure how I'm allowed to worship. This is the physique of an athlete, not an engineer, so I'm slightly confused.

"The abs, you get those from all the engineering?"

Embarrassed, Olan covers his face with his hands and reaches for the blanket tossed aside in the commotion.

"What? I mean, all the aerospace stuff really works your abs, right?" I poke his stomach through the blanket to punctuate my point.

"The gym in the basement provides me with an outlet. For stress."

"Hmm. Maybe I should channel my stress into something other than ice cream?"

"Marvin, you're adorable."

"People don't generally want to fuck adorable. Wait, do you have an adorable fetish?"

"You're trouble," he replies and leans over for a kiss. "I exercise to channel my frustrations. I need an outlet, a safe one, and cardio and weight training help."

"Please, don't ever ask me to run with you."

This makes Olan explode with laughter, and having this effect on him warms the cockles of my heart.

"Deal," he says, pulling his pants up. "Now, as to the business of sleeping…"

"I should go home. I'd be mortified if Illona woke up and was uncomfortable with her teacher here."

"I think she'd be thrilled. Maybe not if you were in bed with her dad. We're not there…yet."

"Where are we, anyway? I mean, I know we're here, in your house, on the sofa, but where are *we*?" I move a hand between us.

Olan takes my hand in his, enveloping it with his strong fingers.

"We're okay, Marvin. We're taking things slow."

"Yeah, here's the thing, I don't usually do this," and I open my free hand to gesture to the entire area we occupy, "with my friends."

He smiles, and I have the sudden urge to bite his cheek.

"No, I get that. But we're good. Let's take things slow and see what happens." His words ease my anxious heart. "And maybe it's best if we keep this between us. For now."

"I think that's wise. We're not breaking any rules," I reply. But he's the parent of a student in my class. Teacher of the Year and all riding on it. Technically, no rules forbid this, but there's no reason to go broadcasting it to the world either.

"We're not?"

"Nope. I checked. Four times. But I agree. Maintaining decorum feels wise. Now, how about one of those guest rooms?" I inquire.

A few minutes later, Olan has taken me to a comfortable room next to his bedroom that I apparently missed the night I watched Illona. We're still on the opposite end of the long hallway to Illona and Cindy's rooms which, given the house size, stretches longer than my entire apartment. Like the rest of the house, the room makes my paltry apartment look like a discount store catalog. The king-sized bed calls me, and I'm quite knackered at this point.

Olan lingers by the door, and I sense his tentativeness to leave. I'd be lying if I said I didn't want him to stay. Or for me to follow him. But his daughter sleeps thirty feet away, and we've had plenty of gratification tonight.

"Do you want to, maybe, lie with me? For just a few minutes?"

Olan gives me an of-course-I-do-but-my-daughter-is-right-down-the-hallway-and-it's-complicated look.

"You can't blame me for suggesting it."

"How about for ten minutes?"

"Sold!" I whisper-shout.

And we do. Olan sets a timer on his watch and lies on his back. He opens his arm, inviting me to scooch down and rest my head on his chest, which is becoming one of my favorite areas of his body. His strong fingers rub my head, moving my hair around in circles, placing pressure on my skull, and the room begins to fade away.

"I should warn you," I say, "whenever my head is rubbed or scratched, I get incredibly sleepy."

"Roll over."

I rotate away from him, and he drapes his right arm around me, squeezing me, pulling me toward him. The light scratching from his hand instantly relaxes me. This can't be super comfortable for him, but he does it anyway. "You sleep, and I'll sneak out and see you at breakfast," he breathes into my ear.

Curled on my side, enveloped in Olan's body, him scratching my head, defines bliss for me. Before I know it, I'm out. The following day, I wake to the faintest taste of cherry ChapStick on my lips. I may be alone in this strange room, but I feel like the sun outside the window rises just for me.

CHAPTER SEVENTEEN

Dear Families,
Next week our class will celebrate Valentine's Day. This is a time to
honor the friendships we've cultivated. Attached, please find a list
of every student's name spelled correctly. If your child would like to
exchange cards, please send one for everyone in the class. We'll have
a small party with treats. If you're interested in contributing, please
let me know.

Thank you,
Mr. Block

"It was lovely, pleasant, perfectly innocent," I say, with Jill sitting across from me at a table in her classroom as we both cut hearts out in various shades of white, pink, and red. Lying to Jill makes my insides crumple and jumble like a skydiver with a faulty parachute. I do not care for it one bit. But Olan is a parent. Teacher of the Year. The school's funding. There's no way I would even be considered if this got out. And we're figuring things out. Once it's figured out, I'll tell her.

"But you slept over."

"In the guest room. We made pizza with his daughter. And watched a movie. In the morning, we had cereal, and I walked home. End of story."

"That sounds remarkably date-ish to me," she argues. She's not entirely wrong.

"I realize it sounds that way, but it wasn't. We are squarely locked in the friend zone, and I'm perfectly fine with that," I fib as Olan's flawless naked body flashes in my head. His gorgeous cock in my hand. My mouth. His body writhing under my spell. Friday night obliterated the friend zone, and my chest tingles at the memory.

"Anyway, how was your weekend?" I change the subject with the deftness of a child spitting out their meal into a napkin and hoping their parents don't notice. Luckily, it appears to have worked.

"Pretty good. I actually have some news."

"News? What? What is it?"

Jill stands and shuts the door. If privacy is required, this must be something spectacular.

"I'm pregnant," she whispers, placing a hand on her stomach.

"What? Really? How? When?" I shout louder than I should.

"Hush it. Yes, really, and I think you know how. I'll spare you the gory details of heterosexual intercourse. I missed my last period, took a home test, and the doctor confirmed it this morning, but we're only in the first trimester and agreed not to tell *anyone* yet. Technically, I'm not supposed to tell you, so not a word, mister. I mean it. Zip it. Nobody." She runs a finger across her lips.

I knew Jill and Nick had been trying for a little over a year. The last time she was pregnant didn't have a happy ending. She'd texted me during Morning Meeting. We never text when we're teaching, so I knew something was up. She was experiencing extreme cramps, and I drove her to the hospital to meet Nick. One of the worst days in Jill's life became one I will always remember for all the wrong reasons. I knew they'd been trying, but after the last time, I don't ask about it unless she brings it up. Jill and Nick expecting again gives me hope.

"Oh my gosh, best news ever! I'm so happy. For you both." I stand and hug her tightly. "I'm not hurting you, right?"

"No, Marvin, you're not hurting the tiny human growing inside of me with a tight hug. Now listen, part of the reason I'm telling you, and nobody else yet, has to do with the bathroom. I will have to pee a lot more often and need you to cover for me."

"Aye, aye, captain." I give my best salute. "Seriously, Jill, you know I'd do anything for you. Anything. I love you so much." The corners of my eyes sting with wetness as a stab of guilt about not being honest with her jabs me.

She sniffles. "I love you too. Now stop making me cry. My hormones are all over the place."

"Anything for you. And the baby. The baby!" I put my hand on her stomach. "Do you mind?" I pull my hand away. "Because I know not everybody loves people touching their stomach with the baby, but a baby!"

"You're not people, you're Marvin, and you're my people, and you can touch my stomach as much as you want," she assures me, grabbing my hand and returning it to her belly.

Thinking about how much Jill wants this, how she's telling me and nobody else, and what I'm keeping from her creates a chasm in my stomach. If things progress with Olan, I'll have to tell her something. Jill and I don't do secrets, and I'm certain she'll be on to me soon. And maybe keeping things hushed heightens the turn-on factor, but I'd love to tell Jill every gory detail because she would relish every single one with me.

Olan: Mr. Block, Illona would like to know if she can bring fruit for the Valentine's party?

Marvin: Mr. Stone, fruit would be lovely. Red fruits would be on theme, but no pressure.

Olan: Apples, strawberries, raspberries. Am I missing any red fruits?

Marvin: Cherries and cranberries but most kids aren't fans. And by kids I mean me. Except for cherry chapstick. 😬

Olan: No cherries or cranberries for Mr. Block. Got it.

Marvin: You have to stop calling me Mr. Block.

Olan: Why?

Marvin: It makes me hard.

Olan: Sorry Mr. Block. 😊

I'm not sure folks who don't teach understand the magic of Valentine's Day in kindergarten. For my students, the cards, stickers, temporary tattoos, and candy, all the candy, have nothing to do with romantic love. They symbolize friendship, community, and belonging. A day to exchange cheap cards, stale candy, and heartfelt smiles to celebrate the little classroom family we've become.

The children pass out store-bought cards with silly jokes in the morning, leaving bags decorated with puffy hearts, cupids, and rainbow stickers to sit on the windowsill. I fill our day with stories and activities about all types of love. Romantic (kissing, ew!), platonic (friends), and familial (family, pets, etc.) love are discussed, and I do believe, even at five, they understand the nuances.

Toward the end of the day, the festivities begin in earnest. The excitement bubbles and bursts from their tiny faces. This resembles a birthday party, but we're celebrating everyone, not a single friend. Cards opened, jokes read and laughed at, candy licked, faces smeared and sticky, and temporary tattoos applied at the sink encompass our party. By most adult standards, our celebration is beyond basic, but to these kids, it's a memory they'll cherish for a long time.

Like each child, I've made a bag for cards too. I rotate between tables to open mine. Most children have given me the same variety they gave to their classmates, but a few have crafted their own, and I read every single one aloud as they gush, blush, and giggle.

"To Mr. Block, thank you for your big heart. Love Ricky," I read.

Ricky dips his head, but his smile overtakes his round face, and he wraps his arms around my waist because whenever words fail to express emotions in kindergarten, the best route is an embrace.

"Ricky, I love it. You wrote this all yourself?"

He nods emphatically.

"And look, you drew me holding your hand, and who is this?"

I point to a drawing I'm unable to identify.

"Gonzo!"

"Of course it's Gonzo. Look at him, it looks just like him."

It looks nothing like him.

"I'm going to take this home and show Gonzo and tell him, 'Ricky drew this lovely picture of you.'"

Another tight squeeze from Ricky.

I pull another card from my bag.

"Mr. Block, thank you for helping me. Your friend, Illona."

"Do you love it?" Illona launches herself onto my lap.

"I adore it, but I adore you more."

She leans into me, and I wrap my arms around her. We have a huge love fest in kindergarten, and my heart, already full, bursts with tenderness. There are cupcakes with pink frosting, all the red fruit minus cranberries and cherries, and strawberry yogurt. The simple spread delights the class, and when I tell them we need to clean up to go home, they collectively groan in disappointment.

As we wait for the bus kids to be picked up, Sophia shouts, "Best Valentime's Day ever!" a classic and charming mispronunciation. Overtaken by her enthusiasm, the entire class begins chanting along with her, and these are the moments I hope they remember.

At pickup, Olan and I have become adept at keeping any hint of desire hidden between us. Dr. Knorse looms over the table, checking signatures, saying hellos, and investigating the scene for any cracks in the surface. I have no desire to provide her with one.

"Princess," Olan shouts from behind a cluster of waiting adults. My ears register him first and instruct my heart to stop with all the fluttering. "How was the party?" She's in his arms now.

"Oh, Daddy, we had cupcakes and fruit and so many cards." She holds up her bag, an explosion of pink and red goodness.

"Happy Valentine's Day." Dr. Knorse's greeting to Olan and the other pickup parents leans festive today.

"Happy Valentine's Day to you, Dr. Knorse." Olan attempts to charm her, and I bite my lip to contain my laughter. "And Happy Valentine's Day, Mr. Block." He grins, and the three of us stand there in what feels like a standoff in a bad western, so I end it.

"You too, have a great night," I reply, and I turn and head back to the classroom to tidy up.

There's been no discussion about Valentine's Day between us because we're taking it slow, and I don't want to push matters in an uncomfortable way. Rushing and forcing things only leads to disaster. Sometimes I watch the children at Choice Time playing with tiny toy cars, and when their little hands slap the top of the metal and thrust it too quickly, the car ends up toppling up in a horrible crash, their squeaky voices erupting in laughter. There's no reason for us to push whatever this is that we're not actually talking about or defining yet.

I bought Olan a simple card and hid it in my backpack. It took some time to find one that was sweet but not overly sappy with some painted hearts and a quote that reads, "Love is when you meet someone who tells you something new about yourself—Andre Breton." I wasn't sure about buying a card with the word *love* in any form, but it turns out for Valentine's Day, love is almost impossible to avoid. And Olan has awoken things in me I never knew existed. The quote fits. In an effort to keep it understated, I only wrote, *Thank you for all the fun,* ♥ *Marvin.* We have no plans to see each other outside of pickup today, and I can always give it to him another time.

Driving home with the card in my bag, I'm tempted to pull over and text him. If I let Olan know I have a card for him, he might ask to meet. Or maybe he'd feel bad for not getting me something. Perhaps he'd think I was forcing things. All not outcomes I'm seeking. The uncertainty accompanying the newness of whatever we are is both exciting and excruciatingly frustrating. Not knowing triggers my anxiety; if I let it fester too much, I'll put myself in a bad place.

I flip to the Eighties playlist on my phone, and the high-hats, pulsing bass line, and the unmistakable male voice croons the opening lines of "Don't You Want Me." Within the safety of my car, I belt out the chorus and bop along to the synths. Damn, The Human League never got their due respect.

By the time the song fades, I'm parked, swaying, singing, basking in the comfort of an absolute classic jam, and thankful for the distraction and de-escalation it brought. Walking up to my building, I give a little half-smile to myself. Ice cream in the freezer, a sappy movie on the TV, and Gonzo snuggling under a blanket with me sounds like a perfect evening after the nutty day at school.

As I go to put my key in the front door, I spot something red resting on the ground, directly under the handle. I bend down to investigate and spot *Marvin Block* written on the small envelope and recognize Olan's handwriting from his notes. That bugger. Shivering in the frigid February air, I rip it open. The front of the card has an illustration from *The Very Hungry Caterpillar* on it. It depicts the opening pages. The moon glows softly, the caterpillar still snoozes in its egg, and the entire story awaits to unfold. It's one of those blank cards you can use for any occasion, and Olan has written, in his less than legible handwriting: *Marvin, thank you for being you and helping me be me. Olan.*

My chest feels like warm apple butter syrup, and I almost forget about the subzero temperature. I read his message again because, oh my gosh. Pulling the card up to my face, I give the front, inside, and back a little peck. I skip upstairs, peel off my coat, begin to get comfortable for the evening, and pull out my phone.

Marvin: You're sneaky.

Olan: You're sexy. I can't stop thinking about you.

Marvin: I thought I was adorable?

Olan: OK, both.

Marvin: Well I have a card for you too. Maybe you should come get it?

Olan: Can't tonight. Heading out on a daddy date with Illona.

Marvin: That is the sweetest. Have fun and I'll give it to you soon.

Olan: Give what to me soon? ☺

Marvin: The CARD. But also, yes, please.

CHAPTER EIGHTEEN

> Marvin: FYI the conference mail is going out this morning.

> Olan: Thanks for the heads up. I want an exemplary slot.

> Marvin: You definitely want a good slot.

> Olan: Now who's being naughty?

> Marvin: Only with you. 😏

Since the night at his house almost two weeks ago, Olan and I text frequently, sometimes multiple times a day. Our communication has taken a first-class ticket out of the friend zone straight to Sexytown. We haven't spent time alone since that night, and frankly, all the stolen glances at school and texts in the evenings have my body feeling like a volcano about to erupt. I worry about saving all his texts. They feel like evidence someone could use against me, but also, they provide immense pleasure and have become an integral part of my spank bank.

Olan: You up?

Marvin: Barely.

Olan: I can't stop thinking about you. Your lips around my dick.

Marvin: Well now I'm definitely up.

It's becoming more and more clear, regardless of how I feel about dating, there's no fighting what's happening with Olan. Thinking about him makes my insides feel like jelly. I am so ready for more kissing, more touching, more of the steamy stuff, and based on the nature of his texts, Olan concurs. Between his commitments with Illona, meetings, and my kindergarten planning, plus preparing for the Teacher of the Year interview and school visit, our relationship has been confined to cell phones and sneaking looks at pickup.

With Valentine's Day over, I begin to shift my focus to parent conferences because teaching means volleying from one event to the next. Scheduling of the conferences benefits from an online system that allows families to select their day and time. I simply send an email with a link, and they do the rest. Unfortunately, the rest of preparing and participating in the conferences feels more complicated.

Between culling through saved work, assessments, and portfolios and attempting to organize it all into some semblance of meaning, I'm typically scrambling to get everything ready on the actual days of conferences.

"Marvin, any conferences you need me to attend?" Kristi makes her rounds, checking in, and I truly do appreciate her wanting to help. In years past, I've had conferences with difficult situations to discuss, and having the guidance counselor attend makes a world of difference. Heavy topics can arise and Kristi's presence and expertise are invaluable. Luckily, I don't think she's needed at any of my conferences this year.

"I'm actually all set this year but thank you for checking."

"How are you holding up otherwise?"

Kristi views her job as not only looking out for the social-emotional well-being of the students but the staff too.

"I'm good, just ready for conferences to be over."

"Well, I know families are thrilled to meet with you. How is Illona settling in?"

"She seems happy. The other kids adore her."

"When is her conference? Should I come to chat with her dad about her adjustment?"

"It's my last late conference on Thursday, not until seven."

"Oh, I need to leave by six on Thursday to pick Alison up at practice."

Of course you do. Thank you, universe, for hockey practice.

"I'll make sure to let him know to get in touch if he has any questions."

"Yes, please do. Hang in there and have a great day!"

And she's off to check on the next teacher. Bullet dodged.

At Pelletier Elementary, we have the good fortune of having two weeks to complete our conferences. Some teachers cram them all into a few days to get them done; others spread them out to lessen the impact. I fall somewhere in the middle, offering five days of early morning and late evening options because I don't have to worry about a family at home and know that time can be easier for many. Another way I go above and beyond, but I usually have one of the highest attendance rates.

Thursday rolls around and I'm so ready for the weekend, which tortures me because it's my last late evening of conferences, and, well, Friday still looms. Olan has signed up for the last slot tonight, and while the thought of seeing him alone, albeit to confer about Illona, helps propel me through a full day of teaching and conferences, I also realize if I look half as exhausted as I feel, that's not super adorable. Think more frazzled and crumpled.

By the time Olan arrives for his conference, I've been in the school building for over twelve hours, with barely time to use the bathroom. My dress shirt is crumpled, my khakis have cookie crumbs on them from an almost-disaster at snack time, and the bow tie I'm wearing refuses to remain straight, which feels fitting. I'm finishing up with Jessica's parents, a lovely couple who own a lobster boat and could be candidates for an outdoor adventure catalog. They worry about Jessica's handwriting reversals, and I assure them it's developmental and we'll keep working on it and offer a few activities they can do at home to help.

They stand to leave, and I spot Olan waiting by the closed door. He's wearing dark olive slacks and a beige sweater in some silky soft fabric my teacher's salary doesn't allow me to be familiar with. At first glance, he takes my breath away. It shows off his pecs in a way that will make focusing more challenging than it already is. He shifts his weight from foot to foot, almost hopping back and forth, and looks like a child waiting for his punishment. Now, he's the adorable one.

"Thank you both for taking the time to come," I say to the Sheltons.

"Mr. Block, thank you for everything," Mrs. Shelton says, and they nod at Olan as they pass in the doorway.

"Mr. Stone, come in. Let me shut the door."

With the door closed, there's a modicum of privacy. However, the classroom door has a long, thin vertical window that anyone passing by can peek in. A sign reading *Conference in Session, Please Knock* adds to the isolation, but we're in school. In my classroom. To talk about Illona. I am a professional educator up for my state's Teacher of the Year. I've had many conferences with attractive fathers. I'm an accomplished educator revered by the community. I can do this.

"Hey there," Olan purrs in his deep voice.

I might be toast.

"Hello, Mr. Stone, come sit." I raise my hands like a gay Vanna White and motion him over to the table where I'm set up. He glances down at the minuscule chair and gives a little chuckle.

"I know, the chairs are small, but the learning is big! And I sit in them all the time, you got this."

Olan peels his coat off, pulls the small seat out, and lowers himself into it, looking a little like an elephant trying to sit on a tiny stool. A sexy elephant I'd like to jump over the table and attack with my mouth. *Oy.*

"Illona, as you know, is a complete delight. In addition to Cynthia, she's made friends with just about everyone else in the class. Moving in the middle of the school year can be scary, and she's shown such resilience. In just the seven weeks since she started, there's no doubt she's become an important part of our classroom community. I couldn't be more pleased."

Olan turns his head from side to side and nods as I speak like I'm delivering the most critical information in the world, nuggets of gold to secure world peace. I'm trying hard not to be distracted by the way his sweater reveals his neck, open enough to let me peek a sliver of skin leading to his chest. My eyes wander down, and if I were a betting man, I'd say there's no undershirt under this sweater. Focus on Illona.

"Marvin, I know you know this, but you are a vital reason our move here has been so successful. Illona thinks the sun and moon rise with you, and I'm not sure she'd be adjusting as well with anyone else. Thank you." He pulls his hands over his heart.

Taking compliments about my teaching never feels natural for me, and for some reason coming from Olan, it feels like swallowing a basketball. A smile is all I can offer in reply.

"Now, let's talk about her academics," I begin, pulling out a folder with all sorts of papers, sticky notes, and artifacts. Yes, let's talk about schoolwork. Perhaps this will stop me from wanting to lick his neck.

"When she arrived in January, Illona knew most of her letters and sounds." I place a sticky note on the table comparing Illona's data from then to now and point to the numbers.

"We worked on the few she didn't know, and she quickly acquired them."

I stop talking and turn my head up, but instead of focusing on the data, Olan stares at me.

"What?"

"Nothing."

"That's not a 'nothing' look. Do you not understand something?"

"No, just adorable."

"Anyway," I say with teasing annoyance, "her writing shows progress too. Knowing all her letters and sounds, she's able to put more down on the paper, and she's much more confident too."

I pull out a sample from January and another from this week for him to analyze with me, and the difference stands out even in such a short time. As I point to the January sample, attempting to explain the missing sounds, Olan puts his hand on top of mine. I gently push it away.

"Mr. Stone, we're at school. In the classroom. There are other people in the building," I whisper-yell.

"I'm sorry, but you're incredibly cute in that bow tie and well, I really want to kiss you."

Olan never fails to tell me exactly how he's feeling, and I appreciate that, but I'm also a sweaty, exhausted mess.

"I don't feel very cute, but thank you."

"Mr. Block, you seem rather stressed right now." He raises his left eyebrow and his devilish look cuts right through me.

"I'm not stressed. I'm exhausted and hungry, and you are my last conference of the evening, and I'd love to give you the information about Illona you deserve to hear."

I attempt my least adorable smile, all teeth.

"I'm sorry. Let's finish up." He's serious now, or at least faking it.

He sits and lets me conclude the conference without interrupting or being seductive, and I'm grateful for his compliance.

"I have this report for you to take home." I take the printed summary report from Illona's folder and hand it over.

"Thank you." He appears to skim it, and I'm not sure if this is to appease me or general curiosity, but I'm happy he's focused on the task.

"Mr. Block, this column, the 'now' column appears to be missing some of the scores from the sticky note you showed me."

Of course, now he's all business. Investigating where he's pointing on the report, I see he's completely correct. My face flashes red. How could I have made such a careless mistake? Perhaps the mental and physical fatigue of this week has caught up with me.

"Oh my. You are absolutely correct. I'm so sorry. I assessed Illona today and must have forgotten to transfer her letter sounds from my record to the computer before printing it." I hold up my sticky note, sweat beading on my forehead.

"Let me just copy them from here." He starts to take the sticky note.

"No, no, I'll print you a new report. It will literally take two minutes," I say.

And I'm already up at my computer, pecking the numbers into the spreadsheet that feeds the report and printing a new page as quickly as my fingers will move. Located in a storage closet at the back of the classroom, the printer shares the space with bins of random items needed to teach kindergarten, much of it left over from teachers who previously occupied the space. I skip over to the printer and wait for the ancient machine to whir to life and print the damn page.

"Hang on," I call from the closet.

As I stand at the printer, attending to the digital readout, hoping for a clue to the progress, Olan's arms suddenly come from behind me. He wraps them under mine and pulls me back toward him, so we're doing a sort of hug from behind.

"Mr. Stone, I'll be with you in just a second. This printer is older than Methuselah and takes a minute to warm up because, well, public education is grossly underfunded," I blather as I gently push him off me.

"Marvin, you need to unwind."

"When we finish, I can relax."

"Why don't you let me help you," he suggests, pressing his entire body up against mine and speaking directly into my ear.

"Um, here? Now? How about no?"

Olan reaches and closes the door to the closet and turns the lock. We're suddenly in almost complete darkness, with only a sliver of light radiating from the printer display.

"Let me flip the light," I blurt.

Olan puts his thick arm up, stopping my hand.

"Let me help you relax. Okay?"

He spins me around so we're face to face. His lips find mine, and even though it's been a couple of weeks since we've been alone, there's no hesitancy or forgetfulness. Only warmth and tenderness and spit between us. Olan delivers a complete knockout kiss, causing the sweat on my brow to fully drip. All the magic from that Friday night returns. I know we should most definitely not be doing this. Definitely not here. Definitely not now. We're secured behind two doors. I'd be lying if I didn't admit there's a small spark inside me that's turned on at the prospect of getting caught. With a deep breath, I attempt to do as Olan instructs and stop my brain from churning.

There's a collision of lips and ears and necks and my heart whirling and skidding until Olan pauses. My eyes begin to adjust to the darkness, and with the splinter of light the printer emits, I can just barely make out his face. His eyes grow large and liquid, and I know he's plotting.

"I'm going to help you relax. More. Are you okay with that?"

His request for consent makes my blood simmer, and I only can squeak out something that resembles "Mmmmh," but he nods at my confirmation. His hands move to my hips, and I can feel the pressure of him tugging my pants. I'm not exactly sure what he's thinking, and even though I know I'm being the epitome of unprofessional, there's no way I want him to stop.

"Now." His hands glide from my hips to the front of my khakis. The ones I only wear for conferences. To look nice for parents.

"Let." He begins to unbuckle my belt, which is two sizes too big and takes a little work to undo.

"Me." The button pops.

"Help." The zipper.

"You." My pants fly down around my ankles.

"Relax." And finally, my briefs.

I'm standing. Naked from the waist down for the first time in front of Olan. In the storage closet of my classroom. At school. My dress shirt is unable to hide my thoroughly aroused self. Olan's never seen me without pants, and even though it's dark, I can't help but wonder if he likes what he's able to make out. My brain wants to hike my pants up and flee, but the rest of my body says, "Nope."

He lowers himself to his knees, and based on previous conversations, I'm fairly certain Olan has never done anything like this.

"Olan, wait. You don't have to do this."

"I know. I want to. I've, I've been wanting to. For a long time."

I wonder if he means with me or in general and the thought of being the first man Olan tastes makes my body ache for him.

"But, have you ever, I mean, done this?" I point to myself, standing at full attention.

"Marvin. Relax. Please."

He pushes my hips back, so they rest against the table where the printer sits, and Olan, for the first time, uses his gorgeous mouth in a way entirely new for him and completely euphoric for me. His mouth feels deliciously hot, slippery, and skilled. And because he's a novice, I offer some encouragement and tips. Like a competent teacher, I do my best to cheer him on with the phrases "just like that" and "a little slower," and Olan lets out small growls, and fuck, how is he doing this for the first time so well? His lips, the lips I've studied with my own, so strong, wet, playful.

I look down at him, the top of his head barely visible in the darkness, and reach out and put my hands on his head and grip him gently. Holding on to him as I see the faint vision of my cock sliding in and out of his mouth drives me wild. I move a hand to his mouth and pop my index finger in, feeling the tiny gap between his two front teeth. I'm so painfully aroused my body hums. Not stopping, with joyful sloppy slurping noises, Olan glances up at me, and my heart lurches in my chest.

"Olan, damn."

"Mmmmh. Your dick, it's bigger than mine."

Ever the engineer, Olan's comparing sizes and probably making mental notes of approximate measurements. Yes, my cock is larger, mainly fatter, but I have zero complaints about his. I want to do something for him. Still, I'm incapacitated by what he's currently doing. It's hard to focus on moving.

"Damn. How did you get so good at this?" I ask, pulling him up for a moment, his face so close I can feel his hot breath on my lips.

He doesn't answer but hesitantly puts his lips near mine, testing my acceptance to receive them. I lean forward and nibble on his bottom lip, and he laughs. I kiss him, tasting myself on his lips and the adrenaline from the moment makes my chest pound. His tongue tastes sweaty and salty, and as I think about his lips around my dick, his hand strokes me, all slick from his mouth, and I pull back because now I need his consent.

I wrap my arm around his waist and bury my hand in the back of his pants, searching until I find what I'm looking for. The slight fuzz I remember welcomes me, and I buff it gently. I carefully explore his ass with my fingers. "This okay?"

He answers by bending over so his mouth makes contact with my dick. But this time, grasping the table for balance, his legs bent slightly at the knee, he pushes himself back onto me, increasing the friction. The surprises never cease with him. Removing my fingers momentarily, I spit on my hand and lean over the best I can, my slippery digits exploring this new frontier. It's been three years since I've been intimate with another man and I'm so damn into this. Olan feels different. There's a trust there and that propels the floodgates open. Apparently, it's driving Olan wild because he's making new noises, lower, deeper, rougher. As he slurps on my dick, he begins rocking back and forth, fucking my fingers, and his damp heat and softness turn my core to putty. I want more.

"Fuck, you're horny," I whisper.

I pull myself out of him and place my hand on his shoulder to keep him in place on the table so he can brace himself, the printer's soft light illuminating his beautiful face. Moving behind him, I reach around to unbutton his pants and yank them down. Based on his reaction to my fingers, I want to give Olan a little surprise.

"Um, what are you doing?"

"Mr. Stone, I think you're going to like this."

Kneeling on the floor, I slowly make contact with my tongue, teasing him with just the tip. Olan jolts forward a bit and shudders.

"Holy fuck, Marvin," he whimpers.

"You like that, Mr. Stone?"

Once again, he answers by forcing gently back. This time my tongue probes and licks and slides, and he starts thrusting back on my face, the hunger in my belly bubbling. Opening Olan's eyes to new experiences dissolves some of my fears. I am starving for Olan, and he's fucking delicious.

"Oh my lord," he moans.

"You taste amazing. Jerk yourself."

He begins stroking himself as I fuck him with my tongue. Quickening my pace, I bob back and forth with the motion of his hips. I reach down to stroke myself, trying to match his rhythm.

"Fucking perfect. Your ass," I hiss.

"Oh god," he whimpers.

My heart quickens, and I push into Olan harder with my tongue because I can tell he's close, and all I can think is, what the fuck is my life right now?

"Marvin don't stop. Please. Don't stop."

Olan's entire body starts to contract, and because my face is buried in him, I sense him tensing up. His muscles quiver and pulse over and over as he explodes and lets out the lowest growl I've heard from him. He's coming undone, and knowing I have a part to play in that makes my cock throb in anticipation.

I'm close but not quite there yet. Yearning to bury my tongue deep inside him, I let go of myself for a moment and spread his cheeks wide. My damn huge Jewish nose gets in the way, but I'm relentless and ravenous for him. Olan continues to push back, helping me delve into his entire ass with my mouth.

Moments later, my own climax approaches. My body shakes, my tongue buried inside him as he bucks against me. I unravel. Trying to prevent a total disaster of a mess and also because I crave for Olan to feel every drop, I swiftly stand and shoot all over his delectable ass, slightly pushing myself on the wetness left from my mouth. Shaking with aftershocks of pleasure, I fall over his back, kissing his neck from behind.

We stand there, hot, sweaty, panting, half-naked, and I'm at a loss for words. The heat of our bodies comforts me as I feel our heartbeats begin to regulate.

"What the hell was that?" he asks.

"It's called rimming."

"Um, I think I like rimming. No, make that love rimming. Yes, definitely love rimming."

I laugh because he's so ridiculously precious.

"Relaxed?" he asks.

"Completely. I think that officially ends your parent–teacher conference, Mr. Stone."

We both chuckle. I grab a roll of paper towels from the shelf, and we begin the task of cleaning up.

Olan grabs my bow tie and attempts to straighten it. Swooning over his sweetness, I remember my pants around my ankles, and a nervous cough lurches from my throat. Pulling his pants up, Olan begins to speak.

"Listen, I know it might not be proper for me to ask this with your pants around your ankles, but Illona and I will be heading to Peaks Island over spring break. Cindy's staying here with her boyfriend. Would you care to join us for a few days?"

"Are you looking for a babysitter?" I cock my head.

"Um, no. Definitely not. I will be there the entire time. I'm looking for you." He pokes my chest.

"What about Illona?"

"What about her? She adores you almost as much as I do. Almost." He leans over and carefully pulls my pants up, buttons, zips, and buckles to completion. Moving his mouth over mine, he seals the deal with a searing kiss. I'm not sure what just happened, but was that even me? Doing that. At school. Who am I? Olan brings something out in me I didn't know existed. Something primal and raw, and I'm fairly certain I love it.

CHAPTER NINETEEN

The first half of spring break, the weather's been on the warmer side, for Maine anyway. Besides nesting with Gonzo, I've been able to get out and take a few walks. After Olan's conference and what we now refer to as the "closet incident," we've been texting even more. A lot more.

When I arrived home that evening, my mind raced about how inappropriate and risky it was to do, well, that, there. At school. But my blood sang, as I reminisced about how damn hot it was. As if Olan knew where my mind had gone, a text from him popped up the moment I got home.

Olan: That was incredible. You are incredible. Now stop worrying.

Even though it was challenging for me, I made a conscious decision not to worry. Or at least to try really hard. These first days of spring break have been delightful, and I'm excited to take the ferry over to Peaks this afternoon to spend the last few days with Olan and Illona.

"Mom, hey, how are you?"

Sarah and I haven't spoken in a few weeks and calling her now will eliminate the chance of her potentially reaching out while I'm on the island. A preemptive strike.

"Marvin, I'm good. How are you? Calling on a Thursday? What's wrong?"

"Nothing's wrong, Mom. It's spring break. I'm not working. I'm home."

"Why didn't you come visit?"

And here we go.

"Mom, honestly, there's so much to do with Teacher of the Year. My interview is next week, and I need to prepare."

"Prepare? Prepare what?"

"It's more about being primed for the visit and interview. Plan my lessons for the day, read over questions and interviews with previous winners, that type of thing."

"And you couldn't do that here?"

"No, not really. Anyway, how are you?"

"Good. Hot. I did my errands early before it gets ridiculously hot, because you know how I hate the heat. But things are good. Nothing new. How about you? Teacher of the Year, very exciting, very nice. What else is going on?"

Now I have a choice to make. If I'm smart, I'll say, "not much else" and talk about school and Gonzo and Jill being pregnant, and we'll have a lovely safe conversation. If I'm a blockhead, I'll tell her about Olan.

"Well, I'm sort of seeing someone." I wince as soon as the words come out of my mouth. I'm a complete *nebach*.

"A boy?"

"Well, technically, a man, but yeah."

"Tell me about him. Tell me everything."

I have no intention of telling her anything close to everything, so I think of safe topics.

"Well, he's an engineer."

"An engineer, that's a good job. He must do well for himself."

"I mean, I guess so. And he's a dad, a single dad."

"A father?" This excites her. "How old is the child, wait is it a boy or a girl, or one of those no gender people, non-finery? And where is this child's mother?"

Deep breath.

"His child is five, Mom, and she's a girl. And it's nonbinary. We've talked about this. And his ex lives in California."

"You know I never remember things. Wait, California, so far away, the poor child never sees her mother?"

To the best of my knowledge, Illona has not seen her mother other than on FaceTime since they moved, and since I don't have a good answer to this, I simply say, "She sees her mom."

"How did you meet him? Was it online? I've read those dating apps are very dangerous, Marvin. Are you being careful? Do you need me to hire a private investigator? What else? Tell me something else about him?"

There's no way I'm telling Sarah how we actually met. To halt this line of questioning, I simply say, "Mom, he's amazing."

"Amazing? You never said that about Adam."

"Well, I guess he wasn't. Isn't. Or not to me."

"Oh, honey. I'm so sorry. About Adam, I mean. Not Mr. Amazing. And he's nice to you?"

"Beyond nice. And, actually, I need to run because I'm meeting him now."

"Okay, call me next weekend. I have more questions!"

"Bye, Mom."

"I love you, honey."

"Love you too."

Oy.

March in Maine means spinning the weather roulette wheel. You never know what you'll get. We've had full-on nor'easter snowstorms and days warm enough to require a fan. Spending spring break on Peaks Island was a crapshoot, but the island's magic beckoned. Strolling to the ferry, my light jacket on but not zipped, I'm slightly nervous about spending three whole nights with Olan and Illona. There have been zero sleepovers since the night I stayed in the guest room. The night I knelt before him and went wild on his gorgeous cock. I can't stop thinking about it. In my hand. My lips wrapped around it. *Oy.* We haven't talked about the sleeping arrangements, and I just hope I can keep it in my pants.

"She knows you're a close friend," Olan told me.

"Okay. But what about the kids at school?"

"I told her she could tell them we're friends. I mean, we are friends."

"True, but…"

"But nothing. She adores you. I adore you. And well, try to relax."

"You adore me?"

"Of course I do. Can't you tell? Now try to relax," he repeated.

"Relax. Maybe you could help me with that?"

Worrying about Illona seems fruitless. Other teachers spend time with students' families they're friends with. We're not doing anything inappropriate in front of her. Deep breaths. I'm going to enjoy this mini-break. Olan found an off-season rental online, which will be my lodging for the long weekend.

I stand outside, ticket in hand, waiting for the noon boat. The breeze carries the smell of fish and salt water, and various boats surround me, awaiting their cargo. As the ferry arrives from the island, less than a third full, a small group of people gathers near the dock.

Typically, in warmer weather, I would climb the stairs and head to the boat's top level—the cozy sun shining down and a cool breeze off the water attempting to blow my hair every which way. But today, barely fifty degrees, I find a seat on the upper inside deck by a window. As the booming horn blasts our departure, the boat picks up speed, and I watch Portland slowly shrink in the distance.

Of all the islands accessible by ferry, Peaks provides the largest variety of shops and restaurants. Cars are allowed on the ferry and island, but most people putter about in golf carts or bikes, adding to the quaint charm.

A short twenty-five-minute ride, and the boat softly collides with the dock. Once the few cars on board depart, I walk off, the island emitting its own quiet, peaceful energy. Immediately off the dock, a few restaurants dot the road, along with a golf cart kiosk. The air feels fresher, calmer, and more nautical. As I'm looking around and wondering if I should text Olan, he and Illona pull up in a darling golf cart. Illona leans over and beeps the horn, waves, and calls, "Marvin! Marvin!"

From the moment I spot him, Olan appears more relaxed than I've seen him. He's wearing a chunky deep blue sweater and jeans. I don't think I've ever seen him wearing denim, and they look good on him. Very good. I approach the cart and they jump off to hug me. Having them embrace me simultaneously, we become a tangle of arms and squeezing. I close my eyes, breathe deeply, and take in the comforting feeling in my chest.

"You're here! For three whole days!" Illona says, still latched on to my waist.

"How was the ferry?" Olan asks.

"Perfect. I always forget how little time it takes, and boom, it feels like an entirely different world."

"Well, technically, it's still Portland," he says.

"I know, but it feels like a different universe."

The quietness and immediacy of the island create a tranquility folks love. It's no wonder Peaks has become a desirable summer destination.

I throw my bag in the back of the cart, and we squeeze into the front together, with Illona sandwiched between us.

"Are you hungry?" Olan asks.

"I'm always hungry."

"Me too!" Illona chimes in.

"Well, we acquired a picnic," he says, and I grin at his choice of words. Even on the island, in his sexy jeans, he's still a nerd.

Olan puts his foot down on the gas, and the little golf cart does the best it can to accelerate with two adults, a child, and my bag in the back.

As we drive through the island, the trees have begun to bloom, and everything smells like sweet blossoms and green and ocean and blue, and I'm eager to spend the next few days here. We curve around a winding road, with homes varying in size, and end up on a small dirt road headed toward the water.

Olan pulls over and parks the cart on the grass near the road, and we tumble out and head down a short pebble path. We turn the corner, and the entire bay comes into view, reminding me why there's nothing like living in Maine. Portland looms in the distance but seems so far, almost like seeing it from an airplane. The calm waves splash more than crash, and right now, we are the only people here.

"Well, this couldn't be more gorgeous," I say.

"It's actually called Picnic Point," Olan says.

"Let's picnic!" Illona sings.

We find a small clearing not far from the entrance and roll out the flannel blanket Olan carries under his arm. Olan and Illona stopped at the café near the ferry and bought, no, *acquired*, various sandwiches, chips, and water. Placing the food out for us, Olan works to make the spread visually appealing by carefully placing sandwiches and bags of chips on a large platter with a giant rooster on it, which I assume he's brought from the rental.

"Turkey, roast beef, or peanut butter and jelly?" He motions to each one doing his best sandwich spokesmodel impression.

"I'll take the PB&J. Anyone want to share it with me?" I say because I've seen how much Illona loves PB&J at school.

"Me!" she shouts.

We sit, eat, chat about the weather and what animal shapes we spot in the clouds. While watching for wildlife in the water, Illona thinks she spots a seal. Although I'm almost certain a fish has merely surfaced momentarily, I'm not spoiling it for her. We finish eating, and Olan suggests, "Let's take a little walk. Down this way, ducks gather. We can bring them our leftovers. Princess, let me fix your hair first."

Illona has removed the tie from her hair, and her long tresses wave wildly in the ocean breeze. She hops over to me and takes my hand.

"Marvin, can you do it?"

"Um, sure," I say, glancing at Olan with an I-have-no-idea-what-I'm-doing look.

Olan grabs a fresh hair tie from his bag and hands it to me with a wink. I wrap the tie around my wrist as Illona positions herself in front of me, her back to me, and says, "Ready!"

Once again, my wide, ignorant eyes find Olan's face. He smiles gently, puts a hand on my shoulder, and whispers, "You got this. I'll talk you through it."

I rest my hands on Illona's shoulders, waiting for instructions. Her hair flies in every direction, making me wonder if Mother Nature is about to make this already challenging task exasperating.

"Okay, since we don't have any supplies but the tie, use your hands to finger comb and gather her hair into a ponytail."

"Like this?" I ask, running my hands through her beautiful long curls. I'm attempting to gather them, but they aren't cooperating.

"Sort of. You've got to put some muscle into it."

"Um, hello. I don't have any muscle."

Illona giggles at this and says, "Marvin, you're being too gentle. My hair has a mind of its own. You won't hurt me."

I tense my arms and hands to grab tighter, pulling my fingers through until I have something resembling a ponytail. "Okay?" I ask.

"Yup. Daddy does it much rougher."

"Does he?" I ask, shooting Olan a look with raised eyebrows.

"Now, twist the elastic around the ponytail two times. That will be tight enough," Olan says.

I follow his directions, and while nothing fancy, Illona's hair is out of her face.

"How'd I do?" I ask.

Illona reaches up and feels the new ponytail.

"Amazing!" she shouts and throws her arms around my waist. Olan places his hand back on my shoulder, and being touched by both of them, I suddenly feel a little *verklempt*.

"You did a magnificent job," he says.

"Now, to the ducks!" Illona yells.

Leaving our blanket and items, Illona grabs Olan's hand, and we walk with her between us. Without warning, she leans over and grabs my hand so she's holding on to both of us, and cue a warm glow overtaking my entire body.

She giggles. "Now it's an Illona sandwich!"

Olan and I begin swinging our arms, and Illona levitates just the smallest amount. She tilts her head back, laughing with such joy. I genuinely hope she's as delighted I'm here as she appears to be. As we turn a bend, a small inlet comes into view, and a faint quacking beckons in the distance. This must be where the ducks gather.

"Daddy, can I?"

Olan nods, and she lets go of our hands. She darts off but stops a few feet in front of us, turns around, runs back, and takes both our hands again. She forcefully places my hand in Olan's like a factory line worker inserting a cog into its gear.

"There." She nods and darts off.

Olan and I stop walking and look at each other.

"Well, that conveys how she feels about you being here. And about us." He motions between the two of us with his free hand.

"What did you tell her?"

"I told her we're friends and I care about you. She said, 'Daddy, Kevin says Mr. Block needs a boyfriend. Maybe you could be his boyfriend?'"

"She did not."

"She did."

I sigh and briefly shake my head. "Why do my students all think I need someone?"

"Well, maybe because they see how hard you work. And they care and worry about you."

"Well, teaching is not for the faint of heart. Everyone thinks teaching kindergarten is all fun and games. I mean, it is fun, and we do play games, but there's nothing easy about it."

"And the award. That seems to add a lot to your plate."

"It does, but it's important."

"Of course. Let's make sure this weekend you get to relax. No pressure to do anything. You can sleep in. Nap if you want. We'll leave you alone."

"Um, I came to see you. Please don't leave me alone. But speaking of sleep, where am I sleeping?" I ask with a sheepish grin.

"Well, the house only has two bedrooms. I intended to give you my bed and take the couch, but when Illona asked me where you were sleeping, and I told her my plan, she asked, 'Daddy, your bed is so big. Why can't Marvin sleep with you?'"

Illona, wading near the ducks, looks at us with her huge, gorgeous smile, and we both wave to her.

"Really?"

"Yup. I told her I'd be amenable to the idea, if you were, and she smiled. She clearly knows..." And he doesn't need to say more.

I squeeze his hand, and he returns the gesture.

"I really want to kiss you right now," he says.

His eyes bore into me and his desire to close the gap between our lips becomes palpable.

"Later. We have all night. Let's go feed the ducks."

Back at the rental, I'm surprised at the modesty of the place. I mean, it's still massive compared to my apartment, but compared to what Olan and Illona are used to, it's quaint. The first floor has one great room with an unassuming kitchen and a living room with a leather sofa. There's a half bathroom off the back of the room near the stairs. On the second floor, two bedrooms lie on either side, with the bathroom in the middle. Way more my style in size and decor, I instantly feel comfortable.

We spend the evening cooking, eating tacos, and playing Uno until the sun has almost set. Olan peers at his watch, and Illona groans. "Not yet. Please. We're on vacation, and Marvin's here."

"Princess, you were up before six this morning. It's time for bed."

"How about I come up and read you a story?" I offer.

"Yes!" She bolts up the stairs, and the water rushes from the faucet.

"You don't have to," Olan says.

"I know. I want to."

Once Illona's had her story, a drink, a hug from me, a check under the bed for monsters, another drink, and a kiss from Olan, we head downstairs for the sofa and hopefully some snuggle time.

CHAPTER TWENTY

We sit on the worn sofa and Olan immediately pats his lap.

"Lie down," he beckons.

I place my head on his lap, and his hands—assertive, but tender—begin massaging my head and playing with my hair. There's no television and the quiet welcomes our conversation.

"This has been one of the best days I've had in a long time," I mutter with my eyes shut.

"I love it out here. Having you here only makes it better."

I take one of his hands, kiss the top of his palm, and gently return it to my head. Lying here, the weight of my head on his lap, I'm supported by Olan in a way I haven't felt in a very long time. Maybe ever.

"Imagine being able to live here, year-round?" I ponder.

"There's a small but active full-time community, but I'm not sure about the school."

"The island has a small school, but it's part of the mainland district."

"Interesting, food for thought. I mean, living here would be amazing."

"Amazing, yes, just, well, not realistic for most," I say, reminded of the thirty-two dollars currently in my checking account.

We chat and cuddle on the sofa until the fire's last embers begin to smoke, and it's finally time to head to the bedroom. Olan takes my hand, pulling me off the couch, my legs leaving small indentations in the soft leather. He tugs me up the stairs, and my heart swells. We stop by Illona's room, her door open a few inches, and he peeks in without dropping my hand. He winks at me as he shuts her door completely. My stomach flips, and I tighten my fingers around his palm. This man, such a loving father, adores his child. And why that turns me on so much feels like a mystery I can't quite crack.

"Do you need the bathroom?" Olan asks.

I brush my teeth and splash some cold water on my face, freshening up and also reminding myself I'm not dreaming. I change into a plain orange T-shirt and flannel pajama bottoms. Back in the room, I'm greeted by Olan. He's only wearing gray sweatpants shorts, the hem struggling against his thick thighs. Can we please thank the universe for giving us gray sweatpants? There should be a holiday celebrating gray sweatpants season. I would gladly fall on my knees and pray to gray sweatpants.

I want to run over and caress his bare chest. To touch every part of him, with my hands and mouth, but he stands, just staring at me, and I want to honor his pace.

"Hello," he says.

"Hey. Um, if that's your idea of pajamas, I am so on board," I say, feeling slightly overdressed.

That chest. Yikes. I'm not typically into muscles, but right now, with them in the room, in front of me, for me, my hands want to live on his warm, firm pecs forever. Olan places his hands on my hips and draws me to him, and we fit like two puzzle pieces coming together as his mouth finds mine. We stand there, hands frozen as our lips dance.

He pulls back just enough to mutter, "Can I?"

His fingers lightly tug at the waist of my pants, and once again, the asking sends me over. I press my mouth to his as my answer, and he pulls them down. Unable to contain or hide how aroused I am, my dick pops up like bread from a toaster and smacks Olan's leg. A short chuckle escapes from him, and we both laugh without taking our mouths off each other. Standing here, kissing Olan Stone, tasting the sweetness of his skin, the light smell of the ocean mixing with the musty house, his hands on me, all of me, as we make these noises into each other's mouths, I'm overtaken by the closeness, something more than a friendship, more than dating, more than sex, and so much more than I anticipated.

He starts to lift the bottom of my shirt. He wants it off. But by reflex, my hands rush to stop him.

"What's wrong?"

He's never seen me without a shirt. No pants, in darkness, the focus solely on my cock, but not completely naked. The thing is, Olan Stone could be on the cover of a men's fitness magazine. He may be nerdy and not entirely aware of the level of his hotness, but what will he think about me without any clothes on? I don't work out. I eat what I want, and the good Lord blessed me with relatively good genes. I've never been ashamed of my body, but with him, I suddenly feel painfully average.

"Look at you," I say, waving a hand over his torso.

"What about me?" He genuinely doesn't understand.

"You're. This." Both hands gesture to his body.

"And you're adorable. Let me. Please." His hands tug at the hem of my shirt.

I take a deep breath, close my eyes, and relent.

Olan lifts my T-shirt off and tosses it to the ground. He runs his hands over my chest, my skin burning under his touch. Pausing to press his thumbs along my clavicle, his fingers finally travel up my neck to my mouth. His right hand strokes my face, and desperate to taste him, I turn, pop his thumb into my mouth, and begin sucking it gently.

"Marvin. You are so fucking hot."

Not adorable. Hot. I can't remember the last time someone called me hot. Has anyone ever? The way he's looking at me, his thumb in my mouth, I might actually consider believing him. And because I know everything we've done so far is new for Olan, I ask him, "What do you want?"

"You."

"Yeah, I kinda got that. But what do you want...to do?"

"Oh."

He lets a breath out through his nose and dips his head, and I swear, Olan Stone makes that sweet bashful face that alerts me he's blushing. Heat radiates from his cheeks, and desire grows in my center. I want to move closer and bite his lower lip just hard enough to make him wince.

He snakes a hand around my waist to my back, lowers it, and pats my backside two times.

"May I?"

"Such a gentleman."

He wants to fuck me. My body shudders, thinking about having him inside me. It's been, well, since Adam, but one thing I know, there's a direct correlation between how turned on I am and how amazing it feels. Right now, my dick aches against my pajamas, a predictor of potential bliss. Taking Olan's hand, I guide him to the chair in the corner of the room. I move my backpack to the floor, right next to the thick wooden leg of the seat. My hands slide between his gray cotton shorts and warm skin and push them to the ground until he steps out of them. His cock, thick and rigid, clearly ready.

I press Olan's chest, urging him to sit and the contrast between the chair's creamy corduroy fabric and his onyx skin reveals even more of his beauty. Like a tourist in a new country, I want to pause, grab my phone, and take pictures to capture the moment. Naked and gorgeous. I want to remember him this way. He tilts his head up to me from his seated position and smiles. The biggest, widest smile, with so many teeth shining at me, and my body relaxes in a way I can't remember ever happening. I'm calm, tranquil, ready.

Unzipping the outer pocket of my backpack, I grab a small bottle of lube and a condom I smartly packed and present them to him for inspection.

"Oh, were you expecting something to happen?" he asks.

"My brief two-week stint at seven as a Boy Scout taught me always be prepared. Wait, also, men in uniforms are hot."

He tilts his head back, opens his mouth, and lets out a laugh. Watching his Adam's apple ascend and descend his throat turns my insides to melting wax, and I take it as an invitation to kiss him there. Apparently, my mouth on Olan's neck works magic because he trembles at the contact.

"Ready?" I mutter into his ear.

"Fuck, yes," he moans. "Your ass, so fucking hot."

His hands cup my cheeks and playing with my ass appears to lull him to euphoria. This Olan, the one with no clothes on, the one who talks dirty, the one who becomes unleashed, I wonder if anyone else has ever seen this version of him. Was he like this with his ex-wife? Did she get to witness him truly letting go? There's sadness in thinking Olan waited his entire life to feel this, but a selfish part of me delights in the possibility I'm the first to witness him this way. I have so many questions for him, but not now. Now it's us, here, together, close.

Kneeling before him, I open the condom and gently roll it down over his shaft. He shivers a little under my touch, and I bend over to kiss his inner thigh, making him tremble. I take the small bottle of lube and rub some of the slickness between my palms, warming it up so as not to shock him with the cold. But even so, when I finally wrap my hands around his cock, his chest and shoulders rise with the new sensation. I lean forward, inches from his face and carefully say, "Breathe."

Once a generous amount of lube coats my hole, I stand and straddle him. My feet planted on the hardwood floor, I brace myself, hands on his chest, and carefully ease myself down. Olan wraps his hands around my neck, pulling my face toward him.

"Easy, we're gonna take this slow," I whisper.

He nods. His eyes wide open, so eager and curious about what awaits. I reach around to guide his cock. Gingerly, I sit, only taking the head at first. An explosion of pain and pleasure erupts as stars overtake my field of vision. Deep breaths and I stand.

"Give me a second," I say.

"Take all the time in the world. I'm not going anywhere."

I chuckle and Olan pulls me down for a kiss, his mouth warm and wet. Our tongues mingle and I lower myself again, pausing at the same point where I previously stopped. Once I've completely welcomed him inside, I pause again, allowing my body to remember how to do this. Breathe, relax, and wait. Having my feet resting on the floor allows me to take Olan in at my own pace. Like tying shoes, something as a kindergarten teacher I'm highly skilled at, muscle memory takes over. Warm, sweet pleasure flows from every nerve in my body as Olan slowly begins to thrust to match my motion. The pleasure makes me mindless, and I reach down to feel his cock sliding in and out of me. He growls at my touch, and I move my hand down to cup his balls and massage them gently.

"Oh, oh damn," he moans.

"Fuck. Your dick feels so good."

Having Olan inside me, my brain goes round and round. Levitating from the pleasure, my heart pounding, I don't want to come down from this high. My head falls forward, my hair following suit. Olan leans in to roll his head back and forth in my curtain of curls, our two frizzy heads of hair meshing together. With so much happening, sensation, and focus, Olan's eyes roll back a little, and I press my lips to his forehead.

"Kissing. Please," he pleads, and I weave down to his lips.

I never thought the kissing, our lips and tongues moving from teeth to cheeks to ears to necks and back again the entire time was something anyone did, certainly not me, and it heightens every nerve and sensation. Moving my body a little faster, Olan responds, thrusting his hips eagerly. My own cock, hard and wet with precum, slaps against my stomach as he moves his hands to my waist, guiding my motion to match his thrusts. As we continue, it's clear Olan's cock actually becomes harder, and the sensation of him inside me blows me open. My heart pounds, this man literally rocking my world, and I cradle his face in my hands while my tongue plays in that tiny gap between his teeth.

Olan takes my hands and returns them to their home on his chest, and I know we're hitting a new level. He's using his body to ask for what he wants. I lick both my thumbs and start massaging his nipples, and he starts to move faster.

"God, you're starving for it," he says.

"Only for you."

Olan unravels me and I want to remember this feeling, being connected, literally as close as we can be. His hand comes up to my head and he grabs my hair, a little tighter than last time, and damn why does that turn me on? I lean forward and place my mouth on his chin, sucking gently as he begins to buck faster.

"You feel so fucking fantastic," I spill into his mouth.

"You're blowing my mind."

I wrap my arms around his neck and crash my mouth on his. There's sweat on the brow of his lip, creating a sweet saltiness to our kiss I devour. I've come unhinged. My entire body shifts, and I want him closer, deeper. Carefully lifting my legs off the floor, I rest them on the soft chair on either side of him. In this new position, he's able to pound me even deeper.

"Right there. All of you. Fuck me. Harder."

With a tinge of surprise in his eyes, Olan draws me to him. There's such emotion on his face, I'm *kvelling* and why do I keep wanting to bite him? I swear I'm not a vampire. He reaches around and places his fingers at the exact spot where he's entering me, delighting in the literal location of our connection. His eyes flash electric and he rocks with more intensity, and damn, the pleasure makes my eyes roll back for a moment. His breath quickens, and I move my lips to his, our tongues another way to nestle inside each other.

"I'm close." He fumbles into my mouth.

"Come for me. Fuck me. Harder. Please."

My hips hurry, trying to make this as pleasurable as possible for him. I bite his lower lip, slightly harder this time, and return my hands to his chest, flicking and pinching his nipples. Olan makes a sound that starts soft and low but builds and finally comes out as "Fuuuuuuck."

I can feel his orgasm inside me, pulsing, throbbing, his face contorted in ecstasy, gasping for oxygen. Slowly, his breathing quiets, and we come to a momentary pause.

"You okay?" I ask.

"You wrecked me. But I'm perfect. What about you?"

"Amazing. That was, you are, amazing," I pant.

"No, I meant, what about…" Olan gently grabs my unyielding erection.

"Oh, well, let's see." I stand slowly and move to the bed.

"If you give me some time, I could be ready to go again," he offers from the chair.

"Not necessary. Come." I summon him with a hand.

Lying on my back, I take his hand and pull him down next to me.

"If you just cuddle next to me, maybe kiss me a little, I can get myself off."

"Okay," and he begins kissing my neck. He moves his lips up to my ear and a jolt vibrates through me. My dick throbs, becoming even harder in my palm.

"How about this," he murmurs in my ear, his steamy breath tickling the inside.

Olan reaches down and gently begins to finger me, slowly at first, until he realizes I'm more than open and willing. I shift my hips and then legs up, allowing him easier access. As his finger moves inside me, I stammer, "Another, please."

"Now, who's the gentleman?"

With my invitation, Olan adds a second, and now between his mouth and hand, frissons of pleasure overtake me. I begin to tremble as the crawling build of my climax approaches.

"Oh, fuck, fuck, fuck. Don't stop," I cry.

Olan moves his mouth to my chest and begins to kiss and nibble, sending my eyes rolling back in complete euphoria. I allow myself the release, shooting all over my stomach and chest, a few rogue drops landing on his shoulder. He props himself up, covered in sweat, skin glistening, and I want to lick him up and down.

"Come here," I say, too breathless to move.

"I want to look at you like this," he says.

"Like what?"

"So fucking perfect."

Embarrassed, I cover my eyes with my left arm. Olan returns to my side, resting his head in the crook of my neck. I turn and bury my face in his hair, the smell of sweat and coconut mixing on his brow. Feeling euphoric and slightly hungry, I place my lips on his hair and mouth at it a little.

"That was... incredible. You are incredible," he says.

"Now you've wrecked me."

I gnaw at his hair like cotton candy.

"Marvin, what are you doing?"

"I'm trying to eat your hair," I mumble.

"You are absurd. Fucking absurd."

I shower and return to Olan lying on the bed, eyes closed, covers folded over, waiting for me. I slide in with my back to him, trying not to disturb him, but as soon as my body touches the sheets, his arms fly up and move to pull me close, tangling with mine. I can't tell where his arms begin and mine end, and the smell of his sweat, slightly sweet, and the clean linens intoxicates me.

He pushes his head forward, his lips brushing my ear, and whispers, "Good night, Marvin."

I crane my neck and turn just enough to kiss him—soft, slow, sweet—and reply, "Thank you for inviting me."

"Thank you for coming. Thank you for everything."

Collected in Olan's arms, the entire back of my body pressed into the entire front of his, being the little spoon makes my head buzz. I lie there taking it all in, and soon his breathing gets heavy, and there's a low rumble from his mouth. He's fallen asleep. I close my eyes and inhale his smell, his warmth, his energy. There's no denying the intense heat between us, but perhaps, more importantly, our connection. Opening my eyes, I peek at his silhouette in the dark one more time and drift off to the best night's sleep I've had in years.

CHAPTER TWENTY-ONE

The rest of the weekend proceeds like a dream. Saturday morning, I wake up alone, but Olan's warmth lingers next to me. Remembering last night, my body aches for him. Having him inside me. Feeling connected in a way I can't recall. Falling asleep surrounded by the heat of his body. A deep breath to center myself, a quick prayer of gratitude, and I'm ready to consider abandoning my current cocoon of bliss.

The noises and voices downstairs clue me in. He's with Illona. Grinding and gurgling noises, the faint aroma of coffee, and something sweet whir my stomach awake. He's cooking. In addition to everything else, Olan Stone got up to make breakfast. Rolling over to where he slept, I shift my head to his pillow. The faint scent of coconut and shea butter remains, and I breathe it in, wishing I could keep my head here a little longer.

"You up, Marv?" Olan pokes his head in, attempting to whisper but failing miserably.

"Excuse me?"

"Ah, you are up. Illona was asking for you."

"Did you just call me Marv?"

He looks down with that bashful face, and I know he's blushing. I want to drag him into bed and kiss every inch of him.

"I like it. It's . . . sweet. You're sweet."

"Coffee's brewing. And we're making waffles. Chocolate chip waffles."

My stomach gurgles at the mention of food. He turns to head downstairs, and I call out to stop him.

"Olan, wait. What about Illona?"

"What about her? She's downstairs waiting for you. Us. Get up, lazy bones."

I wrestle into my orange hoodie and flannel pajama pants and head downstairs. I know Illona knows I'm here. I know she suggested her dad and I share the room. I know all this, yet I have no idea what to expect this morning. At the bottom of the stairs, Illona appears, like a tiger waiting to pounce, throwing her arms around my waist, pressing her head against my side, shouting, "Marvin!"

"Illona, good morning! What's for breakfast?"

She wears pink and purple fleece pajamas with ponies on them. Two braids lie on either side of her head, and immediately I envision her sitting patiently, her dad carefully tending to her, and again, I am moved by how patient and loving he is with her.

"Waffles! Do you want yours with chocolate chips or without chocolate chips?"

I give her an are-you-seriously-asking-me-this-question? look.

"With chocolate chips!" she shouts to her dad.

"Please, and thank you."

We sit around the wooden table which is filled with knots that I trace with my fingers, and pour copious amounts of maple syrup over waffles stuffed with chocolate chips. We talk and sing and laugh, and it feels so correct. At one point, Olan reaches over to squeeze my shoulder, and my body stiffens because I'm hyper aware of Illona. She's caught up singing the latest teen-girl-group sensation power ballad to us. Her eyes land on her father's hand where it rests on her teacher's body and she doesn't flinch. She simply keeps singing. For the first time in a long time, I feel safe. Right. Worthy. Hopeful. Loved.

The weekend continues to play out like the love collage in a sappy romantic movie. We take walks, have another picnic, and introduce Illona to *The Muppet Movie*. Her face and reactions when Kermit rides his bicycle are priceless. On Saturday afternoon, we take the golf cart to the convenience shop for more coffee because Olan underestimated how much coffee a queer Jewish kindergarten teacher spending a long weekend with a student and her phenomenally handsome father drinks. As we exit the store, a strange voice calls, "Olan! Buddy!"

"Ralph, I forgot you live on the island full time," Olan says as they shake hands.

An older gentleman, easily in his late sixties, Ralph wears what appears to be the island uniform: an old baseball hat, old flannel, old jeans, and old sneakers. Peaks Island—where everything's old...but in a quaint isle way.

"Yeah, I'm over on Reed Ave., the far side. And who is this?" He's looking down at Illona, who's grasping her father's hand and standing slightly behind his long legs.

"This is Illona."

"Oh, I've heard all about you. It's so lovely to finally meet you!"

"And this is my buddy, Marvin." He motions to me.

"Marvin is also called Mr. Block. He's my teacher," Illona adds, feeling less timid by the second.

"Well, it's nice to meet you both." Ralph smiles. This man oozes charm and sweetness, and my head races to connect the dots and figure out how they might know each other. Olan doesn't seem to know many people in Portland, let alone out here on the island.

"How long are you here? I see you rented a golf cart. You know I have an extra van. The key is right under the driver's seat mat. I'll text you my address. You can always borrow it. Don't even have to ask. Just come get it."

"That's generous of you, Ralph, but I thought Illona might like the golf-cart experience."

"True, very true. There's nothing like poking around the island in one of those buggers." He nods to our parked cart. "Well, you have my number. If you need anything or if you come back, you know how to get in touch with me."

"Thank you." Olan nods.

Illona waves at Ralph, and I say, "Nice to meet you."

We pile into the golf cart, and as we drive off, Ralph stands and waves kindly. Olan has put his arm around Illona and grasps my shoulder. He's clearly not the slightest bit concerned with this man knowing who I might be. We ride back to the cottage and Illona finally asks, "Daddy, who was that man?"

"Oh, he's a friend of mine."

"Okay," she replies.

"I didn't realize you have friends on the island," I say, fishing for more.

"What can I say? I'm a friendly guy. I have friends in lots of places," he says with a wink.

I wake Sunday morning with my head on Olan's chest because, apparently, even in my sleep, my body has taken to navigating to it like a homing pigeon. Olan's body radiates warmth and smells like the mint soap in the shower. He appears to be sleeping and I do my best to remain still, staring, watching his chest rise and fall with each breath. My heart thumps at the thought of him. Of us. I imagine a world where I'm allowed to wake up next to him every day.

Olan's left eye creeps open and he returns a sly grin. His long fingers move to gently rub my head and tangle my curls.

"What are you staring at?" he grumbles.

"You. Just you."

"I'm slightly obsessed with your hair," he says.

"Yeah, I kinda got that." I turn my head to look at him. "Olan Stone, do you have Jewfro envy?"

"I'll have you know, my afro earned me the nickname Black Einstein in college."

"Um, you realize that is completely hot."

"I mean maybe to you, but not most people. And definitely not me. Please don't call me that."

"One hundred percent hot. And I won't. I promise," I say, tousling his hair.

The sun rises on our last day and heading back to the mainland awaits. Back to life, back to reality. No, not the music. Not now. I don't need it.

Lying here, our bodies tangled tight and the nearness palpable, I want to know more about him. When we're together, I feel so close to him, but there are moments I feel he's holding back. There's a wall up, and I can't figure out why. And if this, whatever we have, can continue, we must start removing bricks from the wall.

"You know, you're an amazing guy," I say.

"Really? How so?"

"Hmmm, let me see. You're the most attentive dad. Watching you parent Illona makes my heart swell. Truly. You're thoughtful and kind. Whenever anyone needs something, you're right there before they can ask for help. And you're sexy as hell," I say, tracing his jaw with my thumb.

"Are you trying to make me blush?"

"No, but if it happens, I'll consider it a bonus. Can, can I ask you something?"

"Of course. Shoot."

"What happened with Illona's mom?"

Olan lets out a sigh. I realize I've hit a sore spot, but I've told him about Adam, and want to know more about him and Illona. She hasn't seen her mother in person since they moved.

"Okay. Let me start by saying Isabella is a wonderful person. We're working on being friends, and it's an adjustment, but I do care for her. Isabella and I met in high school. She saw something in me I don't think I knew myself. I mean, I knew I was intelligent, but I didn't recognize my potential. I never even considered AP classes until she suggested them. And when the time came, she helped me with my Stanford application process. I'd never really been interested in dating, and she knew that. We took things slow. Our relationship slowly developed. Everyone thought we were the ideal couple, which put pressure on us. Well, me."

My head rests on his shoulder as he fiddles with my curls.

"At college, a different kind of pressure surfaced. Being the only Black person in my program, my family's expectations, I made some harmful decisions. All my life, I've never fit in. At Stanford, I finally started to believe I could. Desperate to belong, I let some of the guys in my dorm influence me. Before college, I'd only had one beer. Ever. My father actually gave it to me at my graduation party. I hated it."

My lips curl up thinking about Olan's face after a sip of warm, bitter beer.

"But with these guys, there was liquor. Seemingly, unlimited. The partying got out of hand quickly. Isabella would visit, and, well, I guess I didn't realize just how bad I had gotten until she came. She was worried. Scared. I knew she was right, but the stress kept intensifying. Within a year of my parents dropping me off, I had a problem I didn't know how to fix. Apparently, drinking more was not the solution. I ended up in an outpatient facility, and even though it was challenging, I know it was essential. I was finally sober and part of a twelve-step recovery program, and Isabella and I married soon after graduation and started Stone Aerospace. It took a few years to get our bearings, but once Illona was born, the business really exploded. We spent so much time together working that we forgot to be a couple. I channeled all my energy into work. It wasn't healthy. We just, well, people grow apart. It happens. I still love her, but I'm not *in* love with her. Isabella stuck with me through those tough years, so even when our relationship shifted a couple of years ago, I didn't want to abandon her. Now I understand she's a strong woman. Thinking of her that way was actually silly of me. We're much better off as friends. The truth was, I didn't know how to be sober and alone."

As Olan recounts his story, tension starts building in my head. I'm listening and trying to remain calm, but my heart begins to sprint. Flashbacks to my childhood, stepping over my mother on the floor, the smoke detectors blaring over food left on the stove, my aunt Helen taking me for an entire summer because my mother went to rehab. These images spark in my head, making me dizzy, and my ears begin ringing. I keep my head planted on his shoulder because I can't hide the advancing panic on my face. Taking deep breaths, in and out through my nose, willing myself unflustered.

"So you're sober? That's why you don't drink?"

"Yes. Completely sober."

Wetness dots the corners of my eyes. I do not fancy crying in front of Olan right now. More deep breaths.

"Last year, things started coming to a head with Isabella and the business. I had a slip-up. One drink. One time. I called my sponsor, and he came right away. I upped my meetings. It hasn't happened since. That was almost a year ago. It's part of why we moved. I needed a fresh start, and Portland has an amazing recovery community. Things have been going extraordinarily well. You're a significant part of that, too."

He gives a soft, hesitant smile, and I lift my head to examine him and wonder what else he hasn't told me. I swore—with what I went through with my mother, watching her struggle and how it impacted our relationship and my life—I would never be with an alcoholic, recovering or not. And yet here I am, lying on Olan, his daughter in the room down the hall, things feeling more and more like hanging out is morphing into something deeper. I need to speak, but I'm afraid of what might fumble out.

"I'm not sure what to say."

"You don't have to say anything," he replied. "I've been wanting to tell you, but I was, well, uncertain about it. And honestly, afraid. I took bumping into Ralph yesterday as a sign. He's in the program with me. He's a stand-up guy. We sit together at meetings every Tuesday. He's not my sponsor, but he checks up on me. Bumping into him was a sign for me to talk to you."

"But, Olan. My mom, I'm not sure you understand. My mother is an alcoholic. Yes, she's sober now, but growing up, with a parent like that, it does things and, and, that's why I, I, I..."

Olan sits up and takes my face in his strong hands. I want to pull away, but he holds me firm and turns my head so we're only inches apart.

"Marvin. I'm so sorry. And that's why I take it so seriously. I never want Illona to experience that. Before my relapse last year, and it was one drink, one drink, I hadn't had a sip since college, twelve years. And it was literally one drink, and I knew. I stopped. I called Isabella and my sponsor immediately."

"Is that why you split up?"

"It was a long time coming. A lot of it had to do with running a business together. And my working too much. It wasn't healthy. Marrying the first and only person you've ever dated complicated things, too."

"Wait, so you've never been with anyone but her? Not even a hook-up?"

"No, I told you. Hooking up isn't for me. Only Isabella and now, you."

I try to take this in and process it. I'm a few years younger than him, but even with a six-year relationship, I've dated and slept with my share of men. I know Olan's seriousness and nerdiness might make him, or even others, hesitant, but he's so damn attractive. It's hard to believe I'm only the second person on the planet to be intimate with him.

"And why doesn't Isabella see Illona?"

"They chat and video call. I've urged her to visit. I know it's far, and we're working on being just friends, but Illona needs her mother, too. We're approaching a better place, and I hope that will change soon. Isabella knows she's welcome."

I'm sitting in bed without clothes and I've never felt more naked. My head feels milky, thick, foggy. Images from my childhood careen toward me like a train. Lying on my back is the only reason I haven't passed out. Throwing clothes on, grabbing my bag, and running out feels a tad dramatic, but my urge to flee overtakes me, and keeping this bottled in makes it worse.

"Listen, I probably should go."

"Marvin, please don't. Let's make breakfast. We can talk some more once Illona gets up. She can play in her room."

"No. I really need to go. I'm sorry."

"Don't apologize, and don't go. Please."

I lift my head off his chest and begin to push myself up.

"Olan, I care about you, but please understand. I need to . . . I need space, to process this."

I get dressed, throwing on the T-shirt I wore last night, my hoodie, and jeans, shoving clothes in my bag without much care. Moving swiftly, I do my best to remain unflustered and not appear frantic. Fear of what this means crushes me and the need to be away from Olan overwhelms me. I do not want to have a panic attack here.

"I'll text you. I promise," I say.

"Marvin. Wait."

I stop at the bedroom door. It's quiet. Illona either hasn't woken up yet, or she's keeping herself occupied in her room. Olan jumps up from the bed and stands there, naked. On the outside, he looks so fucking perfect and wonderful, but there's clearly more under the surface I need to process. He jogs over and gathers me in his arms. As a reflex, I return the embrace, but my heart feels hesitant. I pull away, and he gives me a quick kiss, soft, on the lips. Even as my mind flutters and races, my lips respond to his touch.

"Please text me and let me know when you're back."

My lips make a thin, barely-there smile. I nod, turn, and head to the ferry. The early hour means I'm only one of a few as we head back to the mainland. Feeling desolate and confused, I wrap my arms around myself and watch the city come into view under cloudy skies.

CHAPTER TWENTY-TWO

The Sunday scaries have never felt, well, scarier. Not only have I not texted Olan, but my phone has sat untouched all day. I haven't replied to the three messages he's sent nor picked up any of his calls. And he's called four times. Not that I'm counting. Except I'm totally counting.

The revelation of Olan Stone in recovery and having a relapse only a year ago, and him keeping that information from me, along with the fact I'm most definitely catching feelings for a recovering alcoholic, makes my head swell like a tick. How did I get myself in such a mess?

Gonzo, ever attuned to his dad, has been extra cuddly. After peeling off my clothes, silencing my phone, and taking a scalding shower, I crawled into bed and haven't moved since. Imagined music in my head feels inadequate, so I fire up an actual playlist and when "Damaged" by the gone-too-soon Danity Kane comes on, I play it on repeat for longer than probably recommended by medical professionals. Warning: This song may cause severe desolation. The lyrics and message match my mood, and with apologies to Taylor Swift, I prefer my sad music to have some punch to it. Even the blasting bass and dance beat don't faze Gonzo as we cuddle together under my thick comforter and I try to process what this all means.

I'm desperate to reach out to Jill. Keeping everything from her has forced a silent wedge between us I loathe. She's finally expecting, and instead of celebrating and being there for her, I've retreated into a shell with Olan. Olan, who kept this from me. Olan, who knew why I don't drink.

Tomorrow morning, Illona will prance into the classroom, and what if she says something? Asks me what happened. What do I say? How do I act? What about pickup? We agreed to keep our "hanging out" under wraps, but would Olan say or do something at pickup if he felt it was his only recourse? My stomach churns in knots, and bile trickles up my throat.

Of course, the Teacher of the Year visit would be this week. Thursday morning, a pair of educators will come to spend the morning with my class and have a one-on-one interview over lunch. With everything at stake, I should be reading, preparing, and focusing. My head feels dizzy thinking about what this means. It's not just about me winning a silly award. How did I manage to end up with this burden on my shoulders? In my typical ADHD fashion, I push the worry away and ignore it. For now.

By bedtime, I resolve to tell Jill everything in the morning. I can't keep this from her. She'll see it all over my face. If I arrive before her and set up for the day, we'll have as much time as possible. It's better than texting. I need to talk to her in person.

Around seven, my phone vibrates. Olan's persistent, I'll give him that. I look at the phone and my mother's, not Olan's, name and number flash. I don't have the energy for her right now, but I feel lost, close to slipping out to sea, and she's calling, reaching out. Hesitantly, I pick up.

"Hey, Mom."

"Marvy, you're home!"

"Yes, mother, it's Sunday evening. I have to work tomorrow."

"Right, it's night there. *Oy*. What are you up to?"

"I'm trying to relax with Gonzo. He's lying next to me."

"He's such a sweet boy. Give my grand-kitty a kiss from me."

She loves Gonzo as much as a passive-aggressive dig at her lack of grandchildren. Time to shift the subject.

"I will, Mom. What's up with you?"

"Oh, you know, nothing new here. Oh wait, I started a new aerobics class at the Y, and that has been kicking my *tuchus*."

"Well, I'm glad you're getting out and staying busy."

"The ladies are nice, I think I might make some new friends."

"New friends are always good."

"How about you? How are things with that man you're seeing?"

And here we go.

"Things are fine," I lie because it's easier.

"Good. Good. I don't like thinking about you alone."

"I'm not alone, Mom. I have Gonzo."

"You know what I mean."

"I know. But I'm okay, Mom. I have school," I contend, trying to convince myself as much as her.

"Marvin, people aren't meant to be alone. You're not a bear in the arctic. I just want you to have someone. Somebody to look after and care for you."

The irony smacks me upside the head. My mother wants for me what she couldn't give me herself when I was a child. But I don't need anyone to take care of me. Besides occasionally forgetting to eat and tempting fate by driving my car with an almost empty tank most of the time, I'm doing fine.

"I know, Mom, but I have friends too. Friends are like found family."

I think of Jill and close my eyes. Why have I pushed her away these last few weeks? In my heart, I know she'd be overjoyed for me. She has so much happening with the pregnancy, and she must be scared. God, I feel like an ass. Every friendship has bumps, but family powers through obstacles. I need to make things right with her.

"You have nice friends who care about you, I know, but a partner, a spouse, that's something different."

And knowing she's right stabs a schmear knife right into my bagel heart.

"Okay, Mom, I have to get ready for school tomorrow," I fib. There's a plethora of tasks I could engage in, but tonight, Gonzo and I will stay in bed, eat spicy Doritos, leave crumbs in places there should be no crumbs, and blast pop songs about broken hearts.

Pulling into the school parking lot, I'm relieved I've beat Jill here. I need to prepare for the day and know once we begin chatting, my brain won't be in the place to do so. The heavy school door slams hard behind me, creating an echo of noise through the hallway that trails me to my room. I toss my backpack on my chair and scribble the morning message as quickly as possible.

March 18

Dear Friends,
Illona is First.
Taylor is the calendar helper.
We have Library.

Love,
Mr. Block

As I pinball around the room, placing papers and moving bins, I listen for Jill's arrival, ready to leap out into the hallway and pounce on her. But as it gets closer to eight, Jill's still not here. Typically, when one of us calls out sick, we text the other and email sub plans. Even though there's been this space between us, I hope she'd still feel comfortable doing that. I pull out my phone to ensure I haven't missed anything and debate texting her as Kristi pops her head into my room.

"Good morning," Kristi says with something else brewing underneath her smile.

"Hey, how are you?"

"I'm good, Marvin." She shuts the door. The guidance counselor shutting your door to chat is never a good sign. She walks over to a table closer to the easel where I'm standing and sits on it. Her usually cheerful face looks ominous, and I'm starting to worry.

"Marvin, Jill's in the hospital. I just found out this morning. I'm not sure what's wrong, but…"

The baby. Fuck. Tears begin to sting the corner of my eyes as I grab my coat and keys and dart for the door. I'm not sure if Kristi even knows Jill's pregnant, and it's not my place to tell her, so I just blurt, "I've got to go. Which hospital?"

"Maine Med, but, Marvin, you can't leave. The kids will be here in twenty minutes. We don't have a sub for you."

"Kristi, please watch my class. I'll be back soon, I promise."

"Marvin, hey buddy. She's going to be okay." Nick grabs me by the reception desk and gathers me in his arms, squeezing tightly, not letting go. Disinfectant and bleach blanket the area and the whoosh of automatic doors underscores Nick's voice.

"What happened?"

"She had some cramping this morning. They've run tests and the doctor says the baby is fine. This happens sometimes."

"She's okay? The baby's okay?" I let out a huge sigh, and the tears bridled all morning begin to stream down my face. Nick pulls away and gives me a soft smile, and I grab him again because I feel like he might need it, and I absolutely do. With my arms wrapped around his broad shoulders, he squeezes me tightly and mutters, "Yes, they're both fine."

Jill lies in a bed, hooked up to monitoring equipment. In this bare, sterile room, attached to tubes and beeping machines, the noises and disinfectant swirling in the air, she appears smaller, something I'm not used to with her.

"You trying to steal my husband?" she says with a gravelly voice.

"Oh no, this guy only has eyes for you. I've tried." I pat Nick's arm.

I walk over to her bed, and more tears cascade from my eyes. I'm crying about Jill, the baby, the secrets I've been keeping, Olan, all of it.

"Oh, honey, it's going to be okay. Sit down."

"I was so worried about you."

"Marvin, look at me. I'm fine. The baby is healthy. We're okay."

I lean over and bury my face into her chest, and the tears morph into a slow sob.

"Buddy, what is going on? There's something else. What is it?"

I don't want to talk about Olan. Or myself. Not here, not now. But Jill knows me better than almost anyone, and it's impossible to fool her.

"These tears. What's this about?"

"We'll talk later. Not now, not here." I motion to the hospital room.

"Marvin, now you're scaring me. Tell me. Now."

The time and place aren't ideal, but I can't contain it any longer.

"I have to tell you something, but I don't want to upset you. Not now."

"Unless you actually are running away with Nick, I promise I won't be."

"Noted!" Nick shouts from a chair across the room where he's engrossed on his phone.

With a needle poking out the top of her hand, for the first time since I've arrived she moves her palm from her belly and takes mine in hers, looks at me, and says, "Spill it."

"There's something I've been keeping from you, and it's been eating me up because I know it's created distance between us, and I hate that. I've been seeing someone, and I didn't tell you because, well, it's Olan, and I wanted to tell you, but he asked me not to say anything, and I agreed. With him being a parent in my class, and Teacher of the Year, and he's never been with a man, and things were amazing, like beyond amazing, but he told me he's an alcoholic, well in recovery, but still technically an alcoholic, and he had a relapse last year, but it was only one drink, and he actually does appear sober, but I ran out and haven't called or texted him since he told me and I'm so sorry I didn't tell you..."

"Okay, first breathe."

I close my eyes and inhale, attempting to make the air flow down to my diaphragm and releasing it slowly through my nose.

"Wait, Olan, the hot, rich dad?" Nick asks.

"Yes, very hot. Very rich," Jill says. "First, thank you for telling me. I knew something was up but didn't want to push you. Remember, you can always tell me anything. This"—she moves her hands between us—"is a judgment-free zone."

"I know. I'm sorry. So sorry. We agreed not to tell anyone, and I absolutely hated keeping it from you. Things were going so well. Or I thought they were. And now I've fucked it all up. Oh my god, sorry for saying fuck. In front of the baby." I gesture to her belly.

"For fuck's sake, you're good," she says with a sigh. "First of all, why didn't he tell you he was in recovery?"

"I mean, we're not super serious yet. Maybe because of my mom? Maybe because he knew I'd freak out? Which I did. So actually, maybe he was smart to keep it from me. I ran out of there like a nincompoop."

"Wait, ran out of where?"

"He rented a cottage on Peaks, and I went for a few days."

"And you didn't tell me?"

"I know! I'm so sorry. I felt awful keeping things from you. I wanted to tell you, I almost did, but then didn't, and things were, well, moving along with us."

"Wait, have you had sex with him?"

I glance over at Nick and back at Jill and give her my are-we-really-talking-about-this-in-front-of-the-straight-guy? look.

"Dude, it's all good," Nick says. "Actually, I'm about to go look for some breakfast." And he slips out.

"Spill it."

"Yes, yes, we've had sex. A few times."

"Marvin, you had sex with that gorgeous specimen of a man?"

"Um, hello, your husband isn't chopped liver either."

"Valid. Now tell me everything."

"We've had sex, all of it. I mean, one of the times was after his parent conference."

I give a wide-showing-all-my-teeth-oops smile.

"You fucking harlot! I love it. Wait, where were you?"

"In the printer closet."

"That's so hot."

"It was, actually."

"So, what are you going to do now?"

"I mean if I knew that, I wouldn't be asking you. I have no clue. I'm without a clue. I'm Alicia-Silverstone-level clueless." I sigh heavily and hope Jill has some words of wisdom.

"I mean he did tell you. Maybe not as quickly as you'd like, but you said he's sober now?"

"Yeah, for almost a year."

Jill shrugs and says, "Marvin, I know you have all these issues around drinking because of your mom, and I'm not trying to downplay that, but maybe this guy is worth working through them. Maybe Olan is an opportunity to face and overcome some of this. Or maybe not. He did tell you. And he's sober. I don't know. I can't tell you what to do."

"Um, hello, that's literally our thing. You tell me what to do all the time."

"Well, I can't. Not with this. I know what recovery means to you. But also, you haven't dated anyone seriously since Adam. I see your eyes when you talk about him. Do you love him?"

Love? Why did she have to bring up the L-word? My feelings for Olan are growing, but why does it feel difficult for me to admit it, even to myself? Is this because Adam betrayed me? My father abandoning me? I'm not sure.

"Do I love him?"

"Listen, I'm lying in a hospital bed. Don't do *Fiddler* with me."

"I don't know. I love being with him. I love the idea of him. Maybe I love him? Is that enough?"

"You have to decide that."

"You've been extremely helpful," I say, rolling my eyes.

"I love you, too."

Jill squeezes my hand, and I'm overwhelmed with affection for her and our friendship but still incredibly perplexed about Olan. I started to really let my guard down, and this reaction came from my gut. I'm supposed to listen to my gut, right? But then there's Olan and how incredibly wonderful he's been. Why can't someone simply make all my tough life decisions for me?

CHAPTER TWENTY-THREE

A real trooper, Kristi watches my class the entire morning with no sub plans. As I arrive back, she looks slightly frazzled with a few of her thick waves hanging askew. Four picture books and extra recess and Choice Time was her strategy and no doubt the kids weren't complaining. They probably felt like they'd hit the lottery.

Spotting me, the class swarms, enveloping me in hugs and shouts of "Mr. Block!" and I'm reminded, once again, of the deep bond we share. Even though I know they spent most of the morning listening to stories with Kristi and playing, I keep our afternoon light. Mostly because my heart still needs to recuperate from this morning with Jill, and I need to think about sub plans for her class, at least for tomorrow. I'm thankful for the distractions and try my best to keep thoughts of Olan at bay. Having his daughter in my class creates a constant reminder. Maybe it wasn't the brightest idea to have an affair with a parent. I feel like such a *meshugeneh*.

"It was fun having you on the island," Illona says as we walk to dismissal.

"Yeah, it really was."

"You make Daddy smile."

I give her a half grin and sigh softly. Illona appears to act as if nothing unusual happened between her dad and teacher. Specifically, she doesn't mention me having a minor panic attack and busting out without saying goodbye to her. This little victory pleases me so. Arriving at the dismissal area, I need to help Kristi dismiss Jill's students, and the utter nuttiness of making sure her students make it to the correct person helps me avoid any elongated interactions.

Olan stands near the pickup table, wearing a blue and pink flannel, and my stomach tugs at the sight of him. Illona runs and leaps into his arms. He closes his eyes and squeezes her a little tighter than usual. Holding her, his arms flex, tighten and taunt me. He opens his eyes, and we lock gazes, my heart does a quick double thump, and I'm reminded of all he said and all I need to contemplate, but also how damn gorgeous he looks in those navy-blue joggers that show all the curves and lines of his legs. He throws clothes on without much consideration for putting an outfit together and never fails to look photo shoot–ready. Jerk.

Our eyes meet, eliciting a soft half-smile on Olan's face, and I reply with my own. Why is he so damn irresistible? I return my focus to the six students from Jill's class looking for their grown-ups. One thing I'm certain of, I can't ignore Olan forever, but it's only been a day, and I need a little time. The Teacher of the Year team is coming Thursday for a school visit and interview. They provide just the excuse I need to postpone both thinking about and talking to Olan. Right as I return to the classroom, my phone vibrates in my pocket.

Olan: We need to talk.

Marvin: I know. I have the TOY visit on Thursday and need to focus on that. Can we chat this weekend?

Olan: Sounds good. Please remember I care about you. I'm sending you good vibes. I'll be thinking about you.

Marvin: Thank you. 🖤

And with that, I vow to stuff thinking about Olan being a recovering alcoholic deep down into a box until at least Friday after the Teacher of the Year team visits. Letting my emotions take over and derail this opportunity and all it means for the school would be a tragedy.

The kids do what they do best and provide me with diversions left and right to keep my mind focused in the present. On Wednesday, Teddy slips on a wet stone during recess and smacks his tiny face against a swing-set pole. Apparently, even the slightest trauma to the face causes massive amounts of blood, and Teddy, seeing blood everywhere, reacts as any five-year-old would. Like he's about to die. To be fair, his entire face, shirt, and even his hair are splattered red. In order to expedite our travel time to the nurse's office, I scoop him up in my arms and carry him.

Gwen Bell, the school nurse, a stoic creature, greets us. Spending your days dealing with sick children will do that to you. Often, I find it hard to read her because she has this combination of resting bitch/poker face. She may be in a permanent horrible mood, or she may have hit the jackpot, but she's not telling, so don't ask. I sprint into her office carrying Teddy, both of us covered in blood, and she's the only person in the room who doesn't appear alarmed.

"Put him down," she says, pointing to the long cot covered in industrial hunter-green pleather.

The worn fabric creaks under Teddy's small frame. I begin to move away, but the moment we break contact, Teddy wails. Loud and sharp, his cry grabs my heart and my feet freeze. I need to get back to my class, but I also know Jill and the other adults witnessed what happened, the amount of blood, and will cover for me. By this point, the blood has coated so much of us it looks like we've stepped in from a war zone. My head races with worry over the extent of his injury.

"Teddy, I'm going to stay right here," I say, sitting down next to him.

Gwen approaches and begins looking him over, assessing the damage.

"Teddy, I need to clean you up a little so I can help," she warns with a handful of gauze. The moment she begins to approach Teddy's face, he lets out a scream loud enough to cause me to jump a little. Gwen looks at me and raises her eyebrows in a please-help-me-with-this-kid look.

"Buddy, Mrs. Bell needs to clean you up so we can see how to help."

Without cleaning some of the blood, there's no way Gwen can assess the extent of Teddy's injuries. My right arm envelops him, drawing him close. I put my left hand out as an offer, and he immediately grabs it with both of his tiny, blood-soaked hands.

"Here's a trick to help while Mrs. Bell cleans the blood off. Close your eyes. Squeeze my hand, and we'll sing."

Because he's five, terrified, trusts me, and knows I wouldn't steer him wrong, Teddy does what I say. Eyes closed, both of his hands squeeze my one so tightly my fingers go numb. Without prompting from me, he begins to sing.

"The itsy-bitsy spider climbed up the waterspout," his little voice warbles, horribly off-key, but it might be the blood in his mouth.

Gwen looks at me, and for a nanosecond, I swear there's emotion in her eyes because she doesn't usually witness this unique bond between student and teacher. I nod gently, letting her know to proceed.

With the utmost care and lightest touch possible, she begins to wipe Teddy's sweet face. I join him in singing, and reaching the song's end, we start again. By the fourth time we sing, "And the itsy-bitsy spider went up the spout again," for all that's good and mighty, Gwen joins us. Her gruff voice slashes through the room and Teddy's body jolts slightly from the shock, so I draw him a little closer.

By the time Gwen has cleaned him enough to assess the actual injury, we've sung enough refrains of "The Itsy-Bitsy Spider" to give a real spider enough time to spin a web, climb up, and slide down with glee. Thankfully, the cut causing this massive amount of gore isn't actually that severe, and some pressure and a small bandage do the trick. Unfortunately, both Teddy and I are so caked in his blood we both need a change of clothes. Gwen stocks an entire wardrobe of outfit changes for the four- to eight-year-old crowd, but sadly nothing for fabulous grown men.

"You absolutely cannot return to your class like, like, this." She nods up and down my outfit that now resembles a horror movie costume. "You're going to have to go home and change."

As if on cue, Dr. Knorse, alerted by either Teddy's screams or the three of us singing, joins us to make sure a trip to the hospital isn't required.

"I'll watch your class for the afternoon."

"I can run home and back quickly. I can be back for dismissal."

"Marvin, go. I've got you covered," she says, and for the first time, probably ever, Dr. Tori Knorse lets a smidge of her humanity peek through her tough exterior; all it took was seeing a student and teacher smothered in blood.

As I sit on the towel Gwen loaned me for my car seat, my pants squish a little from the not-quite-dried blood. I begin driving, finally the urgency of the situation behind me, and I realize I remained calm the entire time. Teddy needed me to be steady for him, and I rose to the occasion. Why can't I do this for myself in times of extreme stress? Why can't I take care of myself the way I take care of my students? Why can't I let someone else take care of me? I feel my throat thicken, and it's hard, stuck, and cold when I swallow.

I do that alarming thing where I'm driving and paying enough attention to not crash but not completely thinking about where I'm going, and without realizing it, I'm heading to Olan's house instead of my apartment. Covered in Teddy's blood, I look like I'm ready for my stint as an extra in a gory flick as I park my car and stride up to Olan's front door.

CHAPTER TWENTY-FOUR

"Marvin, oh my god. What happened? Are you okay?"

Clearly confused by me standing at this door when I should be at school with his daughter and my entire class along with appearing as if I've just committed a heinous murder, Olan inspects me.

"Can I come in?"

"Of course." He moves to let me in, and even as I stand in his foyer, I'm not sure why I came here.

"What happened? Are you hurt?" Olan asks with concern.

For a quick moment, I forget why I'm afraid to be here. Olan's eyes survey me and I look down at my polo. The blue fabric and blood have combined to create a shade that resembles dark burgundy wine. My head fogs with the memory of Sunday. Olan. Recovery.

"Oh no, I'm fine. It's Teddy. He slipped and split his lip. He's fine, or he will be. I just need to change."

"Come in. Let's get you cleaned up."

Of course, Olan would take care of me. That's why I came, right? He's become a safety net. My heart knew where to go, even if my mind didn't. Without blinking, he stopped whatever he was doing to help me.

"I'm sorry. I didn't mean to interrupt or disturb you. I shouldn't be here. I'll go home," I sputter, turning toward the front door.

"Marvin, come." He grasps my hand—my disgusting, sticky hand—and my fingers tingle with his touch.

He guides me to his bedroom and straight into the bathroom. It's easily four times the size of my tiny bathroom, and the spa-like soaking tub and separate shower big enough for four people are accented by deep coffee-colored tilework.

"We need to get these off you. This okay?" Olan asks, taking my shirt in his fingers.

I nod, hoping he doesn't notice my heart pounding.

Carefully, he helps me undress, and though I didn't come here to be naked in front of him, somehow, the care and tenderness Olan uses makes me view him in an unexpected way. He turns on the shower and waits for it to get warm, gives me a soft kiss on my chin, and leaves me to clean myself.

As I stand under the rain shower, dizziness overtakes my brain. What am I so damn afraid of? The memories of my childhood, my mother's benders, the feeling of being alone and scared—it all comes flooding back. But I'm not a child anymore, and Olan is not my mother. Thank god for that. He's been nothing but caring and patient with me, and I'm acting like a *shmegegge*. And my mother. She's been trying so hard for so many years. I feel foolish for holding on to the past and letting it impact me. Making space for healing with her has to be a priority too. My eyes sting with thoughts of how I'm failing people who care about me.

The water runs crimson at first and slowly turns pinkish before flowing clear. The blood permeated my clothes and apparently was not only smeared on my face but matted my hair. The hot water warms my core, and washing with Olan's soap, smelling his woodsy freshness on me, standing where he typically washes, I'm overcome with deep affection. I've asked him to wait until the weekend to chat about his recovery. About us. Until after the Teacher of the Year visit, which, holy crap, happens tomorrow, and yet, here I am, literally naked, calmed by the sound of water around me. We need to talk now.

Back in the bedroom, a giant gray towel wrapped around my waist, a white T-shirt, green sweatshirt, and a pair of gray sweatpants await me. With my few inches on him, his pants might be a little short, but they don't resemble remnants from the set of *Carrie*. As I approach the bed to get dressed, Olan appears in the doorway.

"Clothes are in the wash. I put them on a heavy-duty cycle, so they might take a little longer, but I can get them to you later."

"Thank you."

"I'll wait downstairs. You get dressed." He steps back into the hallway.

"Olan. Wait."

I walk over to him and put my right hand on his cheek, cupping his face. His dark eyes furrow, and I glimpse a tinge of hope.

"Thank you," I say.

And because I'm human and Olan Stone stands in front of me, so close I can smell that damn cherry ChapStick, I lean over and place my lips on his. He kisses me gently and pulls back.

"I thought you wanted to wait..."

"I'm here. We can talk. In a bit."

It's only been four days since I've seen him. Touched him. Kissed him. Being in his presence causes my body to override my brain. Standing in front of Olan, wearing nothing but a towel, knowing he's here for me, wanting to help me, his compassion and tenderness on full display, my body can't hide how aroused I am. Olan glides forward to kiss me and notices.

"Um, are you having an issue with your towel?"

I bury my face in my hands, and he grabs my wrists.

"Marvin, you're doing it again."

"What?" I garble behind my fingers.

"Being adorable."

Olan slowly kisses my neck, taking his time. His mouth explores the space between my Adam's apple and chest. His warm tongue sends twitches of pleasure to my core as he kisses and nibbles me. I stand in his bedroom, about to be completely exposed in the full light of day, and for the first time in my life, I'm not afraid to be seen. The lights were almost always off or dimmed with Adam, or I was under covers, bare but hiding. Worried. Ashamed. Olan sees me, all of me, and I want to be vulnerable. I pull my hands away and move them to rest on either side of his head.

"What about Cindy?" I ask, appalled at the idea of her discovering her boss and her charge's teacher in a compromising position.

"Shopping, then picking Illona up. I texted her while you were in the shower," he mumbles into my neck, making me flutter.

Why did I come here? Not for this. Or did I? Am I willing to put aside my concerns for a momentary physical connection? I do care for Olan. Deeply. But am I only delaying the reality of the situation? Deep down, I worry about being abandoned. About nobody being there for me. But my body brought me here because Olan shelters me. Clustered in his arms, I feel protected. Whatever risk being with Olan brings, I'm ready to take it. Right now, I want this. I want him.

"Okay," I say.

Olan scans me, starting with my hair and moving down until his face reaches the towel. My dick, throbbing against the fabric, shows him it's more than ready to be rid of the damn thing, and he pulls the bath sheet from my body.

In one quick motion, Olan kneels and devours me, making me gasp. Once again, he shows me how his mouth can cause my eyes to roll back, and I'm left speechless. He's enjoying himself more this time, making low growls and moans as he swallows me.

"Mmmmh. Your cock tastes so fucking good."

He takes it out and slaps it against his face, and I'm, well, flabbergasted.

"Holy crap. You love it, don't you?"

He answers by swallowing it, almost to the base, and moaning, "Mmmmh."

I close my eyes, feeling his lips and tongue around me and listening to him slurp and gurgle. The amount of joy he's displaying from sucking me off makes my blood trumpet. Even though I know I'm the first man Olan's been with, he seems to naturally know where to go and what to do, and maybe he's just been waiting so long that he's finally getting to practice what he's been brooding over. In typical fashion, I'm over-thinking, so I try to relax and relish what's happening.

Olan stands and the urge to kiss him overtakes me. I taste myself on his lips and a shot of adrenaline rushes through me, making me shudder.

"Okay?" he whispers.

"Oh yeah, I love it," I say and pull him back, devouring his mouth.

He opens his eyes, just slightly, and I see—maybe for the first time—his deep brown, almost ebony eyes, so close, and he's looking at me with longing. We know each other deeper, and maybe I can hand over a tiny bit of myself to this beautiful man.

We fumble to his bed as his clothes come off, arms tangled and twisted, me giggling as he tries to keep his mouth on mine and remove his long-sleeved shirt. And as turned on as I am, the entire awkward shift to horizontal feels clumsy and comical and laughing about it, with him, in the moment, makes my skin simmer. Finally, he's stripped, and that chest. I never quite understood straight men's fascination with breasts, but Olan's pecs hypnotize me. I find it hard to keep my hands off them, perhaps this falls in the same lane.

As we lie on the bed, naked, legs entwined, our hard cocks rubbing against each other, my body takes over, and I grind on him. Olan stops, takes my face in his hands, and peers at me. The attention makes me blush, and he gives a little laugh.

"Adorable."

"Yeah, yeah, I know."

"I want you to…" He stops, and his chin drops.

"What do you want? Tell me."

He puffs out a breath from his nose. He's either embarrassed or tickled. I came here for help, but also because I wanted that help from him. If we're going to move forward, we both need to start communicating more openly.

"I can't read your mind. I want to know what you're thinking. It's okay to tell me what you want. It's just the two of us. You and me."

He raises his head and moves a little closer, kissing my cheek, and moving his lips to my jaw, and finally landing on my ear. His breath, deep and searing, whispers, "I want you. Inside me."

Now the absolute wrong thing to do in this moment would be to giggle, smirk, or act silly in any way. So, naturally, what do I do? Let out a loud, raucous laugh that startles poor Olan so much that he jerks away and stares at me in disbelief.

"Oh my gosh, I'm so sorry," I say through more laughter, "I was not expecting that from you."

He buries his face in my chest and starts to make small noises indicating he's cracking up too.

"Listen, nothing would make me happier than to, well, do that, but are you, um, ready? For that? You can't just barrel into it."

Olan keeps his head low. I can't see his face, and he begins talking, but with his lips smashed up against my skin, it's hard to make out what he's saying. I gently reach under his chin to lift his handsome face, and by all that is holy, he's burning up from blushing.

"Don't be embarrassed. It's hot when you ask for what you want."

"I'm ready. I've been...practicing," he says and immediately sinks his face back into me.

"Oh, have you, Mr. Stone? Well, you are full of surprises today."

"I want it. You."

He palms my unrelenting cock and begins teasing the head. My body shudders at his exquisite touch.

"Let's do this slowly."

Olan pulls out a condom and a small bottle of lube from his bedside table, and I spy what I'm fairly certain is a sex toy. How long have those been in there? He hands the condom to me and deadpans, "Maybe we can get tested so we won't need condoms. I'd love to be able to just explode inside each other."

And with that, I fumble the wrapper, sending it tumbling to the floor.

"Um, sure, okay, yeah, that sounds amazing. Now, c'mere. I'm going to get you ready first," I say, ignoring the misplaced condom for now.

I lay him on his back and kiss his chin. Applying some lube to my fingers, and, trying my best to be gentle, I begin softly massaging the tender skin around his hole. He lets out a soft whimper as I circle the opening, teasing him.

"So sweet," I say into his neck, carefully pushing a finger in.

"Marv, fuck, fuck."

Hearing his nickname for me, my heart blooms with endearment. I kiss and nibble his neck and ear, attempting to soothe him. He nods, and I add another finger, causing him to writhe in pleasure, eliciting soft moans. The sounds coming out of his mouth and feeling the hot, desperate way he opens up for me makes my dick throb in anticipation. With three fingers, I reach his prostate, and he begins to whimper softly. As much as I want to fuck him, having Olan at my mercy this way delights me beyond measure. He's panting now, occasionally my name ekes out until finally, he says, "Now. Fuck me now. Please, please."

"Okay."

Reaching to retrieve the condom, I'm so turned on and discombob-ulated, I lose my balance and tumble to the ground with a loud thud. And now Olan's on the bed. Wanting to be fucked. Ready to be fucked. And I'm on the floor.

"I'm fine!" I shout.

"Um, what happened?" Olan's face peeks over the edge of the bed and I have the sudden urge to crawl under it and never come out.

"I lost my balance. Again. Story of my life. One day my headstone will read 'Marvin Block—Adorable Klutz.'"

Olan lets out a low rumbling laugh and I simper because, well, I'm ridiculous and he still wants me.

"But I got it," I say, holding the condom up, like a rescued treasure.

"Good. Now, get up here and fuck me. Please."

My eyebrows almost fly off my forehead.

"Yes, sir."

Back on the bed, my hands remain slick and wet, and getting the damn thing open becomes a frustrating task.

"Let me," he says, taking it from me.

Ripping it open with his teeth in a manner that somehow makes him even sexier, Olan rolls the condom on me. Eager and ready, I lift his legs up, rest them on my shoulders, and slowly rub the tip of my cock on his slippery hole. Knowing I'm Olan's first, I yearn to make it magnif-icent. His trusting me with this confirms my decision to come here in the first place. He's not going anywhere. I apply the smallest amount of pressure, ensuring I'm in the right spot.

"Take some deep breaths. Relax. It's just me. You and me," I say, leaning over to kiss his forehead.

Olan closes his eyes and takes a deep breath. Sensing his nervous-ness, I softly brush my lips on his.

"Let's take it slow," I say with another kiss.

It takes patience and tenderness. I push gently inside him and nuzzle his neck, attempting to help him relax. Once I'm mostly in, I pause and ask, "Okay?"

"Yeah, give me a second."

"Remember, deep breaths," I say, nibbling his earlobe.

He moans gently, and I move my lips to his and hold him close.

"Mmmmh."

Pulling out, I say, "Good, breathe. It takes a few tries."

I press back in and pause, holding myself about halfway in until he smiles and nods. I push all the way, feeling him envelop me, and he lets out a gasp.

"Okay, wait, please," he says.

The manners on this man blow my fucking mind. I want to eat him up. Waiting for his cue, I run my hands on his chest and say, "You are so damn beautiful. Inside and out."

Slowly, with a few deep breaths, Olan's face begins to soften. He unlocks, and I can feel his body completely welcome me. My chest opens up as I melt into him. Being inside Olan feels like the universe opening up and letting me glimpse a hint of the totality of everything. I move slowly at first, steady and careful of his comfort.

"Okay?" I ask.

"Fuck, yes. Fuck. So good."

"Really?"

"Yes, yes, now, fuck me. Please."

He begins to rock his hips with mine and gives himself over to the moment, to me. He grabs my hips and draws me into him with such force there's no denying he's ecstatic. I begin to move with more energy as he paws at me. His hands explore the lines of my back, waist, and hips. I thrust into him, trying my best to fuse our bodies together.

"God, you're so perfect," I say.

He whimpers and clasps my ass, pulling me even closer, deeper. The complete bliss on his face encourages me to lean down. Our mouths connect, and my tongue plays with the tiny space between his front teeth, filling every space in him.

"Your dick feels incredible," he says, his voice low and raw, sending a jolt of adrenaline straight to my core.

"Yeah?"

"It's not like the toy. It's, it's..."

"Real," I say, eliciting a laugh from him.

This Olan surprises me. Something inside him was lying dormant. Dying to burst out. He's unleashed with me, and it drives me wild. I bury my face into his neck and begin licking and sucking my way up to his ear, and the soft noises he makes become lower, louder, and unhinged. Overtaken with desire, I open my mouth and take a bite at his neck, nibbling and gnawing at his salty skin. He's now panting, moving his hips to match my thrusts, using his hands to quicken my movement. His raw enthusiasm galvanizes our connection.

The kissing and thrusting and heat of our bodies dancing in rhythm intensifies, and my breathing becomes short, staccato notes. Aware of the change, Olan squeezes me, wrapping his arms around me, and in this instant, it feels like we're quite possibly the closest two people can get.

I push myself up and move a hand to Olan's cock. He's rock hard and if he comes this way, it will tear at his seams in all the best ways. He twitches with my first stroke, so I start slowly and only speed up to match my cadence once he's settled.

"You like that?" I ask.

"Oh, yeah. Keep doing that. A little faster, please."

"So fucking polite, I want to bite you again."

I'm elated he's asking for what he wants. I suck on my left thumb, getting it nice and slippery, and tease his nipple. Some spit on my right palm before returning to his shaft, and everything speeds up. The bed rocks back and forth in time with us, and I turn to kiss his glistening shin resting on my shoulder.

Olan starts to softly whimper and the spellbound look on his face tells me he's close.

"Please, don't stop, please, please," he begs.

I move my hand and hips quicker, and he lets out a gasp, "Oh, Marvin, I'm gonna, I'm gonna..." and he explodes, his breathtaking cock shooting thick ribbons all over my hand, making the movement even more slick.

He pulls me close and grabs my head, fingers entwined in curls, hot breath in my ear.

"I'm almost there, but I need a minute," I say, pulling out and taking a short respite.

"Come inside me." His words prickle my ear.

"Are you sure?"

I pull my face up, wanting to see him.

"Marv, get back in there," he says, turning over, lifting his leg slightly, his delectable ass an invitation.

Again, he's taking control and it sends me over the moon. I lean down and kiss his right cheek. His ass, so round, so fucking delectable. I want to bite it. Softly, I take a nibble.

"Okay, Mr. Block. Now let's have you fuck me until you come."

Having him talk to me this way makes my cock surge and I move into position behind him. At the moment of reentry, pleasure overtakes me. His head thrown back, my eyes dart between the euphoric expression on his face and the sight of my dick sliding in and out of him.

I use my left hand to lift his leg, sliding my palm up and down the underside of his thick thigh. Finally, my hand descends and feels my dick fervently fucking his gorgeous hole.

"It's not going to take long," I groan, feeling my orgasm rising like a thermometer in the scorching July sun. Those final thrusts liberate not only my ejaculation but something deep inside me. A brick falls from the wall I've carefully constructed to keep myself safe. Now to blast the entire thing to bits. I bury my face in his neck, and my body quakes with blissful release.

"Oh, fuck, Olan. Fuck, you, you, you're so fucking, you."

My arm wrapped around his chest, clutching him close, we lie, small aftershocks making my body tremble against his back. My heart begins to slow with deep breaths, and in this vulnerable, delicate moment, because I'm me, I start chuckling.

"Are you laughing at me?" he asks, turning over to face me.

"Oh my god, no, no. Sometimes, after, I giggle. I can't explain it."

"It's probably the release."

His face is flat and serious and once more the urge to bite him surges in my belly.

"You are such a dork."

My mouth falls on his, still laughing. Exhilarated and numb, we lie on the bed sweaty and sticky, and serenity washes over me. I close my eyes and make a quick wish to stay this way forever.

"You okay?" I ask.

"No. I'm better than okay. I'm spectacular. That was…so different. So much better."

"Better than what?" I ask.

"Than before. Than alcohol. Than everything." His eyes sparkle mischievously. "You know, we still have about an hour until Illona comes home. I have an idea," he mutters.

"I don't think I'm ready for round two yet."

"No, silly."

Popping off the bed, he jogs into the bathroom, his fabulous body on full display. I hear the sound of water cascading and smile. I'm not sure what his plan for us entails, but I'd be more than content to lie here naked with him for the next hour. A few minutes later, Olan appears, still bare but with a shiny, damp stomach and chest, and he grabs both of my hands in his.

"Come on, lazy bones. You're going to love this, I promise."

Reluctantly, I let him help me up, and we saunter into the bathroom. My feet shuffling behind him, hands on his waist, I try to keep my body warm by staying as close to him as possible. He fits perfectly in front of me. We're like two snap cubes clicking together.

Water flows almost to the top as the bath fills. Aromas of lavender and smoke fill the room from five flickering candles, creating a quiet twilight against the walls.

"There's room for both of us," he says, walking me over, not dropping my hand, and assuring I don't lose my balance stepping in. The water steams, I ease in, and the tension from the day begins to fade. Olan joins me, and we rest on opposite ends of the soaking tub, the spout smartly positioned in the middle so we can both lean back. He keeps his knees bent slightly and tugs at my feet, stretching my legs out. Under the water, his hands glide up and down my shins, and I wonder if maybe this would be the ideal place to spend eternity with him instead of the bed.

"We've got an hour," he warns.

"Perfect."

I wasn't planning on it, but I feel so relaxed, at ease, and connected to him in this tub. What I say next surprises even me.

"I want to tell you about why your recovery freaked me out."

Olan's lips draw tight, and he gives a slight nod, urging me to continue.

"Growing up with an alcoholic mom, well, messed with my head. My dad left when I was a baby, and Sarah was solely responsible for me. Turns out, she could barely take care of herself. She would have these horrible benders, always vowing to do better the next day. Promises to take me places, to the movies, shopping, to buy me stupid things we couldn't afford. Broken promises."

Olan continues to rub his hands up and down my legs. His eyes are glistening and my throat catches.

"She'd stop drinking for a few days, and then it would all happen again. Rinse and repeat."

"It sounds like your dad leaving really did a number on her."

"Yeah, I mean, I think that was a big part of it. And over years and years, well, it caused me to have an enormous problem trusting people."

"And then your ex cheated on you."

"Exactly. I'm working on things with my mother. She's doing so well and I know she's moving heaven and earth to repair our relationship. It's really on me now."

"Don't be so hard on yourself. It sounds like years of trauma to deal with."

"Yeah, I'm trying. I know I'm messed up, and I know there are issues I need to tackle, but well, now you know why I bolted on Peaks. I feel like an ass. I'm sorry."

"Marvin, you are not an ass. You have a great ass, but you are not an ass." He leans forward and runs his right hand all the way up to squeeze my butt.

"So, when did she finally sober up?"

"My senior year of high school, she had a nasty night out and drove when she shouldn't have."

Olan winces, his inferences skills on point.

"Thankfully the only casualties were a tall oak tree and her Focus. She was banged up pretty bad in the hospital, and I sat at her bed, weeping, pleading for her to get help. I was leaving for college soon, and the idea of her alone, drinking herself to death, terrified me. I think that frightened her enough to agree to get help. She's been sober since but getting there was a long fucking road."

Olan scoots closer, our legs bending and melding together underwater. He places a hand on each of my thighs and pulls himself until his beautiful face lingers inches from mine.

"Listen, I can't guarantee perfection, but I promise I'd never hurt you intentionally. And I'm not going anywhere. I haven't had a drink in almost a year. And before that—college. I know this, whatever this is, feels new, but you have to trust me. I take my sobriety seriously. When you took off, well, it stung."

My eyes begin to water, and I'm hopeful the steam from the bath might camouflage them a little.

"Olan, I'm sorry. Truly. The last thing I want to do is hurt you."

I give him a soft, gentle kiss. He opens his mouth slightly and I take that as acceptance of my apology.

"One of the reasons I moved to Portland was the strength of the recovery community here. I've got a fantastic sponsor, Jack. We text and chat daily. He knows all about you. I attend three meetings a week. Maybe you could come with me sometime?"

The thought of recovery, AA, it all hits a little too close to home, but I also see Olan, unguarded, and my soul sings loudly. My heart understands he's a good man. My head worries about, well, too much.

"I'd like that. My trust issues mean I sometimes struggle with being vulnerable, but you're starting to weasel your way into my heart. Truly. I'm going to do my best to let you in."

"Well, I did just let you in. Pretty deeply," he says flatly.

"Are you being filthy when I'm trying to be serious?"

He leans in and presses his lips to mine, answering me with a kiss that sends a swarm of butterflies plunging into my stomach.

"Now, can I tell you something that worries me?" he asks.

"Of course."

"You're such a committed teacher. You clearly love your students and take your job seriously, but sometimes, well, I worry you're too dedicated."

"Is this about the award?"

"Partly, yes. I know it means a lot to you and the school, but I just worry you're not taking care of yourself."

"I just want to be the best for the kids. I can work on balance. I'm not perfect, but I'll keep trying."

"Marvin, you don't have to be perfect. Nobody is. Why do you think you need to be perfect?"

"I don't know. Maybe if I'm perfect..." But I can't say the rest: *maybe nobody will leave me.* Instead, I say, "I hear you, and I understand. Once the visit and interview are over, things should settle down some."

"Okay, but I'm keeping my eye on you."

"Please do," I say and move in for another kiss, his lips wet and warm.

"We should get out. They're going to be home soon."

And with that, the reality of tomorrow, the visit, the interview, the award, the funding comes crashing into my head.

"I better get home," I blurt, jumping out of the tub, sending copious amounts of water cascading onto the tile floor, sloshing everywhere.

"Marvin, slow down. Let me help you."

Olan hops out of the bath, grabbing towels from a shelf to lend me a hand sopping up the puddles of water. We both get to work, pushing towels around in grand strokes, attempting to erase the mess I've made being erratic. And, for just a moment, I stop mopping up water and simply stare at him, his muscles damp from the tub, rippling and stretching as he works completely naked.

"What's wrong?" he asks, noticing I've stopped.

"Nothing, it's just, well, distracting." I motion to his nudeness.

He grabs one of the dry towels from the pile and wraps it around his waist.

"Better?"

"Yes. And no."

Dressed, we stand at his front door. This afternoon unfolded in a way I would have never predicted. Leaving school early, covered in blood, being comforted by Olan, bathing with him—the ransacking of

233

my routine would typically rattle me, but with him next to me, close, kind, and supportive, I'm leaning into the reshuffling.

"I'm going to do some reading and preparing tonight, but let's make sure we at least text later. Sound good?"

Olan nods, and kisses me. And instead of turning and bolting, I pause and kiss him back. Our mouths connected, filled with affection, I linger, savoring the moment. Maybe there's hope for me after all?

Back in my apartment, I pop a frozen cheese pizza into the oven as Gonzo lies on the table next to my computer, pawing gently at piles of papers. Tomorrow's visit and interview feel like a big deal. Me, in that luxurious tub, attempting vulnerability with Olan, feels monumental. Talking with him and sharing a part of why I'm so, well, me makes the tightness in my chest loosen, which feels auspicious.

CHAPTER TWENTY-FIVE

Olan: I'll be thinking about you today. You got this!

Marvin: Thank you that means a lot.

Olan: I'll see you at pickup. Maybe we can chat this evening.

Marvin: I'd love that. 🖤

As I walk into my classroom, everything feels heightened today. I wear khaki pants, a powder-blue short-sleeve button-down shirt, and a navy gingham bow tie. All of these items rarely see the light of day because kindergarten teachers do not regularly wear nice clothes. It would make no sense. Refer to earlier stories about vomit and blood and add on encounters with paint, markers, snot, urine, and feces. We're also on the floor. A lot. When the people you need to communicate with are tiny, and you must kneel, squat, and even lie on the floor multiple times a day, you learn swiftly that anything you wear can and will most likely be ruined.

Only special occasions warrant the inherent risk of ruining expensive clothes and today definitely fits the bill. Dr. Knorse informed me she'd be meeting the team at eight thirty since that's when my students arrive. Because I understand how five- and six-year-old brains function, yesterday, I mentioned to my class we'd be welcoming some visitors but kept the conversation low-key.

"Tomorrow morning, two grown-ups are coming to spend some time with us for a bit."

"Why are they coming?" Kate asked.

"Are we in trouble?" Charlie added.

"Nobody is in trouble. You know how I brag about having the best class in the school, well, word got out, and these adults want to come and see how amazing all of you are. We'll just do our normal routine, and they'll watch. They might even participate or ask you questions. All you have to do is be your amazing selves. That's what they're coming to see."

And that was enough. No mention of the award or my interview during lunch. The key lies in giving enough information to prepare them but not too much to cause concern or overthinking. When I started teaching, I gave way too many details about being out or special events, which only brought more questions and worries. When you know better, you do better.

At eight thirty, Dr. Knorse appears at the door with two people. She walks them in, and I pause to greet them.

"Good morning, welcome."

"This is Dr. Hayes and Mr. Ali," Dr. Knorse announces. I know she's counting on this going well.

Dr. Angela Hayes has been my contact with the organization, and all my emails have come from her. A white stout woman—not terribly taller than the students—with auburn shoulder-length hair that she's clearly spent time curling, she wears a purple dress covered in pink flowers. Her round, friendly face smiles wide enough to show teeth. Next to her, Mr. Ali towers over her and everyone else. He's Black and slender with a neatly trimmed mustache. He's wearing a navy suit, minus the jacket draped over his arm, which makes sense on this warmer, almost-April day. He smiles, his eyes darting around the room, taking it all in, and I wonder what experience they both have with kindergarten. Until you've experienced the magical chaos, you have no idea.

"Welcome! Feel free to join us on the carpet or take a seat at one of the tables," I offer, knowing not all adults want to sit on the floor.

Dr. Knorse gives me her best version of RuPaul's good-luck-and-don't-fuck-it-up stare, leaving Dr. Hayes and Mr. Ali in the pit of the lion's den. Of course, I'm a lion tamer, and they are in for quite a show.

Dr. Hayes, clearly the braver of the two, joins us on the carpet. She waddles over, and without prompting Martha and Illona move apart, giving her a wide berth. She lowers herself, legs apart, and about halfway to the ground gravity takes over. Realizing she's about to fall, she juts her arm out at the last moment to catch herself and lets out an "Oh my!" as she lands. She rights herself and does her best to sit with her legs tucked to her side. Martha scoots over even more, again without being asked.

Mr. Ali watches in slight horror and, being even further from the ground, wisely opts to grab a chair and sit on the circle's periphery. Even in a chair, his knees rise up to his chest. Maybe I should've procured some adult-sized chairs for them, but the complete kindergarten experience includes managing tiny furniture.

With everyone mostly settled and my students already showing an enormous amount of patience, I continue with the share portion of our meeting.

"We've been talking about being flexible. Who can remind us what 'being flexible' means?"

A few perplexed looks are dotted between raised hands. Ricky's hand waves wildly, and I nod toward him.

"Being flexible means if you want blocks, but it's full, pick something else and don't throw a fit," he spits out, pointedly looking at both Dr. Hayes and Mr. Ali with a grin.

"Yes, Ricky, that is an example of being flexible. If you make a plan and it doesn't work out, you need another plan. Now, I want you to think of a time you were flexible. Like Ricky's example with blocks. Take a thinking minute, so you're ready to share," I instruct.

Each child's pointer finger goes up to their chin and begins tapping, a strategy I taught them to show they are thinking.

"All right, turn and talk to your partner. 'One time I was flexible was…' and go!"

Each child turns to the one next to them, there's no chaos or confusion as we've practiced this over and over until it became seamless. They begin speaking to each other using the sentence stem provided, and I push myself up to a squat, popping around and listening in to as many partnerships as possible. I glance over and both adults have taken laptops out and are feverishly typing notes. My class, no different than any other day, shines. Only now, the Teacher of the Year folks are here to witness them. Proud doesn't begin to describe how I'm feeling.

I keep waiting for a catastrophe to happen, but no meteors crash into our room, and the ceiling does not cave in. There's almost a disaster at snack time when Mr. Ali helps Kate with her yogurt by ripping the end off, and it spurts all over his shirt. Before I can intervene, Kevin runs and gets the wipes and begins cleaning Mr. Ali up, and again, my heart fills with joy.

Outside during morning recess, I finally steal a moment to chat with them both.

"Mr. Ali, I'm sorry again about your shirt."

"Please, call me Samir, and truly, it's fine. Kevin was there before I could even ask for help. Your class clearly takes care of each other."

"Marvin, both Samir and my experiences lean more toward upper elementary and middle school, so visiting kindergarten opens a whole new door for us," Dr. Hayes adds, pulling her hair back into a tie as the wind whips it around.

"I wondered about that," I reply.

"You clearly have created a community full of respect, love, and learning," Mr. Ali adds.

"Thank you, they're fantastic kids, and I truly do love learning with them."

And with that, I notice Zoe searching for a push on the swings and excuse myself.

The rest of the morning unfolds without much fanfare. Both Dr. Hayes and Mr. Ali sit at tables during Writing Time and seem amazed at how much actual writing kindergarteners do. Pages and pages appear as the children feverishly write. We are working on increasing our volume, and they're nailing it. At lunch, I drop the class at the cafeteria, and quickly check my phone.

Olan's emoji game impresses me. I tap back a heart and my stomach flutters as I think about thanking him later in person. Back in the classroom, Dr. Hayes and Mr. Ali sit at one of the tables chatting. Dr. Hayes sips from a silver water bottle, and seeing me, they pause their conversation.

"Marvin, come sit." Mr. Ali nods toward a chair at the end of the table.

"We like our interviews to feel informal, casual. It's why we try to spend time in the classroom first, to watch you in action, observe your teaching, and now we'll have a chat," Dr. Hayes begins.

My worry about this day melts away with their friendliness and how my students behaved this morning, although the importance of actually winning the award nags at my stomach.

"We both enjoyed our time with your class this morning," Mr. Ali says.

"Truly, it's no wonder you're so well loved within your community," Dr. Hayes continues.

"Thank you. Both. That means so much."

"And our first question is about community. How do you involve your student's families in their education?"

"I took a sexy bath with a parent yesterday, after railing him," flashes in my head, but probably wouldn't be the wisest answer. But the mention of families jolts my brain to Olan and how I'm clearly catching feelings for him and where this appears to be headed. We haven't labeled our relationship but have clearly moved past hanging out. Focus, Marvin, on the task at hand.

"Before the school year even starts, I'm thinking about ways to engage families in their child's education. I offer home visits for those who feel it would help their child, and they have been a wonderful way to build a connection prior to the first day. Daily emails, they're short but offer an outline of what we've read and learned about, topics discussions, that sort of thing. They help families engage with their children about school. And in addition to volunteers, I try to create a few opportunities each year for families to come in and share in celebrations of our learning."

Nailed it. And no mention of nailing Olan.

"Oh, that sounds wonderful. Can you tell us about one of those experiences?"

"Well before the holiday break, we had a community potluck where each child's family was encouraged to bring in a dish representative of their culture or heritage. And in two weeks, we're having a reading celebration where we'll retell *The Very Hungry Caterpillar* as a class, before each student uses a storyboard to retell to their family on their own."

"Fantastic," Dr. Hayes proclaims.

Their faces nod with full smiles, and both of them feverishly type as I speak. The visit and interview have loomed for months, and to have it finally happening, and going so well, makes my heart swell with a mixture of relief and pride. We spend the next thirty minutes chatting about my teaching philosophy, classroom management, engagement, and all the ways I try to make my classroom a special place for students. Shockingly, nobody asks if I'm having a torrid affair with the father of one of my students.

Once Dr. Hayes and Mr. Ali depart, a small pang of guilt pokes at me. Olan and I have kept our relationship a secret because we're worried about how it would be perceived. The truth is there's no rule against it. What other people think about us is none of our business. I know this, yet there's an empty feeling in the pit of my stomach. This isn't only about me. Pelletier Elementary needs this Teacher of the Year win, and I won't do anything to jeopardize it.

CHAPTER TWENTY-SIX

Olan: How did it go?

Marvin: I don't think it could have gone better.

Olan: Amazing and not surprising. Also I wanted to kiss you so bad at pickup. You. In that bow tie. Please wear it for me sometime.

Marvin: Of course. 😎

The next couple of weeks fly by. With the anticipation of the visit and interview over, I lean into life. Dr. Hayes informs me I won't be notified about the selection until the ceremony at the end of May, so I do my best to put it out of my mind and focus on my students, friends, and Olan.

At school, we are busily getting ready for our reading celebration. We spend a little bit of time each day rereading *The Very Hungry Caterpillar*, creating costumes for each part with posterboard, paint, and yarn, and practicing our retelling on the carpet. The kids adore the story, and the chance to craft and use their imaginations only enhances the joy of reading. Having families join us for the afternoon to revel in their children's growth takes work, but the payoff exceeds expectations.

Jill and I return to our Saturday morning gatherings. The scare with the baby is happily only a memory, and her bump slowly begins to grow. We talk about when she might tell her class with Kristi, and she lands on waiting until closer to the end of the school year. Now that she knows about Olan, I can chat with her about him, and honestly, that feels like a huge weight has been lifted. Olan isn't thrilled I confessed to her, but he understands, and I assure him Jill's lips are sealed.

"I get you need someone to talk to about... well, me."

"What about you? Who can you talk to? About me," I ask him.

"Well, there's Illona," he jokes. "No, my sponsor, Jack. We have no secrets."

Even though we're keeping things hush-hush, Olan and I progress in a way I never would've imagined. We spend at least one weekend night together, usually with me staying at his place.

For Mother's Day, Illona flies to California to see her mother, which makes my heart happy. Olan worries about being away from her, but Cindy took her, and that helps calm his nerves. With nobody at his house, he stays at my place for the first time. Gonzo is extremely wary at first and not keen on moving from his spot next to me on the bed, but eventually, with enough treats and chin scratches, he succumbs to Olan's charm. Welcome to the club, buddy.

Waking up on a Saturday morning with both Olan and Gonzo in bed creates a sense of calmness new to me. As I lie there, sandwiched between them, I stare up at the ceiling, and a sense of peace washes over me. Olan begins to stir and mumbles, "Morning."

"Hey, sleepy head."

He opens one eye. "What are you so smiley about?"

"Oh, just love lying here with both my boys." Gonzo crawls over me, lying between us and nudging Olan's hand with his nose.

"Tell me more about little Marvin."

"My dick? Um, I'm pretty sure you could identify him in a police lineup."

"No, silly. Little Marvin, your childhood. You don't talk about it much."

A small lump forms in the back of my dry mouth. "That's because I mostly try to forget it."

"There must be something pleasant you remember. Something that was a reprieve for you."

"Hmmm. Well, there was this dog."

"You had a dog?" Olan's eyebrows hitch up with curiosity.

"No, not a real dog, a stuffed dog. When I was about five, my mother bought him for me after a particularly bad weekend. She was trying to make up for her mess. I loved that stupid stuffed animal. He had shaggy brown fur and a giant black nose. Cuddling and playing with him brought me more comfort than you can imagine. I used to make little forts in my bedroom with blankets and pillows and have these mini adventures with him. So foolish."

"I think it's sweet. What was his name?"

"Ivan. It was on his tag, and I just liked it. It felt like a strong name, and I imagined he would help take care of me."

Olan gathers me in his arms, my head on his chest as he begins stroking my hair.

"Not that you need it now, but I'd like to help take care of you."

"What do you think about that, Gonzo?" Olan's hand pauses petting my head, and moves to Gonzo, who immediately begins purring loud enough to shake the bed.

Gonzo, always a glutton for attention, rolls slightly, exposing his belly.

"He's being a whore for you," I say.

"Just like his dad."

"Only for you."

Since Bloody Wednesday (what I'm calling the day of Teddy's accident), we've been getting to know each other on a deeper level. My feelings for him are developing in a way I wasn't sure was possible. Even in a relatively short time, our conversations become intense. This feels so right.

Saturday night, we cook giant bowls of spaghetti because Olan believes half a box is the right measurement per person. Once the copious leftovers are packed and Illona's in bed, we chill on the sofa, my head on his lap, his hands tangled in my hair, massaging my scalp, my eyes closed from the utter relaxation. I work up the courage to ask a question I've been wondering about for some time.

"So, you've been with Isabella and now me. Do you think you're bi?"

"I'm not sure how I identify. Maybe I'm bisexual. I don't know. Do I need to label myself?"

"No, of course not."

"I definitely enjoyed being with Isabella, at least at first, and now, this." He motions between us. "You. I'm not sure what it means, but I definitely like it."

"Like what?" I poke his thigh.

He leans over, and his face comes closer to mine. "You. I like you. A lot."

He glides his fingers on my face, his thumb resting on my cheek.

I lift my torso and scoot into his lap, my hands on his chest.

"Oh, you like me? I would never have guessed. Would you say we're dating?"

He almost chokes on his laugh, it comes so fast. "Uh, yeah, I'd say we're more than dating, Marvin."

"Oh, we are?"

"You are so damn adorable. Yes, we're dating. Yesterday, Jack was asking about you and I referred to you as my boyfriend."

"Excuse me? Boyfriend? How is your sponsor finding out I'm your boyfriend before me?"

"Are you okay with that?"

"I think so," I say, unable to hide my smile.

And now we're talking about feelings. This isn't about lust or desire but the steady, tender yearning of care. Of a fire you want to keep blazing. And the way he's looking at me, honestly, the way he's looked at me for a while, he doesn't even need to tell me. We spend a good ten minutes without moving much, but the talking leads to kissing. Olan does that thing where he starts nibbling my earlobe, sending an instant shudder of adrenaline to my core, and I murmur, "Let's go upstairs."

It seems odd, but the sex is actually getting hotter. The more we let each other in emotionally, the more I let my defenses down, and being intimate becomes more than a physical act. We connect with our bodies, yes. It's exquisitely hot, wild, and raw, but our hearts also clamp onto each other. The relationship we're building propels the sex into the stratosphere.

A quick shower and I'm back in bed with Olan. He extends his left arm, inviting me into my favorite spot, lying my head on his chest. He gets to stroke my hair, and I get my cheek on his pec, so it's a true win-win situation. Between sex and the hot shower, I'm about to doze off.

"Hey, I need to tell you something," Olan begins.

"Mmmmh," I groan.

"So you know the reading celebration?"

"Yeah, it's next Friday."

"Illona's really excited about it."

"She's a cupcake."

"A cupcake?" Olan's face twists with confusion.

"In the story, the caterpillar eats all this random food—fruit, cake, a lollipop, a salami, and she wanted to be the cupcake. Wait until you see her outfit. She's precious."

"I have no doubt. And I feel like I'm missing a joke here about salami, but I'm going to let it go. Anyway, she's quite excited and actually mentioned it to her mom."

My ears twitch and perk up at this. Illona rarely speaks about her mom to me, and I don't ask questions or attempt to push her into conversation around the topic.

"Oh, well, I'm glad she's fired up for it. That's my goal."

"So, Illona asked her to come, and Isabella wants to. There's no way I could tell her no."

"Of course, she's Illona's mom. She absolutely should come."

My damn head and heart tussle again. There's nothing for me to worry about with Olan. We're so clearly good, more than good, but the mother of his child, his ex-wife, shouldn't be glossed over as nothing.

"There's more. She asked to stay here, and I didn't think I should say no. For Illona."

"Oh." That's all I've got.

Olan props himself up, forcing me to do the same. He puts his hands behind my neck and draws my face close to rest his forehead on mine.

"Listen to me, Mr. Block. You have absolutely nothing to worry about. Nothing. This thing, you and me, I'm all in. So, whatever your adorable little brain is worrying and spiraling about, please stop it right now."

"You don't know me."

But he does. And he's right. And maybe, just maybe, I'm starting to move past catching feelings for this guy to something more.

"Does she know about me?"

I'm not sure it's within my purview to ask, but if she's coming, staying in the house with Olan, I need more information if he wants me not to agonize over it.

"She knows you're Illona's teacher. She knows we're friends, and we hang out outside of school. Often. My gut tells me she's suspicious. Illona talks about you. A lot. It's been years, but I've talked with Isabella about wondering if I might be bisexual. She'd never ask me outright about you. I'm going to tell her, I promise."

"How do you think she'll react?"

"Honestly, I'm not sure. She knows I haven't dated anyone since we split."

"No, I mean about you dating a man?"

"I mean, it shouldn't matter, right?"

"It shouldn't, but that doesn't mean it won't."

"Well, she will have to deal with it regardless. And I want you to come for dinner. After the celebration."

My eyes go wide, and I'm sure my shocked face reveals my uneasiness.

"Marvin, it's a meal. With me. And Illona. And her mother. It will be fine. I promise."

And even though it feels like the universe might be sending me something new to obsess about, I try my best to ignore the urge to spiral. Isabella is Illona's mom. She's Olan's ex. How bad can she be?

CHAPTER TWENTY-SEVEN

Marvin: I'll see you this afternoon.

Olan: I can't wait. I'll try my best to behave.

Marvin: You better. I'm breaking out the khakis and bow tie. FYI

Olan: You're going to make this tough for me. 😏

"You ready?" Kristi asks, thrusting her head into the doorway of my classroom.

"Ready or not! I kid. We've been practicing, and I think we're prepared. Plus, the beauty of kindergarten lies in the cuteness of mistakes."

"Very true. Well, I'll be here. Remember to have fun and enjoy it."

"Thanks," I say and she's off.

The tightening in my chest reminds me I'm meeting Isabella today. My brain tries hard not to think about possible worst-case scenarios. She wouldn't barge in and announce, "Mr. Block is *shtupping* Illona's father!" Right? I rub my hands on my pants and close my eyes. The silence in the room allows me to hear the faint ticking of the second hand on the classroom clock. Tick, tick, tick. Maren Morris's rich country alto voice comes in, Zedd's beats drop, and the wall of sound that is "The Middle" washes over me. This song epitomizes the term *banger*. Whoever thought to combine EDM music with a country singer's sumptuous voice deserves a medal. Or a Grammy. I bounce my leg to the music in my head, and a rich warmth comes over me.

"Marvin. Marvin. Hello?" Jill interrupts the melody in my mind.

"Oh, hey, sorry."

"What song?"

"'The Middle.'"

"Nice choice. Total banger."

"Right?"

"And what are you distracting yourself from? Are you nervous about the celebration? Meeting the ex?"

"Definitely Isabella. Apparently, Olan told her about us. Lord knows what she thinks."

"She will meet you in the best possible environment—your classroom. Marvin, you are literally up for fucking Teacher of the Year. She's going to see you shine like the brilliant star you are. Her daughter adores you. She's going to see how happy you make Olan. What more could she want?"

"That's what worries me. What if she doesn't love how happy her daughter and ex are because of me?"

"Well, that would be about her and not you. Please, just be your charming, cute self and enjoy the celebration."

"Come here, please."

Jill strolls over to me, and I swaddle her in my arms. She's so small it's easy to completely envelop her.

"Thank you for being you."

"You're welcome. And remember, you're providing unlimited free babysitting." Jill taps her tiny bump.

"Duh. Only a Jewish Guncle can teach the baby about noshes and *Drag Race*."

Clearly pumped for the celebration, the class jumps and bounces as they return from lunch. We read a story, and I turn off the lights and guide them through some deep meditative breaths. Of course, this helps me as much as them. One thing I've learned as a teacher, expect the unexpected and roll with it. Whatever happens, the families will forgive us because if all else fails, the kids are ridiculously cute. At one thirty, the room phone rings. The children squeal in anticipation and glee. It's beyond precious.

"Hold on, I can't answer if I can't hear."

They all make "shush" noises, quiet down, and stare at me. Jean lets me know families have started arriving and asks if she can send them down.

"Okay, they're coming," I say in the calmest, quietest possible voice.

A few soft screams erupt, but for the most part, they manage to keep it together. My heart beats loudly for the minute or so until the families are going to stream in.

"Okay, friends, remember, when you see your family, give a wave, but stay on the rug so they can sit at our tables. You'll have time with them afterward with your storyboards."

Relatives begin appearing, entering the classroom with a look of trepidation. People know enough to understand a kindergarten classroom might be a little intimidating, to say the least. But this is organized, well-planned, managed chaos they've been invited to witness.

Charlie spots his family. His mother, father, and two-year-old sister come in first. Popping up on his knees, he waves his arms so fast I wonder if he'll begin to hover like a small helicopter. There's something magical for children about their two worlds smashing together like this, and I take a deep satisfying breath, knowing I not only arranged it but get to witness the glory. More families trickle in with smiles and greetings as they wrangle their adult bodies into tiny seats at tiny tables, and I think, "Welcome to my world."

I spot Olan and my face flushes, and Lord, I pray nobody notices. He's wearing slate dress pants and a rich chestnut sweater. Cindy follows directly behind him. She waves and raises her eyebrows at me in a way that suggests solidarity and understanding. I'm grateful for the friendship she provides Olan and help she affords him with Illona. Behind Cindy, Isabella appears, and even though I've seen her in photos littered around Olan's home, in person, she's simply stunning.

She walks with the confidence that only comes with a certain level of beauty. Shoulders back, her hair flows past them a few inches in shades of brown and auburn, clearly masterfully curated in a salon. The small flaps of fabric on her white blouse move with each step toward the table, and she somehow makes simple jeans dressy, maybe by pairing them with heeled boots. We lock eyes, and she gives me a simple grin that conveys she knows. Everything. *G'vald!*

Because I'm positioned with the students in hopes of keeping them corralled, we won't officially meet now. I offer a small wave to their group. Olan waves back with a beaming smile, Cindy nods her head in response, and Isabella sits with an expression I'm unable to decipher. There's no time to read into anything now. We have a celebration to get through.

"Welcome to our class and thank you for coming this afternoon," I say. "We've been working hard on both our class and individual retellings of *The Very Hungry Caterpillar*. We'll start with our whole group presentation, and then the children will join you at their tables to show you what they've been working on individually. We hope you enjoy yourselves. Let's get started!"

Every child takes a turn, walking across the carpet which we've transformed into our stage, coming forward and reciting their line. They each wear a costume they've designed and created to match their part. The caterpillar in various states of fatness as he gorges along with each food item is represented by a different child before the final reveal of the beautiful butterfly.

Once we begin, phones come out, recording videos and snapping photos. I do my best to stand aside and only assist with prompts if needed. When it's Martha's turn to step forward and say her five words, she bursts into tears and runs toward me.

"Oh, sweetie, are you okay?"

Her face remains buried in my side, and she refuses to budge or speak.

"Listen, if you don't want to do this, we can have someone else say your line. Sound good?"

She nods into my waist.

"Let me take your costume," I say as I gently slip the yarn loop over her head.

"Jessica, can you do it?" I ask her because, as the slice of salami, Jessica's next and I also know she'd love the opportunity to say two lines.

I hold out the large yellow posterboard with holes cut out to resemble the cheese. Jessica skips over, and I pop it over her head. Disaster averted.

With the final line said, the entire class looks at me like we practiced. I nod, and they all say, "The End!" and take a bow. Families clap, and I stand a little taller, knowing how splendid they were.

"Now your learner will head back to their seat and show you the storyboard they created and retell the story by themselves."

We've been practicing this for weeks. As a class, in small groups, with partners, I coached in and helped those who needed it. Today, they get to show off all their hard work. I walk around from table to table, greeting families, listening in, and ensuring each child successfully retells the story. I make a point to visit two other tables before Illona's. Olan may have told Isabella about us, but nobody else in the room knows, and I'd prefer to keep it that way.

An empty feeling in the pit of my stomach nags as I arrive at their table. To procrastinate a little longer, I check in with Teddy and his family first. Teddy needed extra support from me. We had to work in stages, going over the book in smaller chunks over and over and only moving on once he could remember the previous part. Today, he is absolutely shining. I simply stand back and listen. He finishes, lifts his chin up to me and shares a satisfied grin.

"Teddy, you are amazing. I don't know what else to say. High five, friend."

We smack palms, and I turn my attention to Illona, biting my bottom lip. This is it. Isabella and I are about to speak. Time to take a deep breath, show my dimples, and schmooze.

Illona has been waiting for me before starting her retelling, and thankfully this provides a reason to keep our chatting to a minimum.

"Welcome. I'm so glad you all could make it," I say.

Isabella puts her hand out to greet me, and I take it. Her long, manicured fingers wrap around the palm of my hand, and it's hard for me to ignore her pointy pale-pinkish nails. She could poke someone's eye out with those. Or murder them.

"Mr. Block, it's so lovely to finally meet you. Illona hasn't stopped singing your praises. Olan too."

Heat rushes to my face, and I'm quite aware of redness overtaking my cheeks.

"Call me Marvin, please. And thank you, she's been the most wonderful addition to our classroom community. Illona, ready to show your family your storyboard and puppets?"

Nodding feverishly, Illona opens a large manilla envelope and takes out a rectangular piece of posterboard she's painstakingly painted to show the story's setting. A long thick branch sits in the center, with a leaf taking up most of the white space. There's an amber sun on one side and a silver moon on the other. Reaching back into the envelope, she pulls out her puppets. Each version of the caterpillar, pieces of food, chrysalis, and butterfly have all been crafted from construction paper and affixed to popsicle sticks.

Picking up the tiny egg puppet, Illona begins to masterfully retell the entire story, dropping and scooping up each new puppet as needed. Her voice goes up and down as she performs to convey emotions, and she's truly captivating. Isabella has placed her hand on Illona's shoulder, and her eyes crinkle slightly as she listens. Deftly, I sneak a glance at Olan. His eyes meet mine for only a second, and we share a knowing smile. Isabella's eyes dart up and catch us, but she only smiles and returns her attention to her daughter.

Illona finally says, "The End," and everyone gives her a round of applause.

I purposefully saved one group so I wouldn't be able to linger too long. Sometimes planning ahead pays off.

"Wonderful, Illona. Well, I have one more table to visit," I say, turning to leave.

"We'll see you this evening," Olan says.

"Yes, I'm looking forward to it," I reply, fiddling with my bow tie.

"Me too," Isabella adds.

Since he suggested it, I've been fighting this dinner, but on Sunday, taking an early hike together, Olan convinced me.

"Marvin, if we're going to make this work," Olan had said, motioning between us. "It will only benefit us if Isabella is on board."

"Wait, what's this," I teased, mimicking his motioning between us.

He tilted his head. "You and me. I want this to work."

I leaned over and kissed him, lingering longer than probably wise given we were literally on public display, but it was early, and nobody was around.

"Okay. But what if she hates me?"

"Impossible," he replied, touching my nose with his finger.

"Are you making fun of my nose?"

"Me? I worship this nose." He'd placed a kiss on the tip, punctuating his point, his lips soft and wet.

With the celebration over and everyone gone, I lie on the class rug, my body supported by the tile underneath, grateful for the experience but also thrilled it's over. Grabbing my phone from my pocket, I thumb out a message to Olan.

> Marvin: I think that went about as well as possible.

> Olan: Absolutely.

> Marvin: Did she say anything about me?

> Olan: She said you seemed nice.

> Marvin: Nice? Oy.

> Olan: Relax, you don't have to impress her.

> Marvin: Actually I kind of feel like I do.

> Olan: You don't. Come over at six. Can't wait to see you. 😊

And so, I find myself standing at Olan's door—slightly dizzy, but showered and changed from the day, flowers in hand—about to spend more time with Isabella. With her family. As it used to exist. Before Olan moved. Before me. Unlike this afternoon, there will be no escape or distractions as a safety net. My stomach churns, and I've got the *shpilkes*.

CHAPTER TWENTY-EIGHT

"Flowers? For me?"

Olan answers the door, and I'm grateful for even the smallest moment alone with him.

"No, not for you, for Isabella."

He glances back into the house, steps out onto the landing, shuts the door, and his lips smash on mine. Disoriented, I step back, and he catches me with his right arm. It's been five full days since we've been alone, and his pent-up energy flows into me. His tongue traces my bottom lip, and I swear I feel dizzy from his smell. My heart soars as our mouths connect, and for a fleeting second, I wonder if the two of us can spend the rest of the night out here.

"Damn, I missed your lips," he growls, pulling away just enough to speak and then jutting back in to bite my upper lip.

"We should go inside," I mumble as he nibbles away.

"We should."

Out with her boyfriend—and either trying not to intrude or attempting to avoid any drama—Cindy will not be joining us. Honestly, having her here as a buffer would have been nice, but I understand. Given the opportunity, I would flee too. Olan's ordered Thai food, and it's all laid out on the island in the kitchen. In his typical fashion, there's enough food here to feed twice the number of people eating. The salty smells of soy sauce, ginger, and garlic fill the air, and my stomach lurches with a mix of hunger and unease. My fingers play with the plastic wrap around the flowers I'm holding, and I wonder where Isabella and Illona are. I'm not trying to rush the evening, but I also would like to shove this train out of the station.

"Sit." Olan pats a stool. "They'll be down in a minute. What can I get you to drink?"

I rub the back of my neck and lean on the island. I'm sure Isabella not coming down when she heard the bell means nothing about how she feels about me being here. Right?

"Water's great. Wait, do you have any ginger ale? Maybe the bubbles will help the flipping in my stomach."

"Marv, I'm here. Everything's going to be wonderful. I promise," he says, pouring my drink into a glass as Illona's voice travels down the stairs toward us.

"Cynthia said we can do a sleepover if all our parents say okay, so I need to work on Daddy, and I'm going to ask him tonight because he loves my hair this way, so I think he'll say yes..."

I move both hands to the island, bracing myself for impact as they join us.

"Marvin!" Illona runs over and wraps her arms around my waist, and my breath becomes steadier, so I move my hands from the island to return her embrace.

"Hey there, oh my gosh, look at your hair. It's beautiful."

Two thick braids hug either side of her head down to the base of her neck, where the hair spills out into the gorgeous curls I'm used to. It's truly a work of art.

"Mommy did it after school."

Of course she did. "Well, it's amazing," I say, turning to Isabella.

"Truly, I've never seen anything like this." I run my hand over the left braid as Illona unclasps from me.

"I've had years of practice," Isabella says, slipping a hand into her pocket. Unlike me, she's still wearing the same outfit I met her in a few hours ago.

"Well, it shows," I say and give a little laugh even though there's nothing funny about what she said, what I said, or the situation.

"Flowers. I brought you some. Flowers. Um, here," I say, thrusting the flowers toward her.

"Marvin, that was sweet of you. They're beautiful." There's a kindness in her eyes I wasn't expecting.

Olan gestures at the kitchen island. "Why don't we get some food and eat."

"I'm starving!" Illona says, still right next to me.

"Me too," I add.

Olan supplies Isabella with a vase and she arranges the flowers. We spend the next few minutes in relative silence, with everyone piling their plates from the containers spread out on the island. Curries, noodle dishes, and vegetables create a vibrant array of colors and textures, and I do my best to load my plate up while Isabella helps Illona with hers.

"Excuse me." Olan comes behind me for a spring roll, weaving his arm around me a little too close for comfort given the current circumstances. I have to remind myself "she knows," to avoid a spiral into panic.

"Sorry," I blurt as I shift away from him.

Finally, we sit at the table and begin eating. Illona attempts to use chopsticks but succumbs to defeat and grabs her fork.

"So, I know you two met at school, but how did things, well, evolve?" Isabella asks.

Her tone feels light and curious, and Olan doesn't jump in, so I take a quick breath through my nose to reply.

"I give my cell phone out to families for questions, issues, emergencies, that type of thing, and well, I guess Olan had a lot of questions."

"Yup, that adds up. Do you know, when we met in high school, Olan used to sit by himself at lunch? This handsome guy, with all the girls whispering about him, and he was completely clueless. Eventually, I went up to him and introduced myself. Here I am, doing my best to flirt, and all he wanted to do was chat about calculus and engines. For the longest time, I was convinced we would never exit the friend zone."

"Mommy, what's the friend zone?" Illona asks.

"It's when two people are friends. But not more than friends. Having friends is lovely, right? But they don't have stronger feelings like wanting to be together and maybe get married," Isabella says.

"You mean like Daddy and Marvin?"

Out of the mouths of babes. My eyes go wide. Olan actually coughs up a bit of Pad Thai.

"No, sweetie, they are not stuck in the friend zone," Isabella replies.

"Princess, remember we talked about this. I like Marvin."

"He's your friend," Illona says.

"Yes, he's my friend, but more than a friend."

"Is that why you always want to kiss him?"

And now it's my turn to cough up some Pad See Ew. Thankfully, Isabella jumps in.

"Yes, when you like someone more than a friend, sometimes you want to kiss them. And your dad, well, eventually, he got the hint with me, but I had to lead him there. He had no clue what to do."

"Oh my gosh, are you serious?" I ask.

"Hey, hey, I'm sitting right here," Olan says.

As it turns out, Isabella does not want to devour me alive. We end up chatting and teasing Olan quite a bit which makes the blood gather in his ears, but he seems to be enjoying the camaraderie at the table. Illona giggles, hearing stories about her parents in high school, and while my head tells me I should feel awkward about it, my heart loves learning more about his past.

Once we're done, and the table's cleared, it's almost Illona's bedtime. Since the evening has gone reasonably well so far, I don't want to push my luck and I plan to leave once she's upstairs.

"Daddy, can you tuck me in?" Illona pleads, and Olan has no way out.

Illona gives her mom a kiss and me a hug and skips upstairs.

"I'll be back in five minutes," Olan tells us. He gives me a reassuring smile, winks, and follows. For the first time, Isabella and I are alone.

We flank the island. I fiddle with the loops on my jeans, poking my fingers in and out. Isabella lets out a sizeable breath.

"Let's go sit on the sofa," she suggests.

We sit on opposite ends, me squishing myself up against the armrest to put as much space between us as possible. Isabella pulls her legs up underneath herself and grabs a reddish throw pillow that brings out the scarlet tones in her hair. She shoves a stray lock away from her eyes with a sharp movement. It doesn't take a rocket scientist to see how Olan fell for her.

"Marvin, I want to thank you. You've made the best of a challenging situation for Illona. Moving in the middle of the school year, being away from her mother, well, she adores you, and I can't tell you how much that means to me."

I'm not sure where to look. Eye contact would be the polite move, but my skin tingles with discomfort at her compliments.

"Um, thank you. She's a complete pleasure to have in class. You and Olan have one phenomenal kid."

"You're sweet. She's been easy. We're lucky. And Olan, I can't say I've seen him this smitten before. It's nice."

My feet shuffle on the floor, and I give a thin smile as she speaks. I'm trying to loosen up, but failing miserably and am beyond grateful the sweater I'm wearing hides the Noah's-Ark-level flood happening in my armpits.

"We had a difficult time last year. I'm sure Olan's told you. And I'm glad he's back to working his program. Do you know much about AA?" Her head tilts.

"A little. My mother's in recovery."

"Oh, Olan didn't tell me that."

"Yeah, for about twelve years, so I'm pretty familiar with the program."

"Wonderful, that will be helpful to him. After his relapse last year, we had some tough decisions to make. About the business, but also, well, us. When you're getting sober or after a relapse, the program suggests you focus solely on yourself for the first year."

"That makes sense."

"I'm not sure if he told you, but Olan worked way too much. Selling the business was one component of focusing on himself. Part of that first year is no major life changes…like dating."

Now somewhere in my head, I've heard this. Probably years ago from my mother, but it was one of many on a list of no-no's your first year. And Olan had only had one drink, right? Was this vital? And his one-year anniversary since his relapse was coming up.

"But, Marvin, the thing is, I see how happy you make Olan. Truly happy. I don't think I've ever seen him smile so much. You're good for him. No, make that exceptional. He's come so far since his drinking became a problem in college, and now, here, with you, it may not be how I thought things would turn out but seeing him this captivated pleases me."

She lowers her head and presses her palms against her cheeks. Isabella's honesty catches me off guard. I'm not sure why, but I was expecting her to lash out. Her support for the idea of Olan and me together is surprising. Sharing about Olan's past seems to torment her, and I reach out and place my hand on her arm.

"I'm so sorry. That had to be difficult. I totally understand."

"When he was drinking heavily, it was scary."

"I bet."

"He wasn't the person I knew. There were some horrific moments in college. Junior year, his roommate found him unresponsive in his room. They had to take him to the hospital and pump his stomach. Once he started drinking solo, that's when I knew he was in trouble. I was scared for his life." Isabella stares at her hands. She returns her gaze to me, and there's a dampness in the corners of her eyes.

Her words pinch at my chest. It's hard for me to imagine Olan out of control. I know it was a long time ago, but my anxiety gurgles at the thought of him drinking, passed out, and the connections to childhood memories of my mother flash hot in my head. This, whatever we have, maybe it's too soon for him. I couldn't handle it if he relapsed, and I'd never forgive myself if it was my fault. Is handing my heart over to this man wise? Isabella looks at me with soft eyes, and I take a deep breath trying to center myself.

"I know you might find this hard to believe, but I actually want him to be happy. We may not be together, but I'll always love Olan and want the best for him. He's a wonderful father and his health means a lot to me. I'm grateful he found you. Clearly, Illona worships you, but more importantly, you seem to ground Olan. So, thank you."

Suddenly, I feel like a dolt. I assumed she'd find some reason to detest me. Swoop in and cause chaos. Instead, she's been kind and supportive. Color me dumbstruck.

"All set." Olan rushes in. "I'm sorry, she wanted to read me a story. How are we doing?" He plops down between us, ever so slightly closer to me, and rests his hand on my knee.

"We're fantastic," Isabella says.

"I probably should get going. Long day and all." My chest tightening, I force a yawn.

Isabella's words replay in my mind. I never imagined hearing about Olan's past, his drinking, would impact me in such a severe way. My skin feels tight, itchy, cramped, like it doesn't fit me anymore. The urge to flee takes over, and I do my best to appear calm as I attempt to escape.

I stand, forcing my legs not to wobble. "But thank you so much for having me. Isabella, I'm so happy you could fly in, and we got to spend a little time together. Safe travels home."

"Let me drive you." Olan pushes himself up.

"No, it's so lovely out. I want to walk."

My body hums with anxiety, my heart thumping into a knot. I worry a panic attack isn't far off, and the second that thought enters my mind, I feel my dinner creeping up. I can't get away fast enough.

CHAPTER TWENTY-NINE

As I stumble outside into the darkness, my head thick, I do my best to move my feet rapidly, attempting to put space between me and the house. The impending tunnel vision and ringing in my ears let me know I'm going to need to sit soon to get my bearings, but not here, not now. My legs swing back and forth on autopilot. A foghorn in the distance cries out, and I focus my eyes on the light from the few streetlamps. Each time I pass under one, my shadow, long and daunting, follows. With each step, I take huge gulps of air to center myself. Isabella couldn't have been sweeter and more understanding. I know she was only trying to connect and help me understand how far Olan's come. But picturing him out of control burrowed deep and touched a raw nerve. In an instant, I'm twelve again, in that dingy apartment, with all those same feelings of panic and fear crashing over me like waves. Drowning me.

My chest rises and lowers with ferocity. I walk a few blocks and spot a stone wall bordering a large home with gorgeous landscaping full of shrubs and coastal flowers, and plop down. The moment my butt hits the flat rock, I close my eyes, and the opening guitar riff and the do-do-do-do's of the Miracles wash over me. The drums and tambourine kick over the low bass guitar, and when the honeyed voice of Smokey

Robinson starts singing about being the life of the party, my heartbeat begins to regulate, and somehow, through the miracle of Motown, playing "Tracks of My Tears" in my head helps me actually not cry.

By the time the blaring horns of the first chorus end, the pressure in my chest welcomes a large hand on my back, rubbing small circles. The smell of crisp-mountain-spring soap mixed with coconut confirms the owner. I open my eyes to find Olan sitting, his leg pushed up against mine, his breathing matching the snare drum in my head.

"Hey." The word fumbles out of my mouth.

"What happened? You bolted. Why are you freaking out?"

"Nothing happened. I'm not freaking out."

"Marvin, I know your freaking-out face."

"You don't know me."

"Actually, I think I do. Did Isabella say something to upset you?"

"No, she was lovely. She's wonderful. I can see why you fell for her. I mean, I can see why anyone would fall for her."

My feelings for Olan have bloomed. I know he's a magnificent human, our chemistry explodes off the charts, and I've never felt this way with anyone. Most importantly, he's a complete *mensch*, so why can't I focus on the present and not his past?

"It's fine, I'm just tired. It was a long day."

Olan takes his left hand and cradles my chin, turning me slightly toward him.

"Marvin, look at me. Clearly, something upset you. Please. Tell me."

My stomach tightens as his thumb glides up and down my jawline. I thought I was past this, but, um, hello, not there yet. Olan's worked so hard and come so far. Making him feel guilty about his history feels like the ultimate asshole move. Yet here I am. The King of Assholes. Pressure overwhelms me, and I feel the slightest bit of vomit crawl up my throat. As I glance up at Olan once again, the urge to flee bubbles up. I have to say something.

"Okay. Um, well, we were talking. She's supportive. Of you. Even me. She thanked me. Actually, thanked me. She said she's never seen you happier."

Olan leans in, his sweet breath on my face. "She's right."

"We talked about AA and how I can be supportive. She told me how far you've come. What a different man you are. Part of that was sharing how hard it was for her when you were in college. How scary it was, and it, it just stirred up stuff for me. My head started spinning. About my mom. I'm sorry," I blurt.

"Buddy, you have nothing to apologize for. I'm sorry. I wish she hadn't talked about that with you."

"I think she was trying to connect with me. Boost you up in my mind. It wasn't her. It's me. I'm the problem."

"No. You're not. Look at me. Listen to me. You are not the problem. I should have told her to avoid the topic. That's on me."

"The thing is, she was explaining part of your past. And maybe I needed to hear it, even though I know that's not who you are now. It impacts me because of my own stuff. I wish it didn't, but it does."

"Listen, I need you to hear this." His hand moves to the back of my neck, holding me in place and sending the tiny hairs on my nape up. "My feelings for you aren't a joke. This isn't a fling. I really care about you. A lot. I love being with you, but, Marvin...I can't change my past, and if you can't accept that, well, it stings, but..."

"Olan, wait. I'm trying. Really. My feelings for you...I've never felt this way. You make me feel like I can be myself, even the prickly parts, but maybe, even with all that, even though it's not who you are now, maybe because of me, it's...I don't know."

Olan's jaw clenches. His hand still rests on the small of my back, but the time for him to comfort me has passed. He lets out a short sigh, his hand tensing on my back.

"Marvin, that's bullshit. I am doing the work. I'm truly trying here, but I am not perfect. And guess what? You're not perfect, either. You're a brilliant teacher. What you've done for Illona, I can't even put into words, but you, you..."

"What? I what?"

"You care. You care so much," he says, shaking his head. "Sometimes, I think you care too much."

"How is that possible?" I say, my eyes stinging with tears.

"Because you give your job everything and, I mean, I've been there. I was there not that long ago, and I just worry. I know how that impacted my relationship with Isabella."

"Oh."

"Between how devoted you are to teaching and this damn award. I'm not trying to sweep your side of the street, but Marvin, have you ever considered you throw yourself into your job to avoid dealing with, with, things?"

The moment he says it, the truth in his words burns my ears and the fire consumes me. I'm too ashamed by what he's uncovered to reply.

"And how you react any time my recovery comes up. I, I can't change who I was. I mean, if my recovery triggers you in such a way you literally flee every time it comes up, I don't know, maybe this, maybe me, maybe I'm too much."

My mouth parts, and I glide my finger over my bottom lip. Olan's words catch me off guard. Maybe this is too much. Maybe he's too much. Maybe allowing my heart to believe someone else could be there for me was a mistake. My entire body feels dense, and I struggle to find the right words. For once in my life, I don't rush to speak. Instead, I take his hand in mine and hold it open. With my other hand, I draw small circles in his palm. A dog barks in the distance. My heart beats even faster. I inhale through my nose and out my mouth, blowing my breath into the salty night air.

"Maybe we should take some time." My voice quivers. Five days apart this week made me realize how much I care for Olan, and my feelings for him keep growing. Jill asked if I loved him. I think the seeds of love are there, and now this hesitation, this pause...I swallow the despair in my throat. Why am I like this?

Olan looks at me and takes his hand from mine, covering his face. His handsome face, his soft lips, covered and hidden, and he shakes his head just enough for it to register.

"If that's what you want. Okay," he mumbles through his fingers.

My heart trips over itself, and the growing wetness in the corners of my eyes wants to give way to full-on tears. Am I royally fucking this up?

"Listen," he says. "I'm supposed to be working on myself. My recovery. I didn't plan to fall for you, but here we are. This back and forth, though, on and off, I'm sorry, Marvin, but it's messing with me. It's not healthy. For my sobriety. For me. Maybe I was wrong to let it go this far. And god, I can't do this to Illona. It's too much. We're a package deal. I've fought so hard to keep things steady for her. I have to think about her first. If this is how you truly feel, we should probably end this now. Rip the Band-Aid off. I'm sorry."

He doesn't yell, but his voice clearly conveys frustration. I've never heard him so distraught. My stomach drops out from under me, and I have the sudden urge to vomit. The possibility of this being our last time alone ties my stomach in hundreds of tiny knots. His words and matte tone fissure my heart. I'm torn between darting away and lurching toward him, clutching him close.

My hand shifts to the back of his neck, gingerly rubbing. I want to remember him like this, the cherry ChapStick on his lips, the fuzz on the base of his neck where his hair begins before it erupts into the gorgeous crown surrounding his head, all of him, close.

"I'm gonna go," I stammer.

Eager for one last taste, my lips kiss his forehead. I stand up. My head spins at the sudden change in height. I take a few deep breaths and mentally direct my feet to move. I glance back. A few yards away, Olan hasn't moved from the stone wall. His face is back in his hands, and my heart wonders how long until he moves. I turn toward my apartment and trudge home, finally releasing the tears from their cages and allowing them to fly.

CHAPTER THIRTY

Gonzo does his best to comfort me, but my tears confuse him. I've set up camp on the couch with a box of tissues, the comforter from my bed, a bevy of delivery menus, and Gonzo tucked under the covers, nestling in between my legs. Too lazy to get up, I keep a neat pile of dirty tissues on the coffee table until I'm forced up for the bathroom. Vincent would be proud.

I've put an old rom-com on, but not even the familiar story and satisfaction of their happily-ever-after comforts me. Once again, I've managed to fuck up something good. No, not good, amazing. I really should've known better than to fall for a hot dad. It feels like the ultimate rookie mistake, beyond naive. Maybe I'm just not able to love someone the way Olan deserves to be loved. Or maybe I'm not loveable. Fuck. My brain usually keeps me out of such trouble, so why did I let my dick take the lead this time? Getting involved with Olan was a monumental misstep on my part. My head knows that, but why does my heart feel as cold and empty as Elijah's chair?

My phone vibrates on the coffee table and Gonzo stirs slightly. I contemplate grabbing it and throwing the damn thing against the wall because speaking to anyone right now feels like cruel and unusual punishment. As I reach to check the perpetrator, there's a tinge of hope in my stomach. Maybe it's him.

My head is dizzy, and a sudden chilly feeling starts in my belly and expands to my fingers and toes. It is him. Not him. Not Olan. Adam. Why the hell would he be calling in my hour of sorrow?

"Hello?" Why do I answer like I don't know who's on the other end?

"Vin, it's Adam." Hearing his old nickname for me makes my skin prickle.

"Adam, hey, um, how are you?"

I grab a tissue and pat my eyes, hoping he can't somehow hear the puffiness of my face.

"Fantastic. Things are great. Mark and I are headed to a dinner party in a few, but I wanted to give you a quick call."

At least I know it won't be a long conversation.

"Cool, um, what's up?" I ask because why the hell are you calling me now and interrupting my misery?

"I heard you were up for Teacher of the Year, and I wanted to congratulate you."

Gulp. I'm not sure how he found out. There have been a few articles in local papers. Clearly, someone told him.

"I know how much teaching means to you, Vin. You're so damn dedicated. I always knew you were a brilliant teacher. Your kids mean the world to you. I'm so proud of you."

Olan's words echo in my head. You give your job everything. You throw yourself into teaching. This damn award. I reach for another tissue and exhale sharply, away from the phone.

"Oh, um, thanks. Yeah, it was a big surprise. The nomination, I mean. Actually winning the county, I didn't expect it, so it's all a bit of a whirlwind."

"Well, you deserve it."

"Aw, thanks, Adam. That means a lot."

He's attempting to be nice, and I sort of hate him for it.

"How's everything else? Gonzo? You seeing anyone?"

Has he found out? Who would have told him? Is that the real reason he's calling?

"Gonzo's great. He's right here. Still as clingy as ever, but of course I love it. Jill's pregnant. They're elated, and I can't wait to be a guncle."

"Sweet. Please tell her congrats from me."

"And, not seeing anyone. Just me and Gonzo."

Tears well up in my eyes and I blink to bat them away.

"Well, someone will be lucky to snag you. You'll find the right guy. Don't give up."

"Yeah, thanks. Um, well, I should be going." I rush him off because blubbering feels imminent.

"Yeah, me too. But congratulations again, Vin, really. Great job. Okay, take care."

"You too. Say hi to Mark for me," I say because being the bigger person always feels correct.

Adam hangs up, and I smash my face into the throw pillow and sob like a trust-fund baby being cut off and forced to find a job.

"It's getting harder to use your lap as a pillow," I complain.

"You try growing a human being in your stomach and get back to me."

"Touché."

Jill lounges at the end of my couch, her legs propped up on the pile of books I leave on the coffee table to make people think I'm smarter than I actually am. My head rests on her lap. We create a perfect capital L in this configuration, allowing us both to have our feet up as we chat. Gonzo sprawls out on my legs, purring at being included as I stroke him behind his ears.

Between the phone call from Adam and a night of tossing and turning before switching from rom-coms to horribly sad movies—the kind where someone gets really sick and dies—a self-inflicted intervention was necessary. Jill answered my distress call with a half dozen donuts in tow.

"So that's it? It's over?"

"I think so. The moment he said it, I wondered if I was making a horrible mistake."

"I mean, he's incredibly hot."

"Not helping. But also, not wrong," I say with a little laugh. "But he's also one of the best people I've ever met. He's kind and loving; all he wants is for other people to be happy. He's a good man."

"Then what the fuck is your problem?" She smacks the top of my head.

"Ouch! Your baby will come out with a mouth like a sailor if you keep that up."

"God, I fucking hope so. Now quit deflecting."

"It's the drinking. It messes with my head. Whenever I think about him drinking or relapsing, it…it triggers me. I don't want it to, but I can't help it."

Jill aggressively pushes my head off her lap, sending my arms and legs flying up to balance myself so I don't tumble to the floor. My strawberry donut flies across the room, and Gonzo leaps from his resting spot on me and bolts into the bedroom, probably to hide under the bed. Part of me yearns to join him. Catching myself, I sit up and face her.

"What the hell?"

"Listen to me, Marvin, because you need to hear this. People are not perfect. Nick is not perfect. The man is a complete pig and a child. Do you know he forgets to flush the toilet? I'm not talking about pee either. Like a kindergartener. How is he going to remember to feed the baby if he can't remember to flush the toilet? I'm not perfect—okay, I'm damn close, but I am bossy and needy, and well, that's about it. So close. But not perfect."

She drops her hibiscus salted chocolate donut on the coffee table, punctuating the seriousness of the situation before continuing.

"Olan is not perfect. He has a past, but everything you've told me says he's doing the work to be better. He is better. Clearly. You talk about 'the drinking' but, Marvin, is he drinking? Now? No. Your mother isn't perfect. But, Marvin, she was a single parent. And not of her own choosing. I'm not making excuses but try putting yourself in her shoes. She hasn't had a drink in twelve years. I know she hurt you, but can you maybe entertain she's trying to make amends? Your childhood wasn't perfect, but, buddy, show me someone's whose was. Now get ready for the big one. Newsflash: You are not perfect. Olan's right. You put way too much into work. Your anxiety can be crippling. You avoid life because you're petrified. And you, too, have a past, and right now, it's preventing you from your present. Nobody is perfect. But when you find someone whose imperfections complement yours and help you both be better versions of yourselves, you choose to make it work."

As Jill lectures me, my hand travels up to my earlobe, my fingers rubbing it slowly. She doesn't often raise her voice with me, but I don't often go off the rails with a man like Olan.

"But, how am I supposed to..."

"Stop it. Stop making excuses. Meditate. Medicate. Go to therapy. Figure it out. Because if you blow it with a guy like Olan, you'll have to live with that regret for the rest of your life."

"What do I do?"

"Take some time. Not too much time. You need to tell him."

"Tell him what?"

"How you feel, jackass."

I sit with what she's told me for a minute. My damn head keeps getting in the way of my heart. And fear, the worst of all emotions, keeps jutting itself in front of me, crafting obstacles to my happiness. I know Jill's right. I need to figure this out, or I will lose this beautiful man.

"Thank you," I say, and I lean over and do my best to scoop her up in my arms, squeezing her a little tighter and longer because she needs to know just how much I appreciate her.

Once Jill leaves, feeling brave and resolute, I text Olan. I know Isabella doesn't leave until tomorrow, and with how I behaved, I probably should give him some space. But we need to talk. I need to talk.

> Marvin: Can we talk Monday after school?

I set my phone down, scoop up Gonzo, and await his reply.

Sunday morning, Olan still hasn't replied. It's not like him to ignore texts from me, and I'm taking this as a sign I've blown it. I mean, I knew I blew it, but this confirms the magnitude of my blowing it. The Prince of Blowing It needs a crown.

I know staying in bed all day and checking my phone every two minutes won't help, so—much to Gonzo's chagrin—I pry myself out of bed to take a walk. With the ocean breeze and warm May sunshine on my face, the smell of the pine trees dotting the trail as I maneuver through the rocky path, my body revels in the release, and my mind begins to uncoil from the last few days.

This early on a Sunday, there aren't many people out, only the occasional runner, and looking ahead on the trail, not seeing anyone, adds to the peacefulness. The path turns sharply and the dirt under me leads out of the woods and into full view of the bay. This part of the trail always takes my breath away. It literally brings you from undercover out into views of the open water, flecked with moored sailboats. The sight never fails to bring a lightness to my chest.

I head to the water, stretching my arms out wide, taking in the gift of living here. In the distance, a woman jogs toward me. As she approaches, the blur in front of her comes into focus. She pushes one of those strollers with three wheels, low to the ground, made for running. As we get closer to each other, I pause, turn and get a peek at the baby. Snuggled into a blanket, there's a visor to protect them from the sun, and their adorable face stares up at their mom with the sweetest look of complete, unconditional love.

The mother gives me a kind smile as she whizzes past. Spotting a large rock near the water that's perfect for roosting, I sit down and pull out my phone.

"Marvin, what a nice surprise."

"Hey, Mom, how are you?"

Calling my mother unsolicited feels like some sort of personal growth in and of itself. It's not part of our schtick. She calls, I ignore, and return the call eventually. I called her uninitiated right before the Peaks trip. Maybe it's becoming a habit?

"I'm good, just came in from *kibbitzing* with Joanne over coffee. Her daughter is having another baby, which will be grandchild number three."

Now, there's a chance my mother simply wants to impart this information to me and isn't being passive-aggressive. That chance is extremely slim, but today, I give her the benefit of the doubt.

"Well, that's a *simkah*! Please tell her *mazel tov* from me."

That wasn't so hard.

"I will. She's overjoyed." Her voice gets quiet. "But, between you and me, her son-in-law is a complete *putz*." And there you have it. "Rebekah, the daughter, does everything. All the shopping, cooking, and cleaning. She works full-time as a dental hygienist, and, well, you know, that's a hard job, Marvin. Cleaning people's teeth. Who wants to do that? The husband needs to help too."

"He does."

"This is why you gays have it figured out. Two husbands, easy to split the work."

I laugh at her comment and take a deep breath, preparing to change subjects.

"So, Mom, I want to ask you something."

My heartbeat quickens. Difficult conversations with Sarah are never simple. I have to find a path toward honesty without upsetting her too much.

"Of course, honey. What is it?"

"Remember I told you I was seeing someone?"

"Yes, of course, I remember, the engineer, right? With the daughter. How are things with him? What's his name again?"

Now I never told her his name, and I love that what she remembers first about Olan is his job.

"His name's Olan."

"Olan? What kind of name is that? That doesn't sound Jewish."

"That's because he's not Jewish." A sailboat breezes by and I close my eyes and take a deep breath.

"Oh. Well, nobody's perfect. How are things going?"

"That's why I'm calling. Things were going well. Very well. He's a good man, and he cares about me, and well, I think I might have messed everything up."

"You messed things up? What did you do?"

My forehead begins to sweat, and I reach up to brush my hair out of my face. "I didn't do anything. Not really. I asked for some time."

"Time? Time for what? What do you need time for? You're not getting any younger."

"Mom, I'm only twenty-nine."

"I know how old you are. I was there when you were born, remember?"

"Anyway, Olan's in recovery."

The line goes silent.

"He's been sober almost twelve years."

"Okay, that's good. And he has a sponsor and goes to meetings?"

"Yeah, both. But he had a relapse last year."

She pauses a moment. "What happened?"

"I don't know all the details. It had to do with his work, I think. He was also in the middle of a divorce. The pressure was too much, I guess."

"It's hard when you don't have other ways to cope."

"The thing is, every time his drinking comes up, it triggers me."

I don't need to say more. She knows what I'm talking about. While she's not speaking, her breathing gently rumbles into the phone. I close my eyes and begin to pick at the loose skin on my thumb.

"Marvin, I know it was hard for you. What you have to understand is I wasn't in control. I was doing my best. I know it wasn't good enough. Not for you and certainly not for myself. I needed help, and it took me too long to realize it, but eventually, I got it. You know that. It sounds like your friend has realized he needed help way sooner than I did. That's a good thing. And relapses happen. It's part of recovery. One relapse in almost twelve years is actually not so bad. It's how you move forward from it. How you learn and grow. You might be part of what helps him stay sober."

And now the tears begin to well up because, contrary to what I expected, Sarah did not become defensive. No raised voice. She's actually listening and trying to help. The thought of Olan needing me pushes salty drops from my eyes, and now I'm sitting on a giant rock, looking out over the Atlantic Ocean, talking to my mother, and crying.

"Why am I so afraid of..." I'm unsure how to finish because I'm not sure I can name it.

"Of being happy? Of letting someone love you?"

I swallow hard. "Yeah, why?"

"Marvin, you are my precious boy. I love you so much, and I hate if I've hurt you in any way. After your dad left, I...I was lost. I know he abandoned you, but honey, he abandoned me too. Being a single parent wasn't the path I saw for myself, and well, you know what happened. I had no clue what I was doing, and the booze numbed the pain. At the time, I was alone. I didn't realize I had a problem until it was too late. I'm not making excuses."

"I know, Mom."

"You are so loved, Marvy, and you, my *boychik*, are worthy of love."

Her voice breaks a little, and I know this is hard for her. I let out a sob, and I'm fairly certain snot has left my nose. I reach for the tissue in my pocket.

"If I could go back," she continues, "I would do things differently. But that's not how things work. We have to live with our mistakes and try to learn from them and move forward. It sounds like Olan wants that too."

"He does. He has, from what I can tell. He's, he's an amazing guy, Mom. A complete *mensch*."

"It sounds like you actually like him."

"I do. I like him so much."

With those words, I realize my feelings for Olan have cultivated beyond hanging out, beyond liking him. There's love there.

"I think I love him, Mom."

"Oh, honey, that makes my heart so happy. Have you told him?"

"No."

"Why not? Marvin, I love you, but don't be a *shmendrik*."

I laugh because only Sarah Block can call me stupid and get away with it. Because, in this instance, she's absolutely correct.

"Thanks, Mom. I will. Okay, I should probably get going. I love you, Mom."

"I love you, too."

My mother, for all her faults, loves me. She's come so far, and I need to find a way to begin letting go of my hurt. Giving my mom a piece of my heart and not knowing what she'll do with it scares me, but I can forgive without forgetting. My heart feels full as I watch the ferry chug by. There are two versions of me. The one whose anxiety rules and whose childhood trauma still impacts him as a grown man. And there's the version when I'm with Olan. Which one do I want to be? I love Olan. I've actually said it. Now, I have to find a way to tell him.

CHAPTER THIRTY-ONE

Monday, you are a wench. Minutes before recess, the rain begins falling, mocking the tears that poured from my eyes all weekend. We're stuck inside, which never bodes well for our afternoon. Without the outlet of actually running, jumping, and in some cases, slamming their bodies around, my students are tiny balls of accumulated energy. I do my best to get them to move by having a ten-minute dance party and saying things like "who can jump the highest?" or "how high can you lift your knees?" but for many of my students, unless they can zoom around like Gonzo chasing a toy mouse, they're going to remain tiny kernels of unpopped corn.

During Choice Time, I sit on the rug, coaching in to block-play between Cynthia, Ricky, and Kevin because Ricky sometimes finds compromising difficult.

Ricky scowls. "I don't want to make a stupid bridge."

"Try asking him if he wants to work with the two of you or by himself," I whisper to Kevin loud enough for Ricky to hear.

"Mr. Block says I'm supposed to ask you if you want to work with us or by yourself," Kevin fumbles.

Ricky looks at me, and I raise my eyebrows to give him my best make-a-decision-but-make-a-good-one-because-I'm-watching look.

"By myself," Ricky blurts out.

"Okay, and if you change your mind, ask Cynthia and Kevin if you can join them. Sound good?"

He nods begrudgingly.

Kate, Jessica, and Zoe are sitting at a table coloring and writing. Illona is at the table next to them, coloring and writing by herself.

"Hey, friend, what's up?" I ask her.

"Nothing. Just coloring."

"Do you want to join the girls?" I nod to the empty seat at the table.

"No, I'm good here."

Ever since Olan and I started "hanging out," I've been extra careful about making sure my interactions with Illona at school don't put any pressure on her or make her feel uncomfortable. It's part of why I'm Marvin outside of school but Mr. Block here. When my students seem "off," I want to know if there are any emotions I can help them process, but with Illona, I have to tread extra carefully.

"That's fine. Would it be okay if I sat with you for a little?"

She nods. I grab a piece of paper, and because he's my go-to subject, I start drawing Gonzo.

"What's that?" I ask, nodding toward her paper.

"A picture for Daddy."

Her fingers wrap tightly around a green crayon. She's drawn a field and has begun sprouting flowers along the entire length of her paper, with pink, purple, and orange crayons patiently waiting their turn.

"I think he'll love that," I say.

Half of her mouth turns up in a hesitant smile, and she nods. For the first time since this all began with Olan, the unsureness of how dating her father might impact Illona in a negative way washes over me. Why didn't I think ahead? I love all my students, and the prospect of hurting them brings me immense distress.

"Please remember, you can always talk to me if you need to."

"I know."

At dismissal, as I walk the pickups down, I roll my shoulders back and steady my breath in an effort to slow my heartbeat and ready myself to see Olan. We've had the entire weekend apart, and my conversations with both Jill and my mom have helped me finally register how much I actually care for him. No, how much I love him. And I need to tell him. It's time to put my cards on the table and stop being afraid of what-ifs. Olan Stone is the kindest, smartest, sexiest man I've ever had the luck to be with and letting him slip away feels asinine.

We turn the corner, and Dr. Knorse and Kristi stand at the table, offering pleasantries as adults sign the large binders releasing their children to them. I scan for Olan, but he's not here. I spot Cindy and she gives me a kind smile and a little wave. My stomach drops as I raise my hand to return the gesture. Where's Olan?

Illona runs over and takes her hand. Of course, I wouldn't dare ask Cindy anything. My stomach quivers and I scamper back to my cell phone in the classroom as quickly as my legs will carry me. No messages await me. My chest feels like a bear has selected the spot for hibernation.

> Marvin: Didn't see you at pickup. Hope you're OK.

And I wait. I stay longer than typical, prepping the message for tomorrow and gathering materials for a math activity.

"What the fuck are you still doing here?" Jill asks.

At lunch today, I explained how I confessed my feelings for Olan to my mom and how I need to tell him. Soon. Jill knows I'm never here this long after the kids have departed.

"Olan didn't pick Illona up. I texted him, but he hasn't replied."

"Oh, Marvin, damn, I'm sorry," she says, sitting on the table nearest the door.

"I'm not sure what to do."

"I mean, I think you just have to wait to hear from him."

I pull my lips in tight. "Yeah, I guess."

"Look, you're going to tell him how you feel. It's going to be okay."

"I hope so."

"Let's go," she tells me, and I grab my backpack. I want to believe Jill, but my stomach feels shaky and uncertain about why Olan didn't show up and hasn't replied to my texts. Perhaps the Prince of Blowing It will ascend to King.

CHAPTER THIRTY-TWO

Cindy picks Illona up all week. There's no communication from Olan. No reply to my text. No call. No carrier pigeon. No skywriting. Nothing. Not hearing from Olan, not seeing him, makes the tiny cracks in my heart splinter and expand. My body yearns for him. To be close. To kiss his soft lips. To hold him tight. The desire to text, call, or show up unannounced at his house nags at me, but I also want to be respectful of his feelings, especially around Illona and recovery.

"Fuck his feelings. You need to fight for him!" Jill declares over lunch on Friday.

I pick at my cheese sandwich, eating the slices of Swiss slathered in mayo and leaving most of the cold bread. My stomach lurches at the thought of carbs, a telltale sign of heartache.

"Go to his house, bring a boombox and blare a love song over your head. Make a grand gesture, Marvin. This is the point in the movie where you step up and go to battle for love."

"Can we please talk about something else?"

"No. Marvin, you love him. You *love* him. He's Tevye and you're Goldie."

"Wait, why am I Goldie? Why can't I be Tevye? 'If I Were a Rich

Man?' That's my song. He's literally a rich man already. Why would he ever sing that song? Plus, he's much more reserved. He's totally Goldie."

"Fine, you can be Tevye. I don't care. The point is you love him."

"I do. I really do. But is that enough?"

Jill puts her fork down on her half-eaten lasagna, reaches over, and takes my hand.

"Marvin, love is always enough."

Friday morning, as I'm setting up for the day, Dr. Knorse strides into my room. She never pops her head in to say hello or asks if it's a good time. When she needs to talk, she enters, sits, and demands you stop and give her your full attention.

"Marvin, Happy Friday. I wanted to chat about the Teacher of the Year ceremony."

Next Thursday night, we're scheduled to attend the banquet where all the candidates and finalists gather to hear a few marginally famous (nobody outside the state would know them) local celebrities speak, and the winner announcement happens. With everything that's happened recently, the entire Teacher of the Year contest has been the last thing on my mind. At this point, the decision has likely been made. Worrying about it won't do much to help, but I muster up some enthusiasm for her because I know she's concerned about what it means for the school.

"Of course. Did you receive the tickets?" I ask.

The committee mailed tickets and the plan is for Dr. Knorse, Kristi, and Jill to join me.

"Yes, secured in my office. I thought it might be nice for us to meet here and drive over together. The ceremony starts at seven thirty, so we can meet in the school lot at seven."

"Yeah, sure, I'll check with Jill," I say, assuming she's already checked with Kristi.

"Good, very good. I have a good feeling about this. Well, have a great day and weekend." She clasps her hands and leaves.

I think about the banquet. Butterflies swell in my stomach. A few months ago, I was beyond jazzed to be nominated, and the entire process has been rewarding, if somewhat stressful. If I win, there's a whole litany of responsibilities and affairs, some of which require traveling to Washington, D.C., for national events. And there's the funding. Dr. Knorse needs this win. No, the school needs the win. It will impact our entire community. Even though I should be laser-focused, there's no denying I miss Olan.

I've been trying to hide my somberness from the children all week. Fake it till you make it, blah blah blah. I'm certain they know something is afoot because they've been on their best behavior and extra affectionate. More requests to hold my hand usually means they're on to me. Illona seems to be more herself, and that pleases me. I have no idea if Olan said anything to her, but my gut tells me at most, he said something simple like, "Marvin and I are both busy, so we're taking some time to focus on work."

She hasn't said a word to me about her dad, and it definitely wouldn't be appropriate for me to inquire, so I just smile and enjoy my time as her teacher. Walking down to pickup, she takes my hand. I look down, and she smiles up at me, using her tiny hand to squeeze mine.

"Thank you," I say.

"For what?"

"For being such an amazing kid."

We turn the corner. A flush of adrenaline tingles through my body, and the desire to drop Illona's hand and run floods over me. Behind the long metal table, waiting patiently, stands Isabella.

"Mommy!" Illona shouts and darts over to her, latching on to her leg.

Cindy picked Illona up all week, and there was no note or email to me about a change for today, and well, I'm not sure what to make of Isabella's surprise appearance. Didn't she fly home just a week ago? Isn't it expensive to fly across the country? Who am I kidding? These people don't think about things like the cost of airfare. She probably flies first class too. Champagne and caviar dreams and all that.

"Hey, honey, surprise!"

"I wasn't expecting you!"

"Well, I told your dad not to tell you. I wasn't sure I'd arrive in time to pick you up, but here I am." She pushes a stray strand of hair from her face and looks up at me. "Mr. Block, I was wondering if we could have a chat?"

My head feels light, and my ears faintly ring. *Oy gevalt.*

Illona tackles the monkey bars, a recently mastered feat she would gladly perform all day long. Isabella and I stand on the playground's perimeter, far enough away to be out of earshot but close enough to supervise. A few other children play under the watchful eyes of their grown-ups gathered closer to the school.

"Surprised to see me?" Isabella begins.

"I mean, yeah, for sure. Didn't you just go home?"

"I did. It was such a lovely visit. I know I told you this, but I've never seen Olan so carefree. He told me how much he cares for you."

My heart trips at the thought of Olan talking to her about me. About us.

"But a few days ago, Cindy reached out to me, concerned about him. I called, and he told me what happened. I can't help but feel like some of this may be my fault."

"No. Really, it's not. You were so kind and sweet. It was all me. I just heard those things about his past and, I don't know, something crunched inside me. And, well, I'm sure Olan told you."

"He did. And that's why I'm here."

"You flew back? To talk to me?"

She flashes a slight smile.

"I flew back to see Illona. And Olan. This chat is an important add-on. Especially if you're going to be a part of her life."

I pull my lips in and nod. Not sure what to say.

"You know, Illona's here because Olan told me he couldn't do this without her. It's not ideal. I definitely don't love it, but also, I know she's a Daddy's girl and Olan needs her more right now. They need each other. We're figuring it out, but I'm always going to spend as much time as I can with her, even if it means I'll rack up a ton of frequent-flier miles."

She turns to face me, her damn gorgeous hair out of control thanks to the offshore breeze. She grabs a hair tie from her wrist and wrangles it into a tight, high ponytail.

"Marvin, I'm here because I love Olan."

My stomach drops. Does she want him back? Her hands smooth the front of her purple paisley dress until they land on the belt, drawing her waist in. "Olan is such a good man. He cares for you. Yes, he told me, but he didn't have to. I saw it in his eyes. The way he stares at you. He looked at me that way once. We grew apart. It happens. Thankfully, we've been able to remain friends. I'm here as Olan's friend. He needs you."

"I'm not sure what to say."

"Then listen. I want to tell you what happened last year."

My eyes widen. I open my mouth to speak and quickly close it.

"Our business was thriving, but I knew we needed a break. Olan struggled with stepping back, and well, selling seemed like the fastest way out. There were offers to purchase it, but he refused to entertain them. I knew, deep down, the demands of running such a huge company were taking a toll on him. He was relentless. It wasn't healthy."

Isabella glances down. She rubs the back of her neck and then looks over at Illona, offering her a small wave before returning her attention to me.

"He went to an investor dinner while I stayed home with a sniffly Illona. These dinners were often overflowing with alcohol. It's a little insurance to help the investors, well, invest. It had never been an issue for him before, but that night, apparently, the stress and temptation were too much. Our split came not from his drinking but from his dedication to bettering himself. We'd been growing apart. I knew he wasn't happy. He needed to be on his own for a bit."

I'm trying to absorb this but my head is woozy, and I take continual deep breaths to steady myself.

"In hindsight, he knows throwing himself into the company with complete abandon wasn't healthy and at least partly contributed to the relapse. Stepping away, taking some time, and moving, he's clearly so much happier without the stress of running a multi-million-dollar company. But you're a huge part of it too."

"Wow." It's all I've got. This explains why Olan was so forceful about my dedication to teaching. And the award. He doesn't want me to repeat his mistakes. Oof.

I turn my head toward her, lift my chin slightly, and give her the beginning of a smile. She's wrapped her arms around herself and meets my grin with her own.

"You make Olan happy. That's what matters. Olan is the father of my child. We've been friends since high school. I'll always love him."

"But I don't know what to do. He told me no."

"Because he's doing what he always does, taking care of others. He's worried about Illona. He's worried about you. He doesn't want to hurt you. But, Marvin, Olan wouldn't hurt a fly. He's a remarkable man."

"I know," I cry a little too loudly, and some of the other parents shoot us a look. "So, what do I do?"

Isabella is the last person on earth I thought I'd ask advice from, but here we are.

"Next week is his one-year anniversary of being sober since the relapse. Go to his meeting. If you showed up, that would mean the world to him."

"Oh." I'm going to have to think about this. "When is it?"

"Thursday."

An AA meeting. And, of course, it's on Thursday, the same night as the banquet, because the universe clearly enjoys testing me. My head stirs and swells.

"What time?" I ask.

"Seven."

"I guess I need to think about it."

"I won't say anything to him. He doesn't even know I'm here talking to you. It can be our little secret." She winks at me, and I can see the love she truly has for Olan sparkle in her eyes.

"Illona, honey, let's get going!" she shouts across the playground.

"Thank you."

"No, thank you," she replies. She lays her hand on my shoulder and gives me a quick peck on the cheek. Her lips are soft on my skin, and the smell of flowers and money swirls in my nose. She pulls away, and I lift my hand to touch where she kissed, fairly certain she left some of her lipstick there.

She jogs over to Illona, takes her hand, and moments later they're gone. I swear, this afternoon could not have played out any more differently than what I'd expected. My head spins. What should my next move be?

"Marvin? What's wrong?"

Calling my mother two Sundays in a row definitely warrants that reaction from her. It's unheard of, preposterous, but desperate times and all.

"Hello to you too, Mom. I just wanted a chat."

"Oh. Okay. How are you? Did you talk to, what's his name again, Orion?"

I crack a small smile because how she managed to transform Olan into Orion, the God of Hunting, escapes me but also smacks of Sarah Block.

"Not yet." I don't correct her because imagining Olan as a Greek god brings me joy.

"Why not? What are you waiting for, a formal invitation?"

My chest expands with air, and I steady myself. "It's not that simple, Mom."

"Explain it to your mother then because I don't understand."

"Well, the short version—he thinks I'm too attached to my job and not ready to be with someone in recovery." My voice cracks and I swallow hard.

"Oh, sweetheart. I'm so sorry. Are you okay?"

"Not really. I'm trying to be."

"Marvy, it's okay not to be okay."

"I know. Thanks, Mom."

"I'm going to look into seeing a therapist. I think I need help with . . . being okay."

I brace myself. I've always worried my mother would consider her son in therapy as a ringing proclamation of her failure as a mother.

"Good. Why do you think I go to AA meetings? They're like free therapy with free noshes. It's like hitting the jackpot for Jews." She lets out a loud cackle, and I grin because I honestly can't remember the last time I heard her let go and laugh with such abandon.

"His one-year anniversary meeting is this week, and I'm thinking about going."

"Good. You should definitely go. It will be good for you, and he'll share."

"I want to. Or I think I do, but the award ceremony falls on the same night. I'm not sure I can do both."

"Oh. I know you've worked hard, and it means a lot to you. Can't they let you know another time?"

I give a little laugh because, again, Sarah's understanding of how the world works feels slightly askew.

"No, it doesn't work that way. There are many nominees. They won't change the entire banquet for me."

"Have you asked?"

"I can't ask them to reschedule their entire event for me."

"Well, talk to Orion. See what he thinks."

My mother tends to have an answer for everything, and right now, we're starting to turn in circles.

"He's not really wanting to talk to me right now. I don't know what to do. That's actually why I've called you."

"Oh, now I see."

Ten minutes later, we finally get there. Slow and steady. I typically get frustrated with my mother's misunderstandings, but today, I smile and laugh them off between deep breaths. Growth starts with baby steps.

"What does your heart tell you?"

My hand rubs the back of my neck. I focus on the base near my shoulder, attempting to massage the simmering pinch there.

"My heart? I know I love him. I know if I don't do something to try and show him how I feel, regret will seep in through every crack and crevice."

"So, there you go."

"But, it's a really big deal to be nominated for Teacher of the Year. The school needs the win too. It could really impact staffing. Plus, I've worked my *tuchus* off for this as well. You know we don't get a ton of recognition as teachers, Mom, and this is a chance for me to shine a light on what I do."

"I understand. The thing is, Marvy, I can't tell you what to do. What day does this all happen?"

"Thursday night."

"And there's absolutely no way to do both? What time does it start?"

"The AA meeting starts at seven and the ceremony at seven thirty."

"Well, you go to his AA meeting at seven and just leave at seven thirty."

"I'm not sure that will work logistically."

"Sleep on it. You don't have to make a plan right now, but I bet there's a way to do both, even if you're a little late for your award thing. You and Orion, if you're *bashert*, it will happen, meeting or not. Nobody can tell you what to do, Marvy. You need to sit with the question a bit. There's no teacher's edition with all the answers in the back of the book."

"When did you get so wise, Mom?"

"It's called getting old. You'll get there. If you're lucky."

"Thanks, Mom. I love you."

"I love you too, sweetie."

I've got until Wednesday to figure this out. How badly do I want to be at the ceremony? How much does it matter? Dr. Knorse needs this win more than I do. Will they still give me the award if I don't show up? Without the funding, the school will have to make cuts. It would devastate the community. But then there's Olan. The way he looks at me. The way he makes me feel like we belong, like family. Isn't that what matters most?

My mother's words reverberate in my head. Showing up at Olan's meeting would surely get his attention. How can I do both?

Gonzo jumps up on the couch where I've planted myself horizontally. He crawls up to my chest and stares at me as he begins to knead my chest.

"Gonzo, what would you do?"

He tilts his face slightly and headbutts my chin, rubbing his nose back and forth across my cheek. Pure love, covered in fur. Clearly, Gonzo won't tell me what to do either. I let out a big sigh, and Gonzo pauses as the air from my nose blows against his face. He blinks a few times and resumes pummeling my chest.

CHAPTER THIRTY-THREE

My knee bounces with such ferocity I worry the people sitting near me might think we're having an earthquake. Though not common in the area, tremors are not unheard of. The plaid bow tie around my neck grips me a tad tighter than I'd like, and with my propensity to be a fumbling *nebbish*, I wonder if I can actually pull this night off. My week has been filled with sleepless nights and more conversations with Gonzo than are probably considered "normal," but he's such a perfect listener. When I asked him if trying to attend both Olan's anniversary meeting and the award ceremony was plausible, he peered at me and started to lick himself. Down there. Thanks, buddy. So helpful.

Daily walks by the ocean helped more than I anticipated. The water centers me. Calms me. Helps me focus and think. I know I'm supposed to be at this meeting. I've got just under half an hour until I need to jet to the ceremony. I've got this.

"Breathe. Try to relax," I whisper to myself.

The chairs are closer together than I anticipated, and more people fill the space than I expected. There must be close to a hundred people. On television, these meetings are always small gatherings with folks sitting in a small intimate circle. Not here. The walls are mostly bare, and besides row after row of metal folding chairs, there's a long table off to the side with urns of coffee and a mix of store-bought and home-baked treats. I spot some Oreos and wonder if I can nab a few on my way out. My mouth waters at the thought of the crispy wafers and creamy filling. Free therapy and food. My mom was right.

I peek at my watch. The meeting should start any minute, but as I scan the room, there's no sign of Olan. He's not usually a show-up-late type of guy, and sweat begins to bead on my forehead. My plan to be here for Olan's anniversary speech and then motor to the Teacher of the Year ceremony might be doable, but I'd rather my dress clothes not resemble a wet T-shirt contestant once I'm there. I rushed to arrive early, making sure to secure a parking spot near the community center's entrance, so I'll have less ground to cover when I bolt to my car in about twenty-five minutes.

At lunch today, I was petrified about chatting with Dr. Knorse about my plans, but our conversation turned out better than I'd anticipated.

"What do you mean we're not all going together? Why not?" Her chin was high, nostrils flaring slightly.

"I have a personal matter I have to attend first, but I'm coming... maybe a few minutes late, ten at most. I'll be there before they even begin announcing awards, I promise."

"Personal matter? What's going on? Are you okay?" She'd tilted her head and softened both her face and voice ever so slightly. This must be Dr. Knorse attempting empathy. At this point—with only a few weeks of school left, my Teacher of the Year journey coming to an end, and by extension, the school's future all but decided—it was time to come clean.

"Tori." I used her first name and waited for flames to fly out of her ears. But she only nodded.

"I've been dating someone."

Her left eyebrow lifted.

"Olan Stone, Illona's dad."

I winced and waited for her reaction. Nothing. She sat stone-faced.

"We've been seeing each other on and off, and well—"

Dr. Knorse interrupted me. "You're afraid of what people will think?"

"Yes, that's part of it. And I was worried about the award. And our funding. If I did anything to jeopardize the school, I'd feel horrible. I don't want to let anyone down, but there's something I need to do. For him. For us. There's a meeting I can't miss. But I'm leaving at seven twenty-five. I've set my alarm," I say, brandishing my phone as proof. "I'll literally be a five-minute drive away. I will be there."

She nodded. Taking a deep cleansing breath, she said, "Marvin, may I be frank?"

"Of course."

"I know the staff here thinks I'm a hard-ass. Excuse my French. And that assessment isn't unfair. I run a tight ship. My job requires a certain level of harshness, and while I certainly don't want people to dislike me, I can't worry too much about it."

I rubbed my chin as she talked, waiting to see where we were headed.

"Teaching is a demanding job. I want my staff to work hard and do their best for our students, but I also know the importance a personal life plays." Her eyes glanced down for a moment. "Do I love that you've been secretly dating the parent of a student in your class? Not particularly. But there's no specific rule against it. I wouldn't shout about it while Illona's still in your class, but there are only a few weeks of school left. Once she's not your student, it becomes way less problematic."

"So, we're okay?"

She leaned forward and placed her clasped hands on the table.

"We're good, Marvin. You do what you need. But get your ass to the ceremony. Excuse my French. Again."

Over the last few days, I've replayed my mother's words in my head many times. Knowing Olan would be speaking, I'm hoping my attendance might demonstrate my commitment to him. To us. Once I decided being a few minutes late to the ceremony wouldn't impact much, it was a no-brainer to find a way to attend both.

Practically every folding chair in the room is occupied, and people seem to cluster with small groups of friends or at least people they know. I continue to search for Olan to no avail. A man with a friendly face hands me a roll of raffle tickets, and my confused expression prompts him to say, "Take one. We give away books at the end of the meeting. Maybe it's your lucky day."

I rip a ticket off and pass them on, happy to have something to keep my hands busy. I fold, roll, unfold, and refold the ticket with my fingers repeatedly, praying some luck rubs off on me.

A petite woman with blown-out sandy hair steps up to the lectern, lays her hands across it, and addresses the group. Her name is Kay, and she's an alcoholic. I wonder if I'm the only one here who isn't an alcoholic, but my mom assured me anyone can attend this type of meeting. There are administration items I don't quite understand, and a small wicker basket comes around for donations. I panic because I have no cash. I never have cash. If I have cash, I spend it. Immediately. Usually on candy. The man beside me sees me fumbling with my wallet, winks, and tosses a ten-dollar bill in, saying, "I got you."

I blink a few times and reply, "Thank you," my voice hitching. His kindness and generous heart put me at ease.

Kay leads everyone in the Serenity Prayer, and I listen and concentrate on the words. It's one of those prayers I've heard many times, but if someone asked me to recite it from memory, I couldn't. Accept the things we cannot change. Have the courage to change what we can. The wisdom to know the difference.

My mind drifts to my mother. Our small apartment. I can't change my childhood. Neither can she. But she's sober now. And Lord knows, she's trying with me. Olan can't change his past, but we both *can* change how it impacts us. Olan's already begun his work, and now I have the opportunity to release the weight of the past. Not to forget, but to forgive my mother and live my life.

"We're now going to start with anniversaries. First up, one-year anniversaries," Kay announces.

Okay, here we go. The reason I'm here. There are so many people in the room. Maybe Olan's sitting near the front, and I simply can't spot him in the crowd. I crane my neck and dart my eyes around in every direction, searching for his handsome face.

A woman stands up. White and probably in her forties, she smiles at Kay and envelops her in an embrace. Her feathered taupe hair falls just past her shoulders. Something about her face emotes such sincerity, I'm drawn to listen.

"Hello, my name is Linda, and I'm an alcoholic."

The entire room calls back, "Hi, Linda."

"Thank you. Today, I stand here, one year sober, and what a journey it's been. If someone told me a year ago that I'd be standing here, in front of you all, sober, I would have laughed in their face and shouted, pour me another glass of wine."

The room laughs, and I check my watch. Ten minutes and I need to bolt, and still no sign of Olan. My hand twitches with the temptation to text him, but I'm determined to be a surprise. Grand gesture and all that jazz.

"For the longest time, I used booze to avoid my problems. It started with a glass here and there to take the edge off my day, help me relax, and get a good night's sleep. But soon, one wasn't enough. Two wasn't enough. I started stockpiling wine. Cheap bottles. Boxes. I wasn't picky. Joking helped. I called it my 'mommy juice.' Well, I understand now how completely stupid that was. And while the shame began to creep in, I got to the point where it didn't matter. Looking back, there were issues I was ignoring. Big issues."

The room gives a collective sound of agreement, encouraging Linda to continue.

"Growing up, I'd always wanted a family. A few years after college, I met my husband, and when we finally married, I thought, this is it. Now I'll have a family and the perfect life I've dreamed about. But we struggled to have children. The whole process was taxing, financially and emotionally. After years of treatment and trying, we finally got pregnant. And when my beautiful daughter was born, the gift I'd been hoping for, trying for, I thought, okay, now, now everything will fall into place. But it didn't. I had horrible postpartum, not helped by a fussy baby. I felt like a complete failure and discovered the wine helped. Going back to work after maternity leave, the wine helped. Arguing with my husband over something stupid? The wine helped. It helped with everything. Or so I thought. But really, it simply masked what I wasn't dealing with."

Linda's words resonate with me. My mother. Olan. Myself. I may not have a drinking problem, but yowzers, I've been doing my best to ignore my demons. Enough of that nonsense. It's not productive. It's literally holding me back. I steal a glance at my watch and realize I need to get moving, and still no Olan. As I look back up at Linda, my phone vibrates in my pocket. My heart leaps into my throat.

> **Jill:** Get your butt here. The doctor is chomping at the bit.

> **Marvin:** On my way.

I stand to leave, and Linda pauses and stares at me.

"I'm sorry, I have to go…to the bathroom. You're doing great, though. Amazing speech."

I pump my fist in the air to cheer her on, and because I'm thinking about grabbing Oreos and not watching where I'm going, I trip over a chair, falling into a burly man who does his best to catch me.

"Slow down there, buddy."

"Sorry, I have to go."

Fumbling to my feet, I move as fast as my legs will carry me outside and dash to my car. It's seven twenty-five, and the ceremony starts soon. It's a five-minute drive if that. There shouldn't be much traffic on a Thursday evening. I've got this. I'm tempted to text Olan. He wouldn't miss his anniversary meeting unless something happened. Where the heck is he? Dr. Knorse's terse face flashes in my head, and I slam myself into my car, immediately jamming my key into the ignition and turning it, but nothing happens. I try again. One final attempt and the gas light flashes red. My heart falls through my bootyhole. I'm out of fucking gas.

CHAPTER THIRTY-FOUR

Jill: Where the hell are you?

Marvin: My car is out of gas FFS.
I'll walk.

Jill: I'll sneak out and come get you.

Marvin: No, it's only a mile. I can walk.

Jill: No fool. RUN.

And somehow, on a warmer than typical May evening, I find myself jogging to the Teacher of the Year ceremony. Kristi would be so pleased right now. Except, I'm not dressed for it. To be fair, I don't really own any clothes for running. No, instead, I'm dressed up to potentially accept a distinguished award. I kind of hope I don't win the damn thing because, by the time I arrive, I'm going to be a complete sopping mess.

Because, apparently, in addition to the rest of my horrible life choices, I'm completely out of shape, I vacillate between actual running, jogging, walking fast, and something in between I'll call wogging. One mile can't take that long, even for a *shlub* like me. Every damn traffic signal turns to Don't Walk as I approach, and I wonder if someone put a

Kinahora on me. I find myself playing chicken, running across intersections, attempting to make it to the hotel as quickly as possible without being turned into roadkill, Frogger style.

Only two blocks away, a woman in a maroon mom-van careens around the corner, slamming on her brakes, barely avoiding flattening me into a latke.

"Watch it!" she shouts out her window.

"Hey, I'm trying to win a prestigious award here!" I scream back, pointing in the general direction of the ceremony.

Cresting the hill, I finally glimpse the hotel, taller than most buildings downtown, a horrible Eighties beige stucco high-rise. I bolt over, and giant glass doors slide open for me. Spotting the letterboard sign directing to the ceremony, I hurry as fast as my tired legs will carry me to the ballroom. Completely out of breath, I throw the doors open, and the murmur of the reception hums low. Folks are sitting, chatting, eating, and nobody seems to notice me. I should have made a pitstop in the bathroom to freshen up. Dripping with sweat from the impromptu and unwelcome exercise, I resemble a wet rat.

Dr. Knorse stands behind a lectern on the makeshift stage, speaking. "Thank you, Dr. Hayes. As principal of Pelletier Elementary, I'm honored to accept this award on Mr. Block's behalf. He should be here momentarily."

Oh my god. I won. Oh my god. I'm late. For my crowning. Technically, there's no crown, but this is the closest I'll ever get, so I'm going with it. I can't decide if I should turn around and dash to the bathroom to hide, perhaps cooling off my entire head in the toilet or fly up to the stage in my current state of disarray. But holy crap, I won. As reality sinks in, I think about what this means. Yes, it's an honor to be recognized, but more importantly, Dr. Knorse should have no problem securing the funding we need to keep the current staff and programming in place. With the staffing secured to make Pelletier Elementary the best place possible for kids, I heave a big sigh. Clearly, that's the more significant win. My chest swells with pride.

"I actually have someone here who asked to say a few words about Mr. Block," Dr. Knorse continues. "We're so lucky to have a parent of one of his students here tonight. Mr. Stone, would you please come up."

My mouth drops to the floor as Olan stands. He's been sitting at a table near the front with Jill and Kristi, and he glides up to the stage. Butterflies overtake my stomach. Winged friends, now more than ever, I'm going to need you to soar in formation. He's wearing a short-sleeved teal button-down shirt, his skin glowing against it. Of course he's dressed up, and while not prudent, part of me wants to run up and tackle him in a hug. Fuck, he looks tasty.

Trying to go unnoticed, I duck into an empty seat at a table near the back with a group of people I don't know. They all turn and stare, and I push damp hair out of my face.

"Mind if I sit for a sec?"

"Good evening. My name is Olan Stone, and my daughter, Illona, is lucky enough to be in Mr. Block's kindergarten class at Pelletier Elementary. I reached out to Dr. Knorse and asked her if I could say a few words in the event he won, and I'm beyond thrilled to be able to share a little with you about the amazing teacher Mr. Block has been for not only my daughter and her classmates but the hundreds of students he's taught over his career."

He's here. I can't believe he's here. For me. I suck in an impending sob and the strangers around the table glare at me.

"Sorry, these things always make me *verklempt*."

Olan continues and we all return our attention to him.

"I myself know the power of a great teacher. Growing up, I never really fit in. My family didn't know what to do with a nerdy Black boy, his face constantly buried in books about how planes fly. Rather than going outside and riding my bike or playing basketball with the neighborhood kids, I was always at the library. Nobody knew what to make of me. Until high school, when, freshman year, my math teacher, Mrs. Williams, asked me if I'd ever considered joining the math club. I was finally with other people, well, nerds like me, and it was all because of Mrs. Williams. She took the time to get to know me. Understand what made me tick. Why I was struggling."

As he talks, my eyes lock on him, and wetness stings my eyes.

"Mr. Block does that with his students. He sits and listens. He asks questions. He learns about them and uses that information to make connections. Those deep connections help him be the best teacher for his students and that extends to their families. This year, I relocated to Portland with my daughter. Mr. Block was patient, understanding, and, most of all, caring with both her and me while we adjusted. He views his relationships with his students as the core of his role as their teacher. He doesn't simply care. He loves them. Deeply. He's taught me that teaching is an act of love. There's nobody more deserving of this award than Marvin Block, who loves with his whole, big, beautiful heart."

Even as my heart aches with affection, I slink down in my seat a little, attempting to hide from what I'm afraid he might say next.

"Marvin, are you here?" he asks.

The room begins to gurgle with noise, and I slowly raise my shoulders to sit up in my seat and stand. The entire crowd turns and peers at me as I keep my arms glued at my side to conceal my sweat, and I'm, once again, flinging my head to move hair out of my face.

I turn toward him, our eyes meet, and he smiles so enormously, that glorious gap tempting me from across the room. Already a sweaty mess, I'm inclined to sprint up and wrap my arms around him. But I don't. I walk up, calm, cool, and collected, attempting to resemble a person worthy of winning.

Arriving at the long, metal steps up to the stage, I pause, stare down, and take each one slowly. This is not the time to trip and fall.

As I approach, I'm not sure how to greet him. He opens his arms, and I launch myself into him, gathering him up in my arms, squeezing tighter than decorum probably advises.

"I went to your meeting. What, why…" I stammer in his ear.

"We'll talk. After," he whispers back.

"Okay."

I pull away because Dr. Knorse is only a few feet away watching, and well, the whole room is waiting. He pulls me back quickly, holds me close, and whispers, "I love you."

Now would not be the time to be speechless, but my breath has temporarily been stolen by Olan's "I love you." Closing my eyes, I attempt to catch myself. With Olan's rousing endorsement, there's not much left for me to say. Plus, I'm currently two things I detest—sweaty and starving. I thank the committee, Dr. Knorse, and the entire community. Dr. Hayes presents me with a huge plaque, and I head to the table where Jill and Kristi sit awaiting us.

"You really love cutting things close, don't you?" Jill asks as we sit. Her stomach barely bumps out against her stunning orange and yellow floral dress.

"I mean, it wasn't intentional."

"Well, you made it. That's all that matters," Dr. Knorse says, and Lord, she's smiling. I'm not sure I'll ever get used to seeing a grin on her face.

"We were happy to vamp a little until you arrived," Olan says, patting my leg under the table.

I want to kiss him so badly, but we still need to talk.

"I need to use the bathroom. And by use the bathroom, I mean give myself a bath in the sink," I say, gripping Olan's knee tightly under the table and rising to my feet.

"I'll help," he says, standing, and we briskly head to the men's room, the table resuming their chatter.

The moment the men's room door swings closed, I smash Olan against the wall and kiss him with all my pent-up emotions from the last few weeks. He places his hands on my waist and pulls me into him, and god, I've missed being this close. We share a too-brief kiss, I pull away, remembering.

"I went to your AA meeting. Your one-year anniversary...what happened?"

"Oops. I mean, I needed to be here. To support you. You're so deserving and have worked so hard. And I was wrong. About you working too much. Too hard. I get it now. But I still want you to take care of yourself. And I want to help. Take care of you. You can't be the amazing human you are for those kids if you're not okay yourself."

I lean in, about to kiss him again, but ask, "But you missed your anniversary."

"No, I didn't."

He pulls a shimmering bronze chip from his pocket and holds it out. The words "To Thine Own Self Be True" are etched around a triangle with a beautiful number one in the center.

"Ralph delivered it this morning. We'll celebrate my anniversary next month. We can go together. But thank you for going. That means a lot. It's not a big deal."

"Yes, it is."

"I mean, the anniversary is a big deal, but celebrating it next month isn't. Really, people do it all the time. This was only happening once, and I wasn't going to miss it. Although you almost did."

"Every time I almost run out of gas, I tell myself, never again, but, well, it always happens again."

"So, you ran here?"

I lift my arms, and the full horror of my sweaty mess of a shirt reveals itself.

"Yup."

"God, you're adorable."

"And you, you're, well, here. How did you know when…"

"Dr. Knorse. I called her. She told me about your chat. You didn't have to do that."

"I know, but I'm tired of keeping this a secret."

His lips turn up slightly for a moment, and the tiny gap between his teeth peeks out at me. I move in and give him the briefest of kisses because I need encouragement for what I'm about to say.

"Olan, I know what you said about us not being right for each other, and if that's truly how you feel, I'll understand, but there's a reason you picked up your life and moved across the country. There's a reason you picked Portland. There's a reason your daughter was put in my classroom. Maybe part of the reason was so we could meet. None of this"—I motion between us—"happened accidentally. Someone wanted us to, well, be an us. I know meeting you has shown me how beautiful it can be to open up my heart."

He takes a small step back. This is it. His answer. My stomach gurgles with uncertainty about what will come out of his beautiful mouth.

"You're amazing," he says. "I wish you could see yourself the way I see you. Maybe I can help you with that."

"I'd like that."

"And you've shown me it's okay to love what you do and have a personal life too. A work-life balance is attainable."

I grimace. "I mean, I need to work on that too."

"Sure, we all can, I know that. But this running away thing you do worries me. What's going to happen when my past comes up? Because it probably will at some point. Or what if I have another relapse? To be clear, I have no intention of that ever happening, but I can't guarantee it. I can't guarantee anything. Every morning, I get up and pray. I pray to stay sober, and I take that prayer and tuck it away so it stays with me all day. All I can do is promise you today I won't drink. Each day, I make that promise to myself. For me first, but also Illona, and I'll make it for you, too."

My hand reaches for his, and he lets me take it, hold it, cherish it. With my other hand, I gently stroke the one I'm holding because touching him, his skin on mine, makes my soul sing.

"I can't promise anything either, but I won't run away again. I won't. I'm going to start therapy. I need to continue unpacking why my childhood keeps impacting me as an almost thirty-year-old man. I promise to try every day, with you, to be the best version of myself. For you. For Illona. But mostly, for me."

Olan's free hand comes up to my cheek. His fingers find their way into my hair because they always do.

"You missed my mop?"

"I so fucking did."

I laugh at this, and his hands, still in my hair, pull my face toward him, and heat radiates from his skin, the familiar smell of his ChapStick instantly soothing me.

"You won. How does it feel?"

"I'm happy. Mostly for the school, but sure, it feels good. But this feels better," I say, placing my hand on his chest.

"Marvin, whether you won or not, you're still always teacher of the year to your students. They adore you. And so do I. You're my teacher of the year. Always."

Not knowing what to say, I softly place my lips on his. He smiles, making the kiss a little more challenging, but I'm up for it.

"You know we first met in the bathroom. At school," he says, pulling back.

"We did?"

"We did. You peed all over yourself."

"Oh my god, no, I didn't. It was water from those damn sinks."

"Well, whatever it was, your pants were soaked. And now we're in a bathroom again."

"Let's finish dinner and go home," I say, leaning in. My mouth makes contact, and this time, he holds me close, and we kiss with intention in a way that lets me know he's present, ready, and we're in this together.

"I love you, Olan Stone," I say on his lips as I pull back.

"I love you, Mr. Block."

And he does. And I do.

EPILOGUE
Three Months Later

Standing at the counter, Illona does her best to spread peanut butter onto bread, her fingers messy and tacky from tussling with the plastic knife. Gonzo lounges a few feet away, studying her, smacking his lips every few seconds, pining for a taste. I slug down my coffee and smile as her tongue juts out with the required concentration.

"Doesn't it feel good to help make your own lunch?" I ask.

"Actually, no, it doesn't feel good. It feels sticky."

She raises her hands, slathered in peanut butter.

"Come, I'll finish," I say, turning the faucet on for her and tossing her sandwich into a container.

Olan bounds down the stairs holding a brush and a handful of ties. He comes up right behind Illona as she washes.

"My hair!"

"I got you," he says.

Olan readies himself for action. Illona stands with her back to him, petting Gonzo while her dad works his magic. Gonzo purrs and rolls over so his belly can be rubbed. I watch as Olan masterfully separates her hair into sections and begins to braid. He works swiftly, but there's such attention and care. It swells my heart and reminds me why I love his beautiful soul so much.

"Are you ready for first grade?" Olan asks, pulling and brushing.

"I mean, I guess so. It won't be as fun as kindergarten, though, right, Marvin?"

"Sweetie, nothing is as much fun as kindergarten. But first grade is pretty awesome. And Mrs. Chapman is amazing. You're going to love her."

"Well, we know one thing. Mrs. Chapman isn't nearly as handsome as your kindergarten teacher," Olan says, winking at me.

"Daddy!"

"Well, he's not wrong," I say and lean over Illona to give him a quick kiss.

"No kissing before breakfast!"

"Sorry, princess."

I catch Olan's eye. "And are you ready for your first day?" I ask him.

"Ready as I'll ever be. I feel good about this."

Over the summer, with some encouragement, Olan applied for and secured a job as a senior engineer at a local aerospace company. Green-Space hopes to change rocket technology by utilizing greener, earth-friendly fuels, and Olan couldn't be more jazzed about it. The best part? He's working part-time, so most days, we're all able to head to and from work together. Seeing him ease into the professional world in a healthy, balanced way brings me joy. He's taking care of himself, and I know that bodes well for us.

I glance at my watch, and a slight panic takes over.

"Um, we have got to get going. Now."

"I'm almost finished. Just one more twist, add a tie, and voilà!"

"How do I look?" Illona asks me, not quite trusting her dad to assess his own work.

"Gorgeous. Stunning. Lovely. Shall I go on?"

"You're so silly," Illona replies. She pulls me down. Our faces grow closer until she gives me a peck right on my lips, and I swear, receiving affection from her transforms me. I love my students, truly, and I think most of them love me, but this is different. This feels more grounded, more special. I never understood how magical familial love from a child could feel. Olan and I haven't talked about making anything official yet, but we're so clearly a family. It's only a matter of time.

"All right, you two, let's clean this mess up and get going," Olan says, handing us each a brown bag. Breakfast and lunch for me and a snack and lunch for Illona.

Illona and I throw our backpacks on, and Olan grabs his new gray canvas briefcase. It's a gift from me for his new job, and it's classy and gorgeous just like him.

We rush out of the house, Illona skipping ahead of us, and Olan takes my hand and begins a gentle jog to keep up with her, tugging me along.

"Come on, lazy bones. We're going to miss the ferry!"

When Olan told me he was buying a house on Peaks, I was surprised. And worried. I assumed I'd see him less because even though the ferry only takes a short twenty-five minutes, a whole expanse of ocean lies between Portland and the island.

"Marvin, you really are hard-headed sometimes. I'm buying this home on the island for us. I want you to live with Illona and me there."

"Oh. You do?" was my brilliant reply.

We reach the dock, and there's no line. The ferry already swells with morning commuters. We dash on with only a few moments to spare before the loud horn announces our departure.

"Can I?" Illona asks, pointing up the stairs.

"Yes, but be careful. We'll be right behind you," Olan says.

She darts up the stairs to watch the island disappear as we sail away. Where she gets all her energy eludes me, but I wish I could bottle it up for those Monday mornings when I'm dragging.

The ferry rumbles to life, and Olan pulls me down from the first step. He's found a spot right under the stairs and gently pushes me against the cold metal wall of the boat. Without speaking, his lips are on mine, and with the throngs of people on the boat, I'm certain someone might notice us, but I really don't care. His searing kiss, delivered as if his life depends on it, makes my blood roar. I wrap my arms around his back, pull him close, and moan a little into him because this gorgeous man has changed my life.

"Let's go," I say.

"One more."

And he kisses me again, gently this time. What I call his "I love you" kiss. He takes my hand, our fingers entwined as we climb the stairs to the upper deck. We find Illona near the front, and she leaps into my arms for a better view. Her legs wrap around my waist, the strong ocean breeze doing its best to blow our hair like everyone else's, but failing miserably against the tightness of our curls. I squeeze Illona for both warmth and affection as Olan gathers the two of us up in his arms. I lean into him. He's strong and steady, and we head toward the mainland for our collective first days. Together. As family.

BONUS EPILOGUE
Nine Months Later

"Bubbles or no bubbles?"

Olan's perched on the tub's edge, wearing only his gray sweatpants shorts. He knows my propensity toward him in them, and he's no dummy. His thick thighs poke out, and when my eyes travel down to his feet and spy his cute little toes wiggling on the cobalt-blue tile, a warm wave of affection washes over me. Even after a whole year together, I still notice new things about him. He'll sit or stand in a new way, or light will hit his face and illuminate his features so I see him in a whole new context. I still have to pinch myself to remember I get to call him mine.

"Bubbles. Always, bubbles, please."

"You got it."

He grabs the deep lavender bottle and slowly drizzles the soap over the running bath water. The tub in our Peaks house is much larger than the one in Olan's old house in town. Which is to say, it's massive. Olan says the real estate agent told him it was a two-person tub, but I'm fairly certain you could easily fit three people in it. Not that I have any interest in anyone joining us.

"Marv, come here."

I walk over to him, my ratty black T-shirt almost entirely eclipsing my ratty boxers, and he immediately stands and wraps me in his arms. Somehow, just having his arms around me makes the world feel less scary. Even if only momentarily.

"Now listen," he says. "Everything will be fine. They're coming to support me. To see us. Now let's get these pesky items off you."

I start to take my shirt off, but Olan grabs my fingers, stopping me. He pulls our joined hands up to his face and kisses my knuckles, one at a time, sending my heart tumbling, then lifts my shirt. I raise my arms, letting him remove it. His hands pause on the waistband of my boxers, and his mouth finds mine.

"Marvin Block, you are so adorable." The words tickle my lips.

If I had a nickel for every time he called me adorable, I'd have, well, more money than Olan. But money doesn't concern me. Especially not today. Today is Olan's two-year-sober anniversary, and tonight, everyone is coming to his AA meeting. Everyone.

"Well, you, sir, are not adorable. You are hot. A hot nerd. My hot nerd. And right now, we're going to get into this bath and try not to freak out about everyone coming tonight."

Olan pushes my boxers to the ground and says, "Delectable."

My smile grows as he removes his shorts and they drop to the floor. He climbs into the tub, and once again I marvel at his physique. The tendons and muscles in his legs stretch as he steps into the bubbly water. He turns toward me, extends his hand, and says, "My love," and the corners of my eyes sting with wetness. Who's chopping onions?

"So, Isabella has Illona, and they're going to the new Children's Museum. She said they wouldn't come here first, but they'll grab us at the terminal because she wants to take Illona for a new dress before. Cindy's not sure Sam can get the night off, but she's coming regardless. Jill and Nick are now bringing Maria because their sitter canceled this morning." Olan never drops my hand, and I join him, settling into the hot water. Our legs jumble together under the bubbles, and my body begins to loosen. Even as my brain chugs along. "Apparently, the sitter has a bad cold, so now Jill's worried that little Maria has it and doesn't want us all to get sick and almost canceled. But I told her, if Maria isn't sick, then they should come, you want them here, and we're all adults with hearty immune systems."

"Marvin, cutey, you have to relax. Everything is going to be fine."

Somehow, Olan has a way of not worrying. About anything. He's literally the most un-Jewish person I know. But I do love the gorgeous goy.

"I know you're right. But a baby at an AA meeting?"

"People bring babies all the time."

"And Isabella and Jill have never met."

"Oh please, they're going to adore each other."

"I know you're right, I just, well…"

"Like to worry."

"You don't know me," I say and lean over to kiss his nose, brushing a smattering of bubbles away.

"I do know you, Mr. Block. Now turn around."

I swivel around, my back to him, and his hands find my shoulders and begin kneading. He moves up to my neck and even gives my scalp some attention.

"You'll do anything to play with my mop," I say.

"Guilty as charged."

I close my eyes and attempt to push away the train of thoughts barreling through. With a deep inhale, Olan moves his mouth to the back of my neck and finds that spot just below my ear that drives me wild.

"Olan, Isabella is picking us up in an hour and a half."

"I know. It takes ten minutes to get dressed, another ten to walk to the ferry, and another twenty-five to get to the terminal. That gives us forty-five minutes."

"Are you using math to turn me on?

"Whatever works. I'm trying to help you relax."

His hands descend from my head down my back and his fingers walk around my waist until they find my submerged semi-hard cock.

"Olan, we have to..."

"Marvin, Illona is out of the house with her mother. Cindy moved out last week. We're alone in this house, and that might not happen again anytime soon."

I lean back onto his firm chest and turn my head. His magnificent lips move on mine, and fuck, how does he know just how to soothe me? When his tongue enters my mouth, the jolt of adrenaline causes my dick to respond, and he begins slowly stroking me under the water.

Breaking our kiss, I mutter, "You're right. God, I can't say no to you."

"That's my Mr. Adorable. Now I want you to stand and put your hands on the edge of the tub. Please."

In the year we've been together, Olan has learned to ask for exactly what he wants, which drives me wild. Not only the asking but the way he asks. He's so damn polite, and all the pleases and thank-yous make my blood bubble.

"Yes, Mr. Stone."

As I stand, the water rushes off me, and I do as he says, waiting for what comes next. I'm not exactly sure what he has in mind, but I trust him. Whatever he wants, I'm game.

I close my eyes and inhale, the lavender bubbles calming my nerves. As I exhale, Olan's hands take hold, spread my cheeks wide, and my breath catches as his tongue begins to explore.

"Oh fuck, Olan. That's not fair, you're, you're..."

"Shhh. Relax."

And he's back. His tongue penetrates me, and I peek round to see he's on his knees, his cock sticking straight up. Oy, why can't I have longer arms?

The slurping, licking, and complete verve with which he tackles the task at hand makes me even harder. He knows this is a surefire way to get me to come quickly, and given our schedule, I'm not mad about his efficiency.

My fingers grasp at the tub, slipping on the porcelain, and I bite my lip. He pauses to lift my right leg and places it on the edge near my hands, and says, "There, better ingress."

"Olan, I fucking love it when you talk nerd."

He returns to fucking me with his tongue, and simultaneously reaches around and begins jerking me. My dick throbs in his strong hand, and the water sloshes. Low moans escape my mouth, with the occasional "Fuck, Olan" and "God, that feels amazing" adding a little flavor.

He buries his face in me and works my cock, and my rising orgasm approaches, ready to take over.

"Olan, baby, I'm close."

"Hold on, I'm almost there."

He mumbles and groans into me before he accelerates. I take over my own dick so he can attend to himself, and I'm overtaken by the frissons of pleasure ripping through me. Hearing Olan stroke his gorgeous cock sends me over. I shoot all over my hands, my right foot, and the floor. Damn. I feel the sounds from Olan's mouth more than hear them as he moans and joins me in adding to the complete shambles around the tub.

"Oh God, fuck, Olan, we've made a mess."

"A perfect mess," he teases, smacking my ass.

I turn around and bend to kiss him. The taste of me is all over his face, and I relish every bit of it.

"You're fucking delicious," he says, pulling away.

"You love a kosher snack, don't you?"

"I do." He dots my nose with a kiss.

"Now, let's clean up and get dressed."

We walk up to the hall, Illona in between her mom and Olan, and I sprint ahead to snap a quick photo of them.

"Stone family, halt!"

I lift my phone, and they freeze and smile. The gap between Olan's front teeth draws my attention, but I focus on the gorgeous family before me. The one I'm now a part of.

"It's a framer!"

"Can I see, Marvin?" Illona asks.

"We can look inside. Look, we have folks waiting for us," I say as I see Cindy, Jill, and Nick—Maria strapped to his chest and completely asleep.

"Oy vey," Illona says with an eye roll, causing a ripple of laughter to spread between her parents and my chest to expand with pride.

"Finally," Jill says. "What took you so long? Skyrockets in flight?" She winks at me, and my face flashes hot.

"Um, no. The ferry only runs every hour. We're here now."

"No Sam?" Olan asks Cindy.

"He wasn't able to get the night off at the restaurant. He sends his apologies and congratulations."

Illona scoots over and takes Cindy's hand. There is so much love in this group.

There are nods, smiles, hellos, and nice to meet yous, and slowly, tension begins to release from my shoulders.

"Olavin," Nick whispers his nickname for us and puts both fists out. Olan and I each bump one, and I peek at Maria. Her soft hair is finally growing in, much to Jill's relief.

"How long has she been sleeping?"

"Since the ride. The car puts her right out," Nick says.

"Let's hope she stays that way," Jill adds.

"Well, her guncle will be there if she wakes up. With a song." Olan gives me a confused look. "A soft, quiet song. I promise."

He smiles and grabs my hand. "We should find seats," he says, glancing at his watch.

"Listen, we were all waiting for you," Jill quips.

"Okay, okay, let's go!" I say, and arms wrap around shoulders, hands are held, and the gaggle of us head in.

After the introductions and the housekeeping items, Olan steps up to the podium, takes a deep breath, and begins.

"Hi, everyone. My name is Olan, and I'm an alcoholic."

The entire room calls back, "Hi, Olan."

"I'm so happy to be here with you tonight, sober and clear-headed. Today, May twenty-fifth, is my two-year-sobriety date. I want to share a little about my recovery and how love, so much love, helped me."

He smiles at our group, and Maria wiggles in Nick's arms. I lean over and quickly kiss her head, taking in her gentle baby smell while lulling her back to sleep.

"Two years ago, I had a relapse. I'd been sober for twelve years before then, and when I had the drink, one drink, I had a moment where I thought, just keep going. Keep drinking. You've broken the seal. Just do it. I was having a crisis in my personal and work lives, and even though I was going to meetings and working with my sponsor, I wasn't really doing the internal work. I wasn't honest with my ex-wife about my feelings. I wasn't honest with myself. Isabella, I love you, and I can't thank you enough for all the support you've given me."

My hand moves to Isabella's thigh, and she takes it and squeezes it. I will forever be grateful for how she's helped Olan before and since the universe brought him to me.

"My daughter Illona helped me stay sober. Her enormous unconditional love has shown me it's okay to be me. She loves me, just as I am. Period."

Illona squirms in my lap. She lies back and presses the back of her head against my chest. Isabella leans over and kisses her daughter on the forehead, and yeah, I'm getting misty. Sue me.

"In college, alcohol helped me ignore the stress and fears I'd long harbored. The more I drank, the less I worried about my fears. My ex knew I was crumbling. She confronted me, which I was furious about at the time. But that's when I knew I needed help."

Isabella squeezes my hand, and I return her clasp, neither one of us taking our eyes off Olan.

"Today, I know I'm an alcoholic. I know every day, I have to make the choice not to drink. I need to accept life on its terms and surrender to something greater than myself and take it one day at a time. I know myself better than I ever have. Two years ago, when I relapsed, I felt like I'd thrown away all I'd gained and needed to make some changes to ensure it never happened again. You know they say in the first year not to make any big life changes, and I tried to stick to that, but sometimes life has other plans for you. Not only did I sell my business, but I moved across the country with my daughter. I chose Portland because of the recovery community, so thank you all for welcoming and helping me. By moving here, something else happened. Something I wasn't looking for or expecting. I met someone."

Olan's eyes land on me, and my heart slows to a crawl. He pauses for just a moment, blinks, and continues.

"But today, I know that falling for someone wasn't too much. It was actually just enough. It was everything I needed and more than I ever thought possible. Marvin—my partner—has helped me love and accept who I am and who I want to be, and it's the most freeing experience in the world. He is here tonight, and I want to thank him for how much he's helped me. Marvin, would you come up here, please?"

Heat rises to my face as I'm keenly aware everyone in the room has turned to look at me. Olan didn't mention this. What kind of mishigas is he up to?

I'm frozen in the metal folding chair. Jill pokes my side. "Go on, you shmendrick. Go up!"

My feet feel like spaghetti, but I hand Illona off to her mother. Isabella's face cracks into a giant smile, and I manage to stand and head to the front of the room. Olan extends his hand and takes mine.

"Marvin Block, meeting you was no accident. Someone up there"—he points to the ceiling—"meant for us to be together. It's, it's...what's that word again?"

"Bashert," I whisper.

"Yes, bashert. Meant to be. Soulmates. Marvin, you have changed my life, and I will never stop telling you how much you mean to me. How much I love you. Oh, and how adorable you are."

A small laugh rolls around the people watching, and when I inhale I feel the seed of a sob gurgling.

"Sharing my life with you is the greatest gift I could ever ask for."

Still holding my hand, he begins to lower himself, and dear Lord in heaven he's kneeling. Chills overtake my entire body, and that simmering sob comes barreling out.

"Marvin Block, you are the love of my life, and nothing would make me happier than spending the rest of it with you. Will you please marry me?"

The blood has rushed from my head, and I'm not sure speaking is possible. The room sits silent, and oh crap, I'm supposed to answer.

"Since you said 'please.' Yes. Yes! Yes, of course, I'll marry you!"

He stands, and I melt into his arms. The entire room claps and cheers, and I hear Nick scream, "Go, Olan!"

Illona dashes up to hug us both, and I'm overwhelmed with emotion. Tears stream down my face as her dad holds her between us, and we wrap her in an embrace.

This is true family. What I've always wanted. What we've always wanted. Here. Now.

ACKNOWLEDGMENTS

Creating a made-up world has been a true highlight of my life. But I couldn't have done it without much love and support.

Mom—Even though my first word to you was *NO!* you still believed in me and were my first cheerleader. You've never stopped buoying me up. I love you.

Amy Spalding—Without your humor and insight, this story simply wouldn't exist in its current form. When I grow up, I want to be you.

Jay Leigh—Writing can be damn lonely. Having you as a writing bestie, thought partner, and all-around sherpa through the process has been invaluable. Jay, Breathe.

Courtney Kae—I'm not sure a sweeter human exists. Your encouragement and support mean the world to me.

A.J. Truman—My brother from another mother. Thank you for everything.

Ashley Bennett, Clio Evans, and Max Walker—I'm grateful for your friendships. You all inspire and support me in a special way. I love you!

Ruby Barrett and K. Sterling—My muses for how strong characters, amazing stories, and high steam come together. I bow to thee.

A.M. Johnson—thank you for providing a personalized podcast for me. I adore you to bits.

Nate Lyon—We talk on different topics, on different apps, at the same time. You always make me laugh and keep me humble.

Elise Vaz—My first editor in life.

Manda Waller—You took my ratty shoes and shined them up for the ceremony, and for that, you are an absolute goddess.

ACKNOWLEDGMENTS

Stevie Finegan—I am eternally grateful for your belief in my stories (and me) and your hard work.

Alex Logan and the entire Forever team—Everyone told me you are the best, and everyone was correct! Thank you for all your time and dedication to sharing my stories with the world.

Dave—My love. My heart. My soul. To you. To us. Thank you for showing me true love every day and always pushing me to be my best.

And last, to you, dear reader, for taking a chance on me, picking my book up, and entering the world I created. It's all fiction. I swear.